Teach Yourself VISUALLY™

QuickBooks®

Elaine Marmel

V·isual
A Wiley Brand

Teach Yourself VISUALLY™ QuickBooks®

657.9042
M351

Published by
John Wiley & Sons, Inc.
10475 Crosspoint Boulevard
Indianapolis, IN 46256

www.wiley.com

Published simultaneously in Canada

Wiley publishes in a variety of print and electronic formats and by print-on-demand. Some material included with standard print versions of this book may not be included in e-books or in print-on-demand. If this book refers to media such as a CD or DVD that is not included in the version you purchased, you may download this material at http://booksupport.wiley.com. For more information about Wiley products, visit www.wiley.com.

Library of Congress Control Number: 2014940488

ISBN: 978-1-118-91520-2 (pbk); ISBN: 978-1-118-91521-9 (ePDF); ISBN: 978-1-118-91522-6 (ePub)

Manufactured in the United States of America

10 9 8 7 6 5 4 3 2 1

Trademark Acknowledgments

Contact Us

For general information on our other products and services please contact our Customer Care Department within the U.S. at 877-762-2974, outside the U.S. at 317-572-3993 or fax 317-572-4002.

For technical support please visit www.wiley.com/techsupport.

Credits

Acquisitions Editor
Aaron Black

Project Editor
Maureen S. Tullis

Technical Editor
David Ringstrom

Copy Editor
Scott D. Tullis

**Manager, Content Development
& Assembly**
Mary Beth Wakefield

Publisher
Jim Minatel

Editorial Assistant
Jessie Phelps

Project Coordinator
Patrick Redmon

Proofreading
Judith McMullen

Indexing
Riverside Indexes, Inc.

About the Author

Elaine Marmel is President of Marmel Enterprises, LLC, an organization specializing in technical writing and software training. Elaine has an MBA from Cornell Universtiy and previously worked on projects building financial management systems in both New York City and Washington, DC. She has authored over seventy books predominantly on business productivity software. Elaine left her native Chicago for the warmer climes of Arizona (by way of Cincinnati OH; Jerusalem, Israel; Ithaca, NY; Washington DC; and Tampa, FL) where she basks in the sun with her PC, her latest cross stitch project, and her dog, Jack.

Author's Acknowledgments

My sincere thanks go to Katie Mohr, who gave me the opportunity to write this book—and here's to many more, Katie, because it has been a pleasure to work with you. And Maureen and Scott Tullis are the best project team ever...I can't thank you enough for your dedication to this project. And thanks go to David Ringstrom, who helped keep me technically accurate.

How to Use This Book

Who This Book Is For

This book is for the reader who has never used this particular technology or software application. It is also for readers who want to expand their knowledge.

The Conventions in This Book

① Steps

This book uses a step-by-step format to guide you easily through each task. Numbered steps are actions you must do; bulleted steps clarify a point, step, or optional feature; and indented steps give you the result.

② Notes

Notes give additional information — special conditions that may occur during an operation, a situation that you want to avoid, or a cross reference to a related area of the book.

③ Icons and Buttons

Icons and buttons show you exactly what you need to click to perform a step.

④ Tips

Tips offer additional information, including warnings and shortcuts.

⑤ Bold

Bold type shows command names, options, and text or numbers you must type.

⑥ Italics

Italic type introduces and defines a new term.

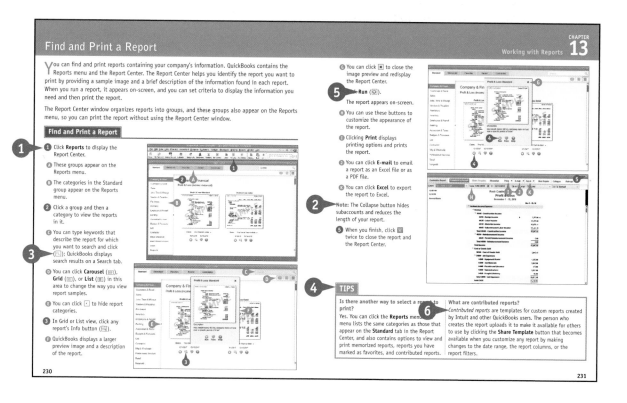

Table of Contents

Chapter 3 — Preparing to Invoice

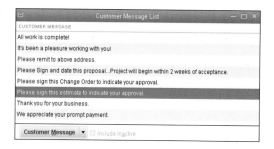

Chapter 4 — Setting Up Customers and Vendors

Table of Contents

Chapter 5 Set Up Payroll Background Information

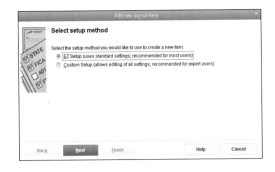

Chapter 6 Handling Payroll and Tax Reporting

Chapter 7 — Tracking Time and Mileage

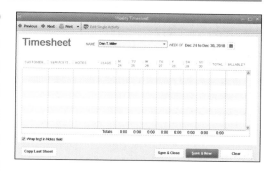

Chapter 8 — Invoicing and Recording Payments

Table of Contents

Chapter 11 Working with Bank Accounts

Chapter 12 Performing General Tasks

Table of Contents

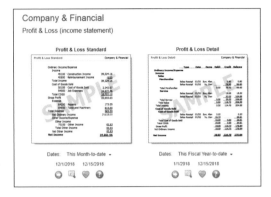

Chapter 15 | Managing QuickBooks Data

CHAPTER 1

Getting Started with QuickBooks

Before you can start using QuickBooks, you need to collect some background information, such as your company's chart of accounts and outstanding invoices for customers and vendors. You also need to decide on a date to start using QuickBooks. After you create a company, you can establish preferences for the way QuickBooks behaves.

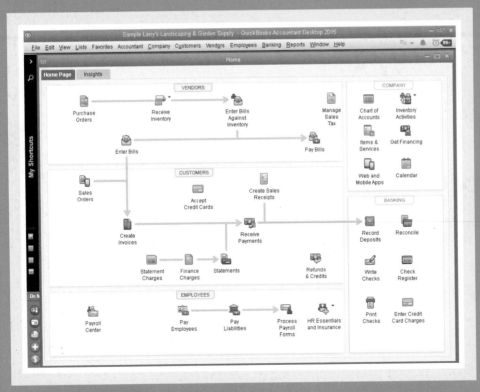

Prepare to Use QuickBooks

Most likely, your company will have been operating, if only for a short time, prior to the time you start using QuickBooks. Make sure you select the right edition of QuickBooks for your business, and gather some background information so that you can create and set up a QuickBooks company.

Desktop editions of QuickBooks for the Windows operating system include QuickBooks Pro and QuickBooks Premier, both aimed at businesses with 20 employees or less, and QuickBooks Enterprise, for businesses with more than 20 employees.

Features of QuickBooks Editions

The following table shows the features for each QuickBooks edition:

Edition	Features
QuickBooks Pro	Print checks, pay bills, invoice customers and track their payments, create purchase orders and track inventory, process payroll, generate reports, and perform tasks associated with job costing and time tracking.
QuickBooks Premier	All the features of QuickBooks Pro as well as the ability to build and track inventory assemblies, generate purchase orders from sales orders, and create a business plan.
QuickBooks Enterprise Solutions	All the features of QuickBooks Premier, as well as, for example, consolidating reports from multiple companies and more robust security for granting permissions to individual QuickBooks users.

Establish a Chart of Accounts

Every business uses a Chart of Accounts to organize accounting information. You need a copy of your company's Chart of Accounts and the balances in each account as of the day before you start using QuickBooks.

NAME		TYPE	BALANCE TOTAL	ATTACH
10100 · Checking		Bank	46,969.10	
10300 · Savings		Bank	17,910.19	
10400 · Petty Cash		Bank	500.00	
11000 · Accounts Receivable		Accounts Receivable	93,007.93	

Select a Starting Date

Decide on the first date you intend to use QuickBooks. This date determines the "as of" date of historical information you need to collect. Try to start using QuickBooks on the first day of an accounting period — either on the first day of your company's fiscal year or on the first day of a month. If you start using QuickBooks on January 1, you do not need to enter any historical payroll information. See Chapter 6 for details.

Employee Information

You need the names, addresses, and background information found on the W-4 form for your employees. You also need a list of the various payroll benefits offered and payroll taxes your company pays.

If you do not start using QuickBooks payroll to pay employees on January 1, plan to start payroll on the first day of any quarter, and gather payroll information for the current year for each employee. You must enter this year's payroll information to ensure that your payroll reports are accurate. See Chapter 5 for details on setting up payroll background information.

Vendor Information

Pull together the names, addresses, and background information, such as payment terms, for your vendors. Also make sure you know whether each qualifies as a 1099 vendor; if you are unsure, ask your accountant to help you make the determination. See Chapter 4 for more on setting up vendors. You also need a list of the outstanding vendor bills you have not paid as of the date you start using QuickBooks. You enter those bills in QuickBooks the same way that you enter new bills. See Chapter 10 for details on entering bills.

Customer Information

Gather the names, addresses, and background information, such as payment terms, for your customers. Also have available the sales tax information that your municipality requires you collect from your customers. See Chapter 3 for information about setting up sales taxes in QuickBooks, and see Chapter 4 for setting up customers. You also need a list of outstanding customer balances as of the date you start using QuickBooks, along with the invoices that comprise those balances. You enter those invoices in QuickBooks the same way that you enter new invoices. To enter invoices, see Chapter 8.

Inventory and Product Lists

You need a list of the products and services that you sell. QuickBooks refers to products and services using the word *items*. See Chapter 3 for information on setting up inventory, non-inventory, service, and other items.

Bank Account Balances

Have available the last bank statement you received for each bank account your company uses, and make sure that you reconcile those bank statements. You also need a list of all outstanding checks and deposits that have not yet cleared the bank as of the day you start using QuickBooks. See Chapter 2 for details on setting up an existing checking account.

Create a New Company

Most likely, your company will have been operating, if only for a short time, prior to the time you start using QuickBooks. To use QuickBooks, you create a company data file to store information about your business using the QuickBooks Setup wizard. Although the wizard can walk you through creating everything you need to use QuickBooks, most people rarely have time to enter all that information at one time. You can leave and restart the wizard, or you can manually set up QuickBooks at your leisure.

Create a New Company

1. Open QuickBooks.

2. In the No Company Open window, click **Create a new company**.

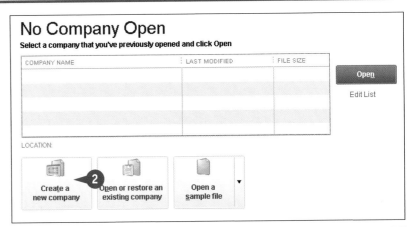

The QuickBooks Setup wizard appears.

3. Click **Express Start**.

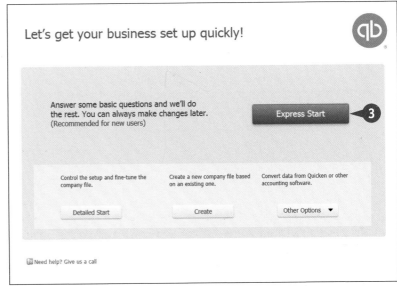

4 Type your company name.

5 Click ▼ and select your industry.

6 Click ▼ and select your company's legal organization.

7 Type your tax ID.

8 Click ▼ and specify whether you have employees.

9 Click **Continue**.

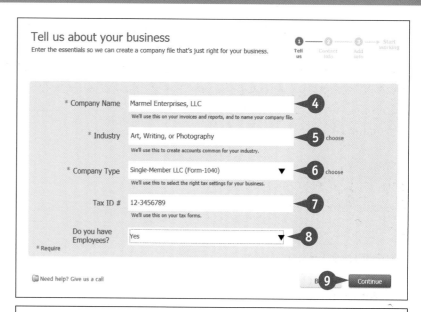

Tell us about your business

Enter the essentials so we can create a company file that's just right for your business.

① ———— ② ———— ③ ———→ Start
Tell   Contact   Add   working
us   Info   info

* Company Name Marmel Enterprises, LLC ◄ **4**

We'll use this on your invoices and reports, and to name your company file.

* Industry Art, Writing, or Photography ◄ **5** choose

We'll use this to create accounts common for your industry.

* Company Type Single-Member LLC (Form-1040) ▼ ◄ **6** choose

We'll use this to select the right tax settings for your business.

Tax ID # 12-3456789 ◄ **7**

We'll use this on your tax forms.

Do you have Employees? Yes ▼ ◄ **8**

* Require

Need help? Give us a call   B **9**   Continue

10 Type in contact information for your company.

11 Click **Create Company File**.

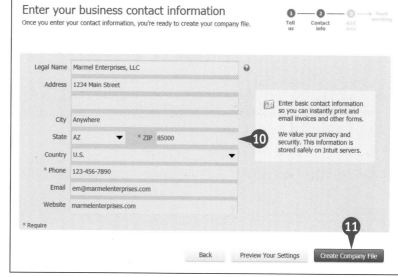

Enter your business contact information

Once you enter your contact information, you're ready to create your company file.

① ———— ② ———— ③ ———→ Start
Tell   Contact   Add   working
us   Info   Info

Legal Name Marmel Enterprises, LLC

Address 1234 Main Street

City Anywhere

State AZ ▼ * ZIP 85000

Country U.S. ▼

* Phone 123-456-7890

Email em@marmelenterprises.com

Website marmelenterprises.com

* Require

Enter basic contact information so you can instantly print and email invoices and other forms.

10 We value your privacy and security. This information is stored safely on Intuit servers.

Back   Preview Your Settings   Create Company File **11**

TIPS

If I want to use the wizard to add information, how can I restart it?

Click **Help** and then click **Quick Start Center** to redisplay the Ready to Start Working? window. Then, click **Return to Add Info** in the upper right corner of the Quick Start Center window to add customers, vendors, employees, products and services you sell, and bank accounts.

Do you have any advice for the filename I supply when I save my company?

Use a filename that reflects your company name. That way, if you start another business, you can easily distinguish one company file from another.

continued ▶

When you use the Express-Start method to create a company data file, QuickBooks requires only five pieces of information: Your company name, your industry, your business's legal organization, your ZIP code, and your phone number. QuickBooks uses the other information you supply — legal name, address, email address, and web address — on reports and forms that you print and send to customers and vendors.

If you return to the wizard to set up customers, vendors, and employees, QuickBooks presents a gridlike format into which you enter information.

Create a New Company (continued)

QuickBooks creates your company file and displays a screen that walks you through setting up other information.

12 Click **Start Working**.

The Ready to start working? window appears, explaining actions you can take.

13 Click ☒ in the upper right corner of the window to close it.

QuickBooks displays your company on-screen; see the section "Understanding the QuickBooks Window" to navigate the window.

Understanding the QuickBooks Window

The QuickBooks window contains several features that help you work efficiently while creating and editing transactions in QuickBooks.

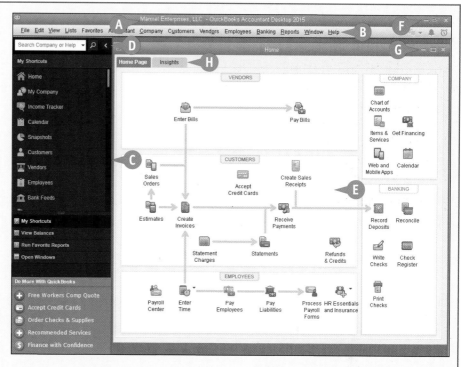

A Title Bar

Displays the name of the program and the current QuickBooks company.

B Menu Bar

Lists the menu names.

C Left Icon Bar

Contains buttons that open commonly used windows commands, such as the Customer or Vendor Centers. See the sections "Using the Customer Center" and "Using the Vendor Center" for more information. You can also choose to display the Top Icon Bar; see the section "Select an Icon Bar."

D Left Icon Bar Collapse

You can click this arrow (◀) to collapse the Left Icon Bar and view more of other open windows, such as the Home page.

E Home Page

A navigation tool that includes buttons you can click to open windows you use to record transactions. Using QuickBooks preferences, you can control whether the Home page appears each time you open QuickBooks.

See Chapter 14 for details on controlling Desktop preferences in QuickBooks.

F Program Window Controls

Buttons that you can click to minimize (▬), reduce the size (▭), or close (✕) the QuickBooks program window. If you click ▭ to reduce the size of the QuickBooks program window, you can click it (▭) a second time to maximize the window so that it fills the available visible space on your monitor.

G Window Controls

Buttons you can click to minimize (▬), maximize (▭), or close (✕) a window. If you click ▭ to maximize a window, you can click it again to reduce (▭) the size of the window.

H Insights tab

This tab displays a financial summary of your company.

Select an Icon Bar

QuickBooks contains two different icon bars: the Left Icon Bar and the Top Icon Bar. By default, new companies display the Left Icon Bar, which you can collapse to a small bar running down the side of the screen. Collapsing the Left Icon Bar gives you more screen real estate for working in windows.

Alternatively, you can opt to display the Top Icon Bar, which takes up much less space while remaining visible at all times. The screens in the rest of this book show the Top Icon Bar.

Select an Icon Bar

1 Click **View**.

2 Click **Top Icon Bar**.

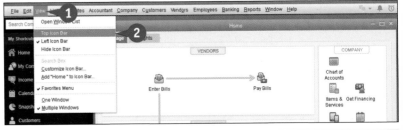

A QuickBooks removes the Left Icon Bar from the window and displays the Top Icon Bar.

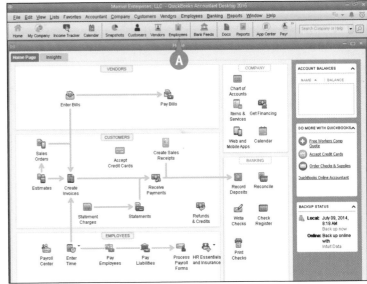

Using the Customer Center

Y ou can use the *Customer Center* to perform various customer-related tasks, such as adding new customers, creating transactions, printing reports, and so on. In addition, you can export information to and import information from Excel and send information to Word to create various customer-related letters. Using the *Income Tracker* in the Customer Center, you can view and manage sales information.

You can view detailed information and print reports for particular customers from the Customer Center, and opt to view only those customers that meet certain criteria, such as customers with overdue invoices.

Using the Customer Center

1 Click **Customers** to display the Customer Center.

A Click ▼ to select criteria for displaying customers in the list below.

B Click in this list to select a customer or job.

C Detailed information for the selected customer or job appears in these areas.

D Click these tabs to view different types of details for the selected customer or job.

E You can use these buttons to take actions related to customers or jobs.

2 Click the **Transactions** tab.

QuickBooks displays the Transactions tab of the Customer Center.

3 Click a type of transaction.

F QuickBooks displays those types of transactions in these areas.

4 Click ⊠ to close the Customer Center.

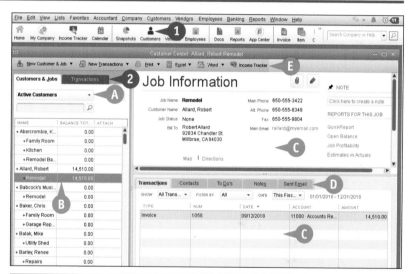

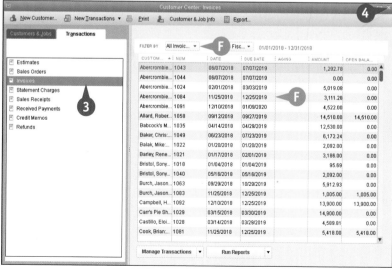

Using the Vendor Center

You can use the *Vendor Center* to perform various vendor-related tasks, such as to view, add, or edit vendors, create or edit transactions, print reports, and exchange data with Excel and Word. For any selected vendor, you can view transactions, contact information, to-do's or notes you have created, and email messages you have sent. You can also view vendor information based on a particular type of transaction. The Vendor Center functions in much the same way as the Customer Center.

Using the Vendor Center

1 Click **Vendors** to display the Vendor Center.

Ⓐ You can click ⏷ to select criteria for displaying vendors in the list below.

Ⓑ You can click in this list to select a vendor.

Ⓒ Detailed information for the selected vendor appears in these areas.

Ⓓ Click these tabs to view different types of details for the selected vendor.

Ⓔ Use these buttons to take vendor-related actions.

2 Click the **Transactions** tab.

QuickBooks displays the Transactions tab of the Vendor Center.

3 Click a type of transaction.

Ⓕ QuickBooks displays those types of transactions here.

4 Click ✖ to close the Vendor Center.

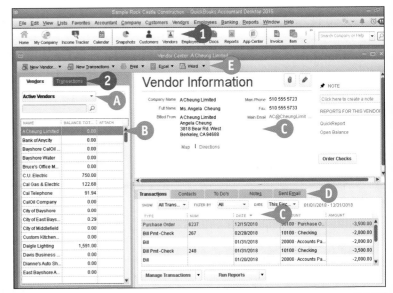

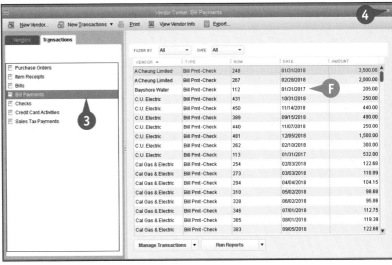

Using the Employee Center

You can use the *Employee Center* to create employees, manage employee information, print employee-related reports, enter time for employees who report work performed based on time spent, and exchange employee information with Excel and Word.

The Employee Center contains three tabs: the Employees tab, the Transactions tab, and the Payroll tab. This section covers the Employees tab and the Transactions tab. You use the Payroll tab to pay employees and for various payroll liabilities. For details on using the Payroll tab to perform these tasks, see Chapter 6.

Using the Employee Center

① Click **Employees** to display the Employee Center.

Ⓐ You can click ▾ to select criteria for displaying employees in the list below.

Ⓑ You click in this list to select an employee.

Ⓒ Detailed information for the selected employee appears in these areas.

Ⓓ Click these tabs to view different types of details for the selected employee.

Ⓔ Use these buttons to take actions related to employees.

② Click the **Transactions** tab.

QuickBooks displays the Transactions tab of the Employee Center.

③ Click a type of transaction.

Ⓕ QuickBooks displays those types of transactions here.

④ Click ✖ to close the Employee Center.

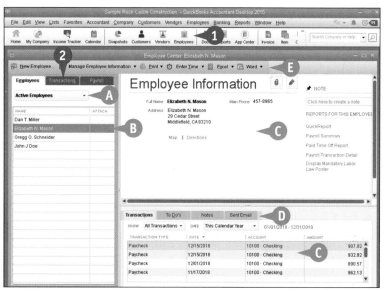

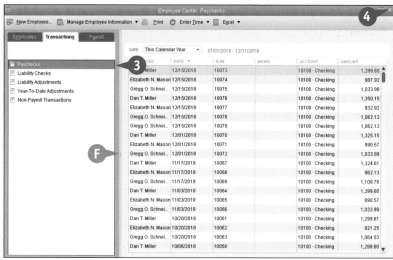

Set Accounting Preferences

You can control several facets of QuickBooks' behavior related to accounting. For example, you can use only names or a combination of names and numbers on the Chart of Accounts. And, if you use account numbers, you can control whether QuickBooks displays a complete account name or simply the lowest subaccount name. You can also use *class tracking,* a QuickBooks feature that helps you further delineate income and expenses. See Chapter 2 for information on accounts, subaccounts, and classes.

Set Accounting Preferences

1 Click **Edit.**

2 Click **Preferences.**

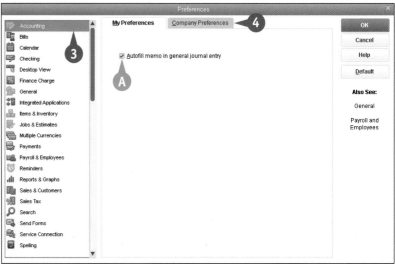

The Preferences dialog box appears.

3 Click **Accounting.**

The My Preferences tab appears.

A You can click the **Autofill memo in general journal entry** option (☐ changes to ☑) to automatically display memo information from the first line of a journal entry on all subsequent lines.

4 Click the **Company Preferences** tab.

5 Click the options you want to activate (☐ changes to ☑):

B These options control your use of account numbers.

C This option assigns class tracking for transactions.

D You use these options to automatically assign journal entry numbers and display warnings when posting to Retained Earnings.

E These options display warnings for transaction dates in the past or future.

6 Click **Set Date/Password**.

F You click this check box (☐ changes to ☑) to exclude transactions from closing date constraints.

7 Click 📅 to set a closing date.

8 Click in these boxes to assign and confirm a password.

9 Click **OK** twice to save your settings.

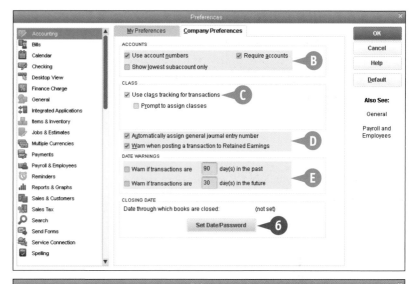

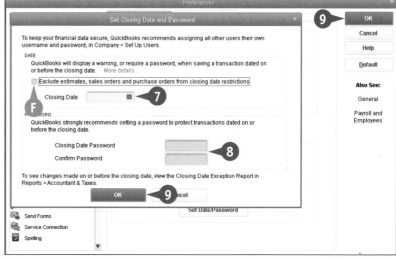

TIPS

Why do two tabs appear for Accounting preferences?

In the Preferences dialog box, two tabs appear for each set of available preferences. My Preferences are those settings that you can customize for your own use without affecting other QuickBooks users. The options that appear on the Company Preferences tab affect everyone who uses QuickBooks.

What is a closing date?

Closing date defines transactions that you can or cannot edit. You set a closing date to avoid changes to account balances prior to that date. If you set a closing date without setting a password, QuickBooks warns you when you try to change transactions dated prior to the closing date, but still lets you make the change.

Set Checking Account Preferences

You can control how QuickBooks behaves in relation to checking accounts and transactions they affect. For example, you can select default checking accounts to use whenever you open any window from which you write a check, pay a bill, or make a bank deposit.

By default, the payee name, the date, the total amount, the first 16 lines of the information in the memo field, and the amount field print on checks. If you store account numbers for payees, QuickBooks can insert those account numbers automatically in the check memo field.

Set Checking Account Preferences

1 Click **Edit**.

2 Click **Preferences**.

The Preferences dialog box appears.

3 Click **Checking**.

The My Preferences tab appears.

4 Click the check boxes (☐ changes to ☑) to select default checking accounts to use with each form.

5 Click the **Company Preferences** tab.

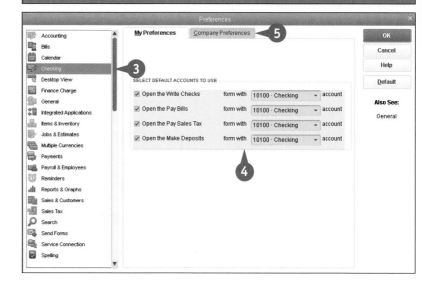

6 Click the options you want to activate(◯ changes to ◉ or ▢ changes to ☑):

A This check box controls the information that prints on check stubs.

B This check box changes a check's date to the date that you print the check.

C This check box positions the insertion point in the name field on checks, bills, and credit card charges.

D This check box automatically enters the account number stored with the payee's record in the check memo field.

E These check boxes select default checking accounts for payroll-related transactions.

F These options select a mode for bank feeds.

7 Click **OK**.

QuickBooks saves your Checking preferences.

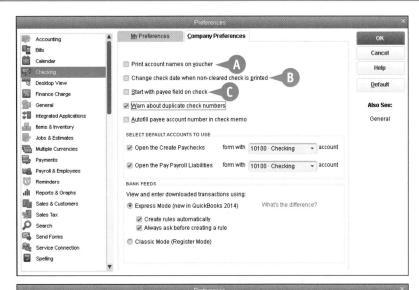

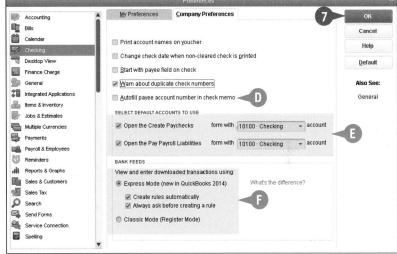

TIPS

What are bank feeds?

Using bank feeds, you can download transactions into QuickBooks from your bank or credit card provider. Note that some financial institutions do not offer bank feeds. Others offer additional services; with some banks you can use QuickBooks to transfer money between two accounts online. *Bank feeds* are, typically, fee-based services, and to use them, your bank must offer the service and access to the Internet from QuickBooks.

Why would I not want to check the Warn About Duplicate Check Numbers box?

QuickBooks takes longer to record a check because it searches your company data file for other occurrences of the check number. If you have a large company data file, enabling this option significantly affects performance.

Set General Preferences

Setting *General Preferences* enables you to control features that affect the QuickBooks program as a whole. For example, you can set the default date displayed for new transactions to either the current date or the last date you entered. You also can let QuickBooks automatically fill in transaction information from the last bill, check, or credit card charge you created for a particular name from a particular account.

To discourage theft, you can make QuickBooks save any transaction before anyone prints it; that way, nobody can print a check without saving it.

Set General Preferences

1 Click **Edit**.

2 Click **Preferences**.

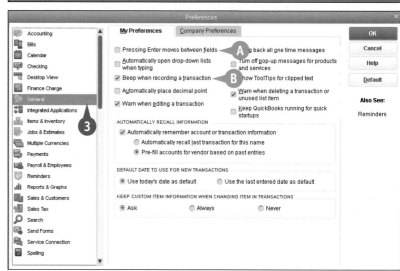

The Preferences dialog box appears.

3 Click **General**.

4 Click the options you want to activate (⬤ changes to ⦿ or ☐ changes to ☑):

🅐 This option enables you to press `Enter` or `Tab` to move from field to field on transactions.

🅑 This option sounds an audible confirmation when you save transactions.

C These options display a warning when you try to edit or delete a transaction or delete an unused list item.

D This option loads QuickBooks when you start your computer.

E These options automatically fill bills, checks, and credit card transactions with data from the last transaction you entered for that name.

5 Click the **Company Preferences** tab.

6 Select the options you want to activate (◯ changes to ◉ or ☐ changes to ☑):

F These options record time entries using either a decimal or minutes format.

G This option displays four-digit years instead of two-digit years.

H This option prevents updating of name information if you change it on a transaction.

I This option helps reduce the risk of theft.

7 Click **OK** to save your preferences.

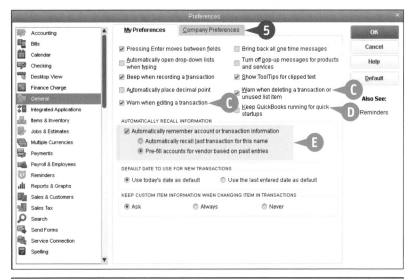

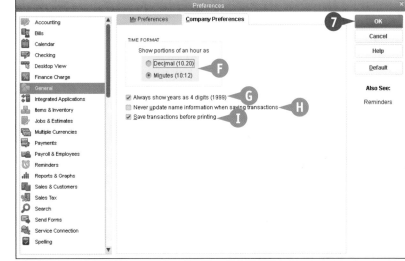

TIPS

What does the Show ToolTips for Clipped Text option on the My Preferences tab do?

Some fields are not wide enough to automatically display all the information they contain. When you click this option (☐ changes to ☑) and position the mouse pointer over one of these fields, the entire content of the field appears in a tool tip.

How does the Automatically Place Decimal Point option work?

When you click this option (☐ changes to ☑) and type a number with no decimal point, QuickBooks inserts a decimal between the second and third digits from the right end of the number. For example, 2995 becomes 29.95. When you do not select this option, 2995 becomes 2995.00.

Open an Existing Company

If you set up more than one company in QuickBooks because, for example, you run more than one business, you can switch between companies by opening an existing company. Another scenario might be if you want to open one of the sample company data files that ships with QuickBooks, or if you want to test something.

The name of the currently open company appears in the QuickBooks title bar. During the process of switching companies, QuickBooks automatically closes the current company for you. After you open another company, that company's name appears in the title bar.

Open an Existing Company

1 Click **File**.

2 Click **Open or Restore Company**.

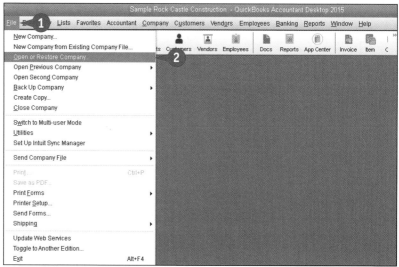

The Open or Restore Company dialog box appears.

3 Click the **Open a company file** option (⊙ changes to ⦿).

4 Click **Next**.

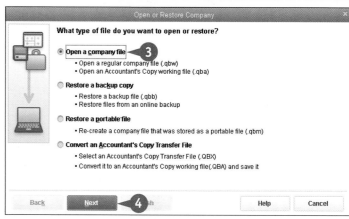

The Open a Company dialog box appears.

5 Click a QuickBooks company.

Ⓐ The company name appears here.

6 Click **Open**.

The company opens.

Ⓑ The company's name appears in the title bar.

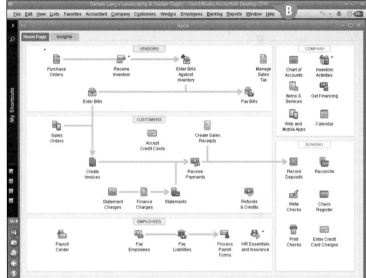

Is there an easy way to open a company I opened previously?
Yes. Click the **File** menu, hover the mouse over **Open Previous Company**, and click the company from the list that appears. From that list, you also can select **Set Number of Previous Companies** to display the Set Number of Previous Companies dialog box. Use this dialog box to control the number of previous companies that appear on the Open Previous Company menu; you can choose any number between 1 and 20.

CHAPTER 2

Setting Up General Information

When you first start using QuickBooks, you can set up background information to manage various aspects of your business. In this chapter, you learn, among other things, to set up new accounts and establish their opening balances, and to create classes and custom fields.

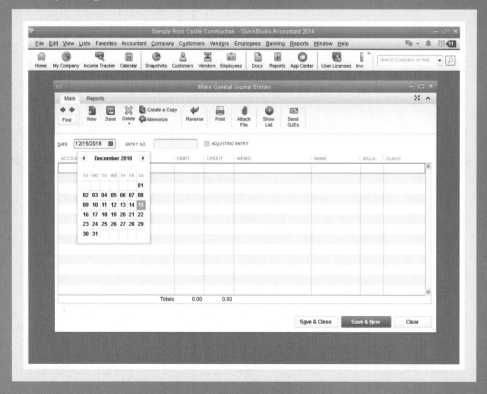

Create a New Account

Although QuickBooks creates basic accounts when you create a company, rarely are these accounts sufficient or totally accurate for your business. You need to add or change the asset, liability, equity, income, cost of goods sold, and expense accounts that QuickBooks creates.

You can also use *subaccounts* to break down an account. For example, you might want to set up an account called Utilities and then create subaccounts to track electric, telephone, gas, and water utility expenses. You can also set up subaccounts to track separate phone line expenses.

Create a New Account

1 Click **Lists**.

2 Click **Chart of Accounts**.

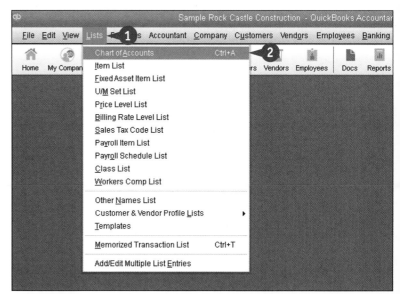

The Chart of Accounts window appears.

3 Click **Account**.

4 Click **New**.

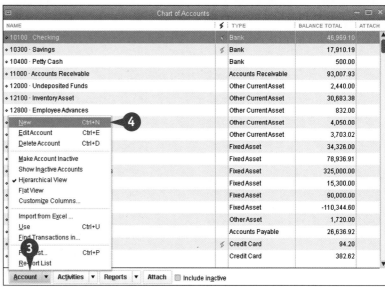

The New Account window appears.

5 Click an option to select an account type (changes to).

6 Click **Continue**.

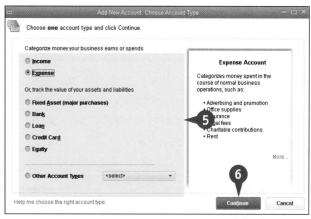

7 Type a name for the account here.

All other fields are optional.

A Most people assign an account number and use a numbering scheme that helps to easily identify the type of account.

B You can click this option (changes to) and select an account ( ) if you are creating a subaccount.

Note: If you see an Opening Balance field, leave it blank.

8 Click **Save & Close**.

TIPS

How do I edit or delete an account?
Follow steps **1** and **2** in this section and then click the account you want to edit or delete. Follow step **3**. For step **4**, click **Edit** or **Delete**. You can delete an account only if your company data file contains no transactions associated with it. To stop using an account, use the same steps but select **Make Inactive** in step **4**.

What kind of numbering scheme should I use?
Typically, a numbering scheme would be as follows:

Accounts Starting With	Represent
10000	Assets
20000	Liabilities
30000	Equity
40000	Income
50000	Cost of goods sold
60000 or higher	Expenses

Enter Opening Account Balances

To set up accurate opening balances for each account, first establish the date you intend to start using QuickBooks, and then get a Trial Balance report from your accountant as of the day before you intend to start using QuickBooks.

Most people use two journal entries to set up opening balances. The first should include all income and expense accounts, and the second journal entry should include all Balance Sheet accounts *except* bank accounts, credit cards for which you record every transaction, Accounts Receivable, Accounts Payable, and Payroll Liabilities.

Enter Opening Account Balances

1 Click **Company**.

2 Click **Make General Journal Entries**.

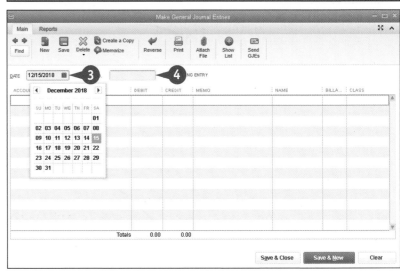

The Make General Journal Entries window appears.

3 Click 📅 to select the date for the entry.

Note: To enter opening balances, select the day before your QuickBooks starting date.

4 Click in this box and type a number for the entry.

5 Click ▾ to select an account.

6 Type an amount.

Note: Most income account balances are credits and might appear as negative numbers; follow your Trial Balance report.

A You can type the purpose of the journal entry here; QuickBooks assigns this text to each line of the entry.

B QuickBooks displays the unassigned amount needed to balance the entry as you work.

7 Repeat steps **5** and **6** for each income and expense account.

8 Assign the amount needed to balance the entry — to **Opening Bal Equity**.

9 Click **Save & New**.

10 Repeat these steps for all Balance Sheet accounts *except* the ones mentioned in the introduction.

11 Click **Save & Close**.

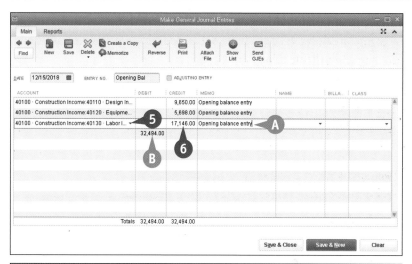

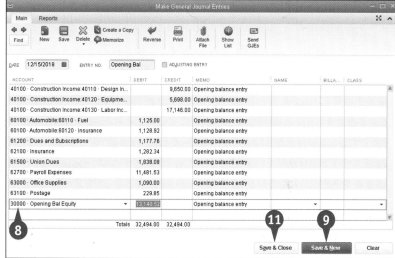

TIP

How do I create opening balances for Accounts Receivable, Accounts Payable, bank accounts, and payroll liabilities?

For Accounts Receivable and Accounts Payable, you enter outstanding invoices and bills the same way you enter new invoices and bills; see Chapters 8 and 10 for more details. Using this technique also helps you retain aging detail and record payments easily. To create opening balances for checking accounts and credit cards for which you record transaction details, see the section "Set Up an Existing Bank Account." To create payroll liability beginning balances, enter paychecks, as described in Chapter 6.

Set Up an Existing Bank Account

To correctly set up a bank account in QuickBooks, you enter the correct opening balance for the account along with all transactions that have not yet cleared the bank. For more information on reconciling bank accounts in QuickBooks, see Chapter 11.

The *opening balance* number for a bank account should be the ending balance that appears on your last bank statement. If you did not reconcile your last bank statement, please do so before completing this section. This section assumes that you set up a bank account with a zero balance using the steps in "Create a New Account."

Set Up an Existing Bank Account

1 Click **Lists**.

2 Click **Chart of Accounts**.

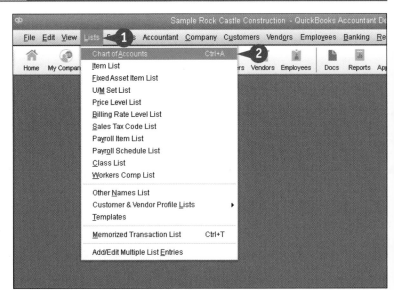

The Chart of Accounts window appears.

3 Click the bank account you want to set up.

4 Click **Activities**.

5 Click **Use Register**.

The register for the account appears.

6 Click 📅 to select a date that precedes your QuickBooks starting date.

7 Click here and type the ending balance on your last bank statement.

8 Click ▾ to open the Account list.

9 Select **Opening Bal Equity**.

10 Click **Record**.

11 Click 📅 and select the date of an outstanding check.

12 Type the check number here.

13 Type the amount here.

14 Click ▾ and select **Opening Bal Equity**.

Ⓐ You can click the Memo area and type the purpose of the outstanding transaction.

15 Click **Record**.

16 Repeat steps **10** to **14** for all outstanding checks and deposits to finish setting up your checking account.

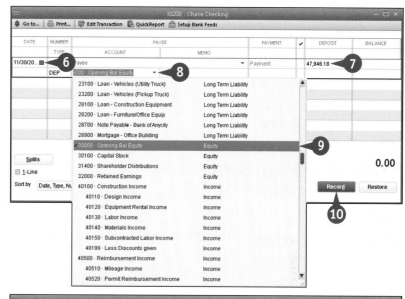

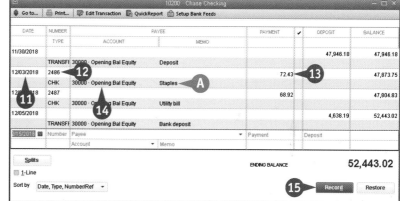

TIPS

Should I enter a payee?

You can, but this can be confusing. If you type anything in the Payee field, QuickBooks prompts you to add what you type to a list. Most users find it confusing to simultaneously set up new names and enter outstanding transactions. Instead, type the descriptions for these opening balance transactions in the Memo column.

What does the Splits button do?

The Splits button opens a window where you can assign different amounts of the transaction to different accounts. However, do not use the Splits window while entering opening balance information; instead, assign all amounts to the Opening Bal Equity account to ensure that you can, eventually, easily reconcile the bank account.

Create Classes

You can use the *class tracking* feature to further delineate income and expenses. To determine how to best use classes, think about the way that you want to report income and expenses. If you operate in several locations, set up a class for each location. Or, use classes to track income and expenses for different lines of business; attorneys might set up classes for litigation, real estate, and estate planning. Use classes for only one purpose, and make sure you assign a class to every transaction.

To create classes, turn on this feature in Accounting preferences; see Chapter 1.

Create Classes

1. Click **Lists**.

2. Click **Class List**.

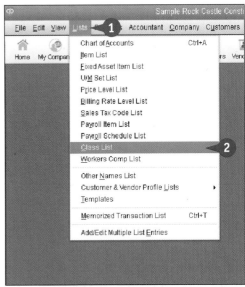

The Class List window appears.

3. Click **Class**.

4. Click **New**.

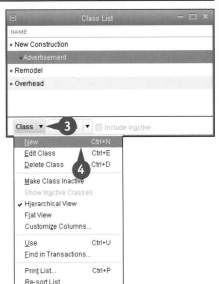

The New Class dialog box appears.

5 Click here and type a name.

A You can click the check box (☐ changes to ☑) to assign a subclass and then click ▼ to select the parent class.

6 Click **OK**.

B The new class appears in the Class List window.

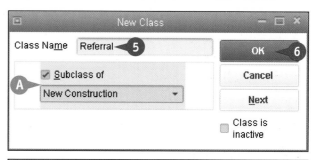

How should I choose between using classes and using subaccounts?

As you add subaccounts, your Profit & Loss Statement becomes longer and, potentially, more difficult to read. Classes segregate the tracking information onto its own report. Remember, though, that you can have the best of both worlds and track two types of information using classes and subaccounts.

How can I view the results of classifying transactions?

Display the Profit & Loss by Class report; see Chapter 13 for details. To easily assign classifications to unclassified transactions, display the Profit & Loss Unclassified report and double-click any amount to see a list of the transactions that comprise the amount. Double-click a transaction to open it and assign the transaction to a class.

Create Other Names

You can use the *Other Names List* to store information that does not fit into any other QuickBooks list. Lists store information that you use repeatedly, and QuickBooks contains lists for customers, vendors, and so on.

Occasionally, you must record *cash transactions* for people who do not really fit into any list. For example, sole proprietorships write checks to owners for the owners' draw, but owners are not customers, jobs, vendors, or employees. Also, you record ATM withdrawals by writing a check, but no payee really exists. In these situations, use the Other Names List to record cash transactions.

Create Other Names

1 Click **Lists**.

2 Click **Other Names List**.

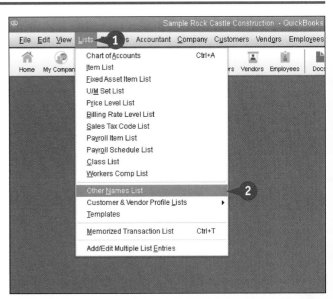

The Other Names window appears.

3 Click **Other Names**.

4 Click **New**.

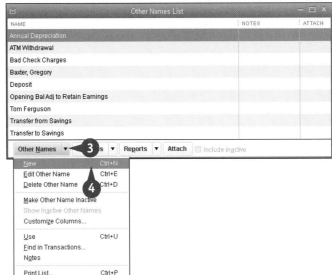

The New Name dialog box appears.

5 Click here and type a name for the list.

Note: All other fields are optional.

6 Click **OK**.

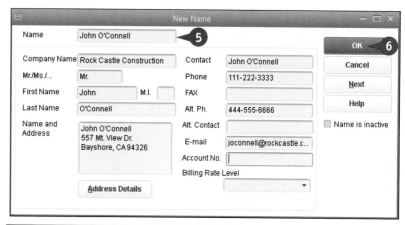

A The new name appears in the Other Names window.

TIP

What are notes, and how do I create one for an entry in the Other Names List?

You can store miscellaneous information that does not fit elsewhere in a note:

1 In the Other Names List, double-click in the Notes column beside the name.

2 In the Notepad dialog box that appears, type your note.

3 Click **OK** to save your note.

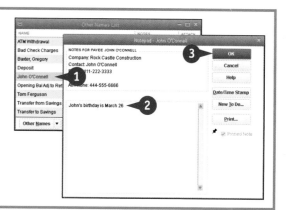

CHAPTER 3

Preparing to Invoice

When you create an invoice in QuickBooks, you include items. Some are goods and services that you sell, and others, such as sales tax items, sales tax group items, and discount items, help you make the invoice appear the way it should. This chapter shows you how to create items so that you can prepare invoices.

Create a New Item

Items are the things you buy from vendors and sell to customers, but items go beyond inventory in QuickBooks: You create items for anything you need to include on invoices you send to customers as well as on bills you receive from vendors. For example, you create items to represent services, sales taxes, discounts, and other charges you need to include on an invoice or vendor bill.

A portion of the steps you use to create items are the same, regardless of the type of item you intend to create. This section presents those steps that do not change.

Create a New Item

1 Click **Lists**.

2 Click **Item List**.

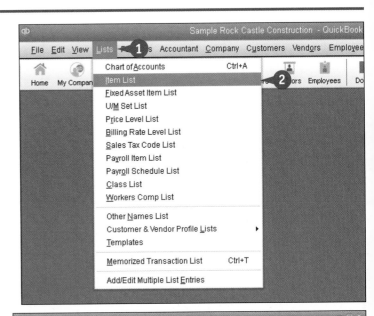

The Item List window appears.

3 Click **Item**.

4 Click **New**.

QuickBooks displays the New Item dialog box that appears in most tasks in this chapter.

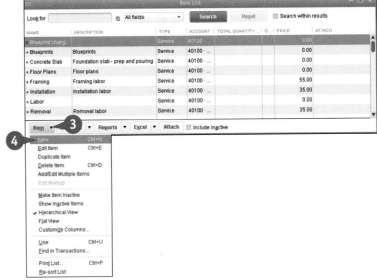

Create a New Subtotal Item

When you create a transaction such as an invoice or a purchase order, you place items on the transaction. QuickBooks automatically subtotals the items that appear on the transaction, applies taxes if appropriate, and then totals the transaction. However, you may want to subtotal the transaction before applying taxes to, for example, give a discount to a customer or apply a special handling charge. In cases like these, you use a Subtotal item. The Subtotal item, which you can place anywhere on the transaction, adds all items above it until another Subtotal item appears.

Create a New Subtotal Item

1 Complete the steps in the section "Create a New Item" to display the New Item dialog box.

2 Click ▼ and select **Subtotal** in the Type list box.

QuickBooks displays the fields you need to create a subtotal item.

3 Type a name for the Subtotal item.

Note: You can use both numbers and letters.

4 Type a description for the item.

Note: This description appears on transactions.

5 Click **OK**.

Ⓐ The new Subtotal item appears in the Item List window.

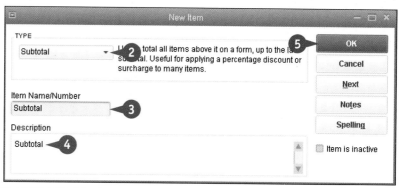

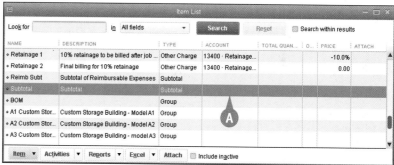

Create a New Discount Item

To give your customers discounts, you use a Discount item when entering sales transactions in QuickBooks. You can apply either a dollar amount or percentage discounts. You can discount an entire transaction, a portion of a transaction, or a single item on a transaction. QuickBooks calculates the discount for the item that precedes the Discount item on the transaction.

You do not use the Discount item when recording a timely payment from a customer or to a vendor; QuickBooks calculates timely payment discounts based on terms you establish for the customer or vendor.

Create a New Discount Item

1 Complete the steps in the section "Create a New Item" to display the New Item dialog box.

2 Click ▼ and then **Discount** in the Type list box.

QuickBooks displays the fields you need to create a discount item.

3 Type a name here.

4 Type a description here; the description appears on transactions.

5 Type the discount amount or percentage here.

Note: Include the percent sign to create a percentage discount item; type only the value to create an amount discount item.

6 Click ▼ to select an account.

7 Click **OK**.

A The new Discount item appears in the Item List window.

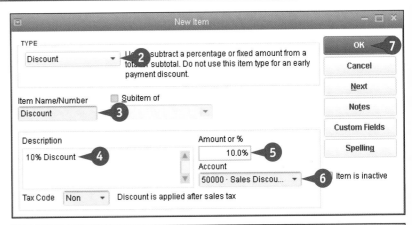

Create a New Group Item

You use a *group item* to sell or buy certain items together, as a group. If you always buy or sell doorknobs whenever you buy or sell doors, save time by using a group item that consists of a door and a doorknob. When you enter the group item on a transaction, QuickBooks enters two items simultaneously. See later sections in this chapter to create items to buy or sell.

You can include both taxable and nontaxable items in a group. If the group includes taxable items, QuickBooks calculates sales tax for the individual items in the group.

Create a New Group Item

1. Complete the steps in the section "Create a New Item" to display the New Item dialog box.

2. Click ▾ and select **Group** in the Type list box.

   QuickBooks displays the fields you need to create a group item.

3. Type a name here.

4. Type a description here; the description appears on transactions.

A. You can click this check box (☐ changes to ☑) to print items and amounts individually on transactions.

5. Select the items to include in the group.

6. Click **OK**.

B. The new Group item appears in the Item List window.

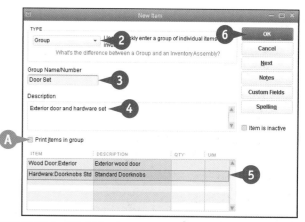
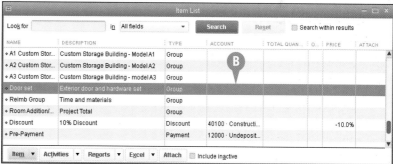

Create a New Payment Item

You use a *Payment item* to record a payment made at the time you make a sale. In most cases, Payment items represent a prepayment for an item or a down payment. A Payment item reduces the customer's outstanding balance.

You can group payments with other undeposited funds, or place the money directly in a bank account. If your bank prints individual lines on your statement for five items you deposit using one deposit slip, you can deposit the money directly into a bank account. Otherwise, group payments with other undeposited funds.

Create a New Payment Item

1 Complete the steps in the section "Create a New Item" to display the New Item dialog box.

2 Click ▾ in the Type list box and select **Payment**.

QuickBooks displays the fields you need to create a payment item.

3 Type a name.

4 Type a description; the description appears on transactions.

5 Click ▾ and select a **Payment Method**.

Note: Payment methods make balancing your bank statement easier by grouping your deposits so that checks appear in one deposit, Visa charges in another deposit, and so on.

6 Click a deposit option (◯ changes to ◉).

7 Click **OK**.

Ⓐ The new Payment item appears in the Item List window.

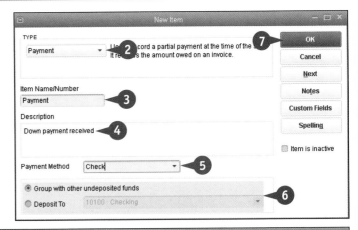

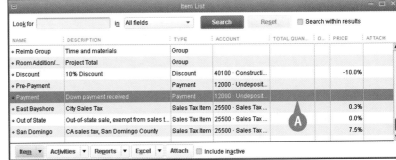

Set Up Sales Taxes

If your company must collect sales tax on the items it sells, you set QuickBooks preferences to enable sales taxes. You identify whether you owe sales tax as of the date of the sale or the date you collect payment, along with the frequency with which you pay sales taxes.

You assign QuickBooks sales tax codes to customers or various items to specify their tax liability. QuickBooks automatically creates two sales tax codes for you, but you may need others to help you categorize sales for sales-tax-return reporting purposes.

Set Up Sales Taxes

Sales Tax Preferences

1 Click **Edit**.

2 Click **Preferences**.

The Preferences dialog box appears.

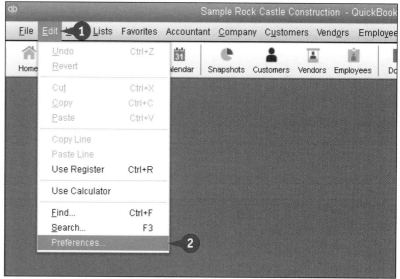

3 Click **Sales Tax**.

4 Click the **Company Preferences** tab.

5 For the Do You Charge Sales Tax option, click **Yes** (◯ changes to ◉).

6 Click an option in this area to select the basis on which you owe sales tax (◯ changes to ◉).

7 Click a payment frequency (◯ changes to ◉).

8 Click ▾ for these options and, from the lists that appear, click **New**.

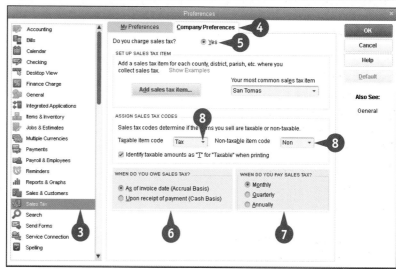

continued ▶

A s part of setting sales tax preferences, you create the sales tax item that you expect to use most often and the vendor to whom you remit sales tax. A sales tax item stores the rate you must charge your customers for a particular sales tax authority's jurisdiction, and you set up additional sales tax items as needed.

In Chapter 4, you learn how to assign sales tax codes and items so that when you sell an item to a customer, QuickBooks can determine whether to charge sales tax and categorize the sale properly.

Set Up Sales Taxes (continued)

Create a Sales Tax Code

The New Sales Tax Code dialog box appears.

9 Type a code using no more than three characters.

10 Type a description.

11 Click either the Taxable or Non-Taxable option (○ changes to ◉).

12 Click **OK**.

QuickBooks saves the new sales tax code and redisplays the Company Preferences tab.

Note: If necessary, reopen the list and select the sales tax code you use most often.

13 Click **Add sales tax item** to add the items you use most often.

Create a Sales Tax Item

The New Item dialog box appears.

14 Click ▼ and select **Sales Tax Item**.

15 Type a name.

16 Type a description.

17 Type the rate charged by the jurisdiction.

18 Click ▼ and then click **Add New** to add the sales tax authority.

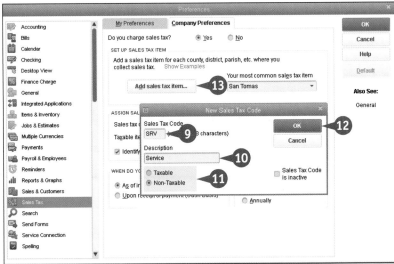

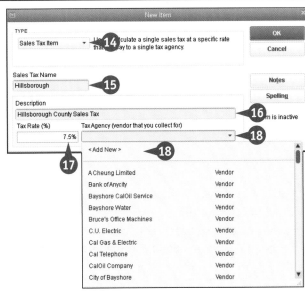

Create a Sales Tax Authority

The New Vendor dialog box appears.

19 Type a Vendor Name, Company Name, and address.

20 Click **Account Settings**.

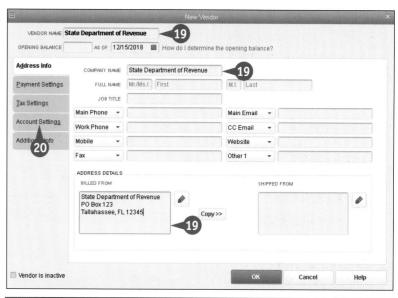

21 Click ▾ to select the sales tax payable account.

22 Click **OK** three times.

QuickBooks saves the vendor, sales tax code, sales tax item, and your sales tax preferences.

23 Click **OK** when QuickBooks asks if you want to make all existing customers, inventory, and non-inventory parts taxable.

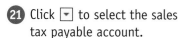

TIPS

How do I set up sales tax items and codes without using the Preferences dialog box?

For sales tax items, follow the steps in the section "Create a New Item." Select **Sales Tax Item** and then follow steps **15** to **17** in this section. For new sales tax codes, click **Lists** and then click **Sales Tax Code List**. Then, click **Sales Tax Code** and then **New**. Complete steps **9** to **12** in this section.

What reports show me sales tax information?

Use the Sales Tax Revenue Summary and the Sales Tax Liability reports, which show complete information for each sales tax item.

Create a New Sales Tax Group Item

In many states, you must charge your customers a combination of sales taxes, and Sales Tax Group items simplify this task. Your state may have a sales tax rate, and individual counties and cities may have separate, additional rates that you must charge the customer. Grouping individual sales tax items that you set up using information in the section "Set Up Sales Taxes" ensures that you charge the correct amount of sales tax, that your customer sees one entry for sales tax on the invoice, and that QuickBooks produces accurate reports that support sales tax reporting.

Create a New Sales Tax Group Item

1 In the New Item dialog box, click 🔽 in the Type list box and select **Sales Tax Group** to display the fields for creating a sales tax group item.

2 Type a name.

3 Type a description to appear on transactions.

4 Select a sales tax item.

5 Repeat step **4** for each sales tax item in the group.

6 Click **OK**.

Ⓐ The new Sales Tax Group appears in the Item List window.

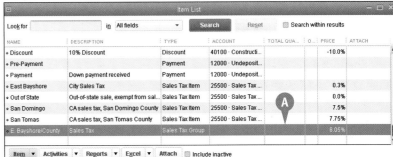

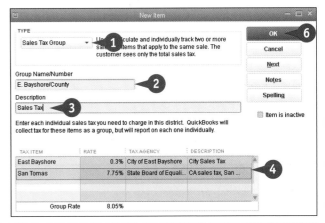

44

Create a New Service Item

You create *service items* in QuickBooks to account for income generated by intangible things you sell, such as subcontractor labor, consulting, and legal advice. You can optionally supply a rate you charge for the service; QuickBooks displays the rate on sales transactions, and you can change the displayed rate.

If your business is not a corporation, and you pay business owners, partners, or subcontractors for work they perform, set up separate service items, because you need to record the cost of the owner's or partner's work against an equity account, and the cost of the subcontractor against an expense account.

Create a New Service Item

1 In the New Item dialog box, click ▼ in the Type list box and select **Service**.

2 Type a name and description for the Service item; the description appears on transactions.

3 Click ▼ to select a tax code.

4 Click ▼ to select an income account.

Ⓐ This option (☐ changes to ☑) creates an item to use when subcontractors or partners perform the service; you can also type purchase and sales transaction descriptions and select expense and income accounts.

5 Click **OK**.

Ⓑ The new Service item appears in the Item List window.

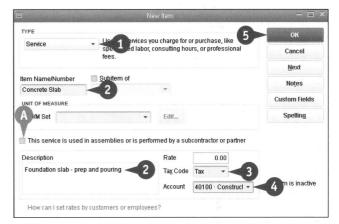

Create a New Inventory Part Item

Inventory items are tangible things that you own and keep on hand to sell to customers.

When you create an inventory part item, you establish the correct inventory, *cost of goods sold (COGS)*, and income accounts for QuickBooks to update when you buy or sell the item. If you are setting up QuickBooks for the first time, do not type either the quantity you own or the value. Instead, record inventory adjustments to establish the starting quantity and total value of the item. See Chapter 10 for details on entering inventory adjustments.

Create a New Inventory Part Item

1 In the New Item dialog box, click ▾ and select **Inventory Part** in the Type list box.

2 Type a name or code for the item.

3 Type a description that appears on bills, and QuickBooks assigns the same description to sales transactions.

4 Click ▾ in these areas to assign a COGS account, tax code, and income account.

5 Click ▾ to assign an inventory asset account.

Ⓐ You can type the minimum available quantity at which you want QuickBooks to remind you to reorder.

6 Click **OK**.

Ⓑ The new Inventory Part item appears in the Item List window.

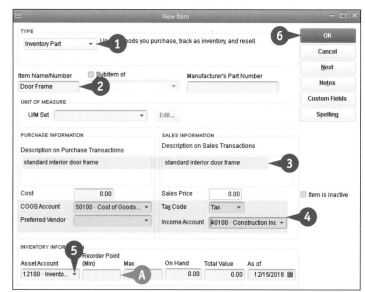

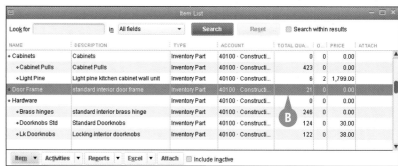

Create a New Inventory Assembly Item

Create a New Inventory Assembly Item

QuickBooks Premier and QuickBooks Enterprise users can create *inventory assembly items* consisting of several existing inventory part items. QuickBooks calculates the value of an inventory assembly item by summing the values of the component parts.

For each assembly, you identify whether the item is taxable and establish cost of goods sold (COGS), income, and inventory asset accounts. Optionally, you can provide a sales price and a quantity at which QuickBooks reminds you to build the assembly item; see Chapter 10 for details. If you purchase the assembly to resell it, you also enter an optional purchase description and vendor.

Create a New Inventory Assembly Item

1 Complete the steps in the section "Create a New Item" to display the New Item dialog box.

2 Click ▾ in the Type list box and select **Inventory Assembly**.

3 Type a name or code and a description that appears on invoices.

4 Click ▾ to assign a COGS account, a tax code, and an income account; optionally you can supply a sales price.

5 Click these areas to select an assembly component, and type the quantity of the component.

6 Repeat step **5** for each component.

7 Type the minimum on-hand quantity at which QuickBooks should remind you to build the assembly.

8 Click **OK**.

A The new Inventory Assembly item appears in the Item List window.

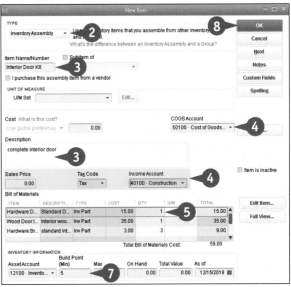

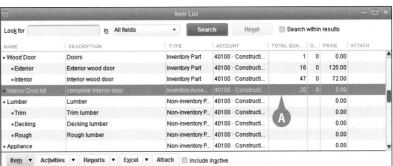

Create a New Non-Inventory Part Item

Y**ou create *non-inventory parts*** for goods you purchase that do not qualify as inventory. Typically, items your company purchases to use to run the business, like office supplies, are non-inventory parts. If a customer asks you to place a special order for an item that you do not regularly sell, treat that item as a non-inventory item.

In addition to setting up selling information, you can set up the purchasing information if you use the item for a job, so that you can charge the customer for the item and produce job profitability reports.

Create a New Non-Inventory Part Item

1 Complete the steps in the section "Create a New Item" to display the New Item dialog box.

2 Click ▾ in the Type list box and select **Non-Inventory Part**.

3 Type an item name.

4 Type a description to appear on invoices.

5 Click these areas to select a tax code and an income account, and to set an optional selling price.

A You can click the check box (☐ changes to ☑) to create a non-inventory part for jobs.

6 Type a description for the purchase transactions.

7 Click ▾ to select an expense account and a preferred vendor.

8 Click **OK**.

QuickBooks saves the non-inventory part.

Create a New Other Charge Item

Y ou create *Other Charge items* for situations that do not fit into any of the item categories described in this chapter. For example, you can use an Other Charge item to charge a customer an insufficient funds fee if the bank returns a customer's check due to insufficient funds in the customer's account. You also can use an Other Charge item to create a reimbursable expense when, for example, you pay delivery charges for an item you ordered on behalf of a customer, and you intend to invoice the customer for the delivery charges.

Create a New Other Charge Item

1 Complete the steps in the section "Create a New Item" to display the New Item dialog box.

2 Click ▾ in the Type list box and select **Other Charge**.

3 Type an item name.

4 Type a description to appear on invoices.

5 Click these areas to select a tax code and an income account, and to set an optional selling price.

Ⓐ You can click the check box (☐ changes to ☑) to create a reimbursable expense Other Charge item.

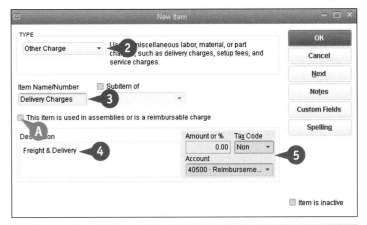

Ⓑ If appropriate, you can type a description for purchase transactions.

6 Select an expense account and, if appropriate, a preferred vendor.

7 Click **OK**.

QuickBooks saves the Other Charge item.

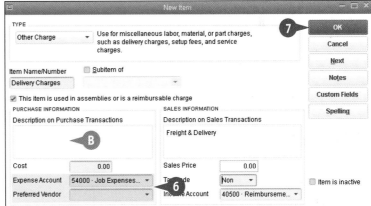

CHAPTER 4

Setting Up Customers and Vendors

To set up customers and vendors, you provide details about each customer and vendor. You also should establish preferences for a variety of customer- and vendor-related information, such as payment terms and methods, customer and vendor types, price levels, and shipping methods.

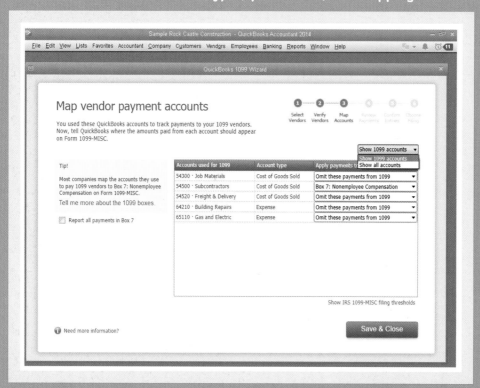

Set Preferences

You can set preferences that affect sales and customers, jobs and estimates, items and inventory, and 1099s.

For sales and customers, you can select data entry defaults for sales forms and sales orders, and enable the Collections Center and price levels. If customers require pricing in advance of a project, you can turn on the estimate feature and set preferences for jobs and estimates, including describing the job statuses your business assigns to each job. You can enable inventory and purchase-order features to warn, for example, about duplicate purchase order numbers or when insufficient inventory exists to make a sale.

Set Preferences

Set Sales & Customer Preferences

1. Click **Edit**.

2. Click **Preferences**.

   The Preferences dialog box appears.

3. Click **Sales & Customers**.

4. Click the **Company Preferences** tab.

5. Set sales form preferences here.

6. Click to select sales order preferences and to enable the Collections Center (☐ changes to ☑).

7. Click this option to enable price levels (◯ changes to ◉).

8. Click **Jobs & Estimates**.

Note: When QuickBooks prompts you, click **Yes** to save your settings.

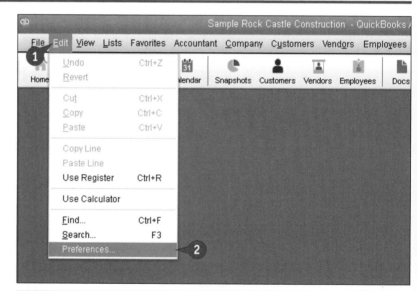

Set Jobs & Estimates Preferences

1 Click the **Company Preferences** tab.

2 Type job status descriptions here.

3 Click **Yes** (◯ changes to ◉) to enable estimate preparation.

4 Click **Items & Inventory**.

Note: When QuickBooks prompts you, click **Yes** to save your settings.

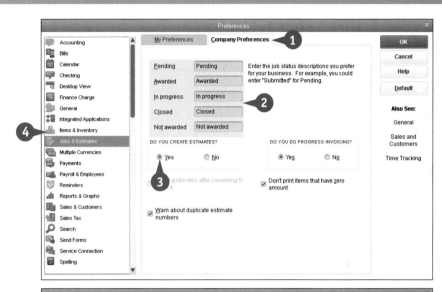

Set Items & Inventory Preferences

1 Click the **Company Preferences** tab,

2 Click these options (☐ changes to ☑) to enable inventory and purchase-order features and to set inventory and purchase-order warnings.

3 Click **Tax: 1099**.

Note: When QuickBooks prompts you, click **Yes** to save your settings.

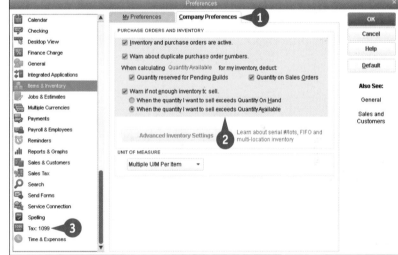

TIPS

What is the Collections Center?

The *Collections Center*, available through the QuickBooks Customer Center, helps you manage collecting payments from your customers by listing all overdue and almost due invoices. You can send email reminders to one customer or many customers, and the Collections Center tracks customer notes about your collection efforts.

What is progress invoicing?

When you do not use *progress invoicing,* you create an invoice for the full amount due. When you use progress invoicing, you invoice for selected portions, for a percentage, or for differing percentages on selected lines of an estimate. Progress invoicing also enables you to display, on the invoice, the amount of the estimate that you previously invoiced the customer.

continued ▶

Set Preferences (continued)

If you use 1099 vendors such as subcontractors in your business, you can set up QuickBooks to track payments to those 1099 vendors. That way, you can print and file 1099-MISC forms when your payments to those 1099 vendors exceed limits established by the Internal Revenue Service.

Most businesses need to track only nonemployee compensation, but the types of payments you must track and report depend on your business. Check with your accountant or local IRS office to determine if you need to track other types of payments to 1099 vendors.

Set Preferences (continued)

Set 1099 Preferences

1 Click the **Company Preferences** tab.

2 Click **Yes** (○ changes to ⦿) to enable 1099 tracking in QuickBooks.

3 Click here to map 1099 accounts.

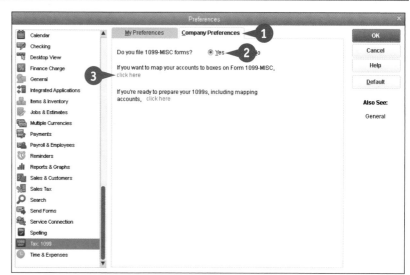

The QuickBooks 1099 Wizard appears.

Ⓐ If no accounts appear, click ▾ and select **Show all accounts**.

4 Click an account you use to pay vendors.

5 Click ▾ and select a 1099 option.

6 Repeat steps **4** and **5** for each account you use to pay vendors.

7 Click **Save & Close**.

QuickBooks saves all changes to preferences.

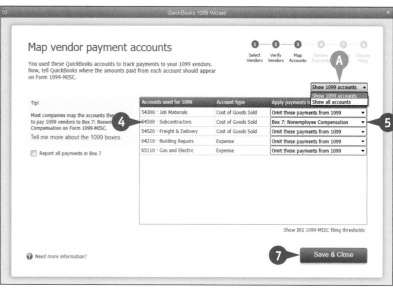

Create Profile Information

QuickBooks contains a number of *profile lists* pertaining to customers and vendors, and you use these profile lists to establish elements to describe each profile. For example, you can set up profiles for sales reps, customer types, vendor types, job types, payment terms and methods, customer messages, and shipping methods.

To set up the various profiles, you open each profile list using the same steps. This section shows you how to find the various profile lists, and subsequent sections in this chapter show you how to create an element in a profile list.

Create Profile Information

1 Click **Lists**.

2 Click **Customer & Vendor Profile Lists**.

3 Choose the appropriate list for the type of profile you want to create.

Note: This section shows the Sales Rep List window.

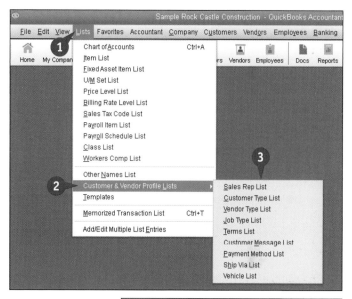

The profile list window opens.

4 Click the left-most button at the bottom of the list window.

Note: The name of the button typically matches the name of the profile list window.

5 Click **New**.

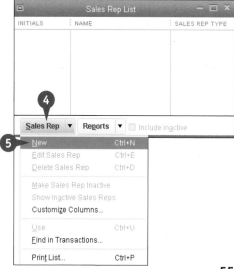

Create Sales Rep Records

You can use sales reps to identify who is primarily responsible for managing a customer's orders and to help track commissionable sales. Before you can create a sales rep, the rep's information must appear in the Vendor List, the Employee List, or the Other Names List. See the section "Create a New Vendor Record," Chapter 5, and Chapter 2 for details.

Sales representatives can be salaried or hourly employees who might also receive commissions. Alternatively, they can be individuals who receive a commission for selling your products but are not employees of your company for payroll tax reporting purposes.

Create Sales Rep Records

1 Complete the steps in the section "Create Profile Information," selecting **Sales Rep List** in step **3**.

2 Click ▼ to select a name to add to the sales rep list.

Ⓐ You can change the sales rep initials here.

3 Click **OK**.

Ⓑ The new sales rep appears in the Sales Rep List.

Create Customer Types and Subtypes

In many businesses, it is helpful to categorize customers so that you can better serve them. In QuickBooks, you use the Customer Type List to create categories that you can assign to customers.

Suppose, for example, that you run a lawn service business in Tampa, Florida, and you have both commercial and residential customers in Tampa and in Clearwater. You can create Commercial and Residential customer types and subtypes Tampa and Clearwater — the localities you service — to help distinguish between commercial and residential customers in each locality you serve.

Create Customer Types and Subtypes

1 Complete the steps in the section "Create Profile Information," selecting **Customer Type List** in step **3**.

2 Type a name for the customer type.

A You can click the check box (☐ changes to ☑) to create a subtype and then click ▾ to select an existing customer type.

3 Click **OK**.

B The new customer type appears in the Customer Type List window.

Create Job Types

Like its cousin the Customer Type, the Job Type helps you classify jobs you perform. Using job types, you can group and subtotal comparable jobs on reports and use the information to help you identify the most profitable types of jobs.

Suppose, for example, that you run a lawn service business, and you offer services that include mowing, fertilization, and installation. You can create job types for each service and, if necessary, you can create subtypes to further categorize job information.

Create Job Types

1 Complete the steps in the section "Create Profile Information," selecting **Job Type List** in step **3**.

2 Type a name for the job type.

Ⓐ You can click the check box (☐ changes to ☑) to create a subtype and click ▾ to select an existing job type.

3 Click **OK**.

Ⓑ The new job type appears in the Job Type List window.

Create Payment Terms

Y ou use *terms* to describe when you expect to receive payment from a customer or when a vendor expects payment from you. QuickBooks supports standard terms, which are based on calculations from the transaction date, and date-driven terms, which rely on specific days of the month; QuickBooks automatically creates commonly used terms.

This section demonstrates setting up date-driven terms of 2% 5th Net 20th, which means that you can discount 2 percent of the invoice or bill if paid by the 5th day of the next month; otherwise, the full amount is due on the 20th of the next month.

Create Payment Terms

1 Complete the steps in the section "Create Profile Information," selecting **Terms List** in step **3**.

2 Type a name for the terms.

3 Click the **Standard** or **Date Driven** option (○ changes to ◉) for the type of terms you want to create.

4 Type numbers to describe the terms.

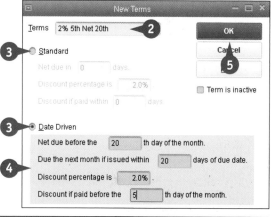

5 Click **OK**.

Ⓐ The new terms appear in the Terms List window.

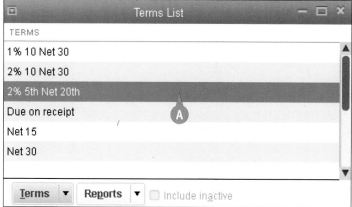

Create Payment Methods

Payment methods represent the different ways you receive money from your customers, and you can optionally assign a payment method when you record a receipt from a customer. Although QuickBooks automatically creates the most common payment methods, you might need to add one.

If you assign a payment method to each receipt, you can create bank deposits for each payment method. If you accept credit cards and assign payment methods, you can match your daily receipts for each credit card to the deposits from each credit card company. And, your deposits in QuickBooks will match the deposits reported on your bank statement.

Create Payment Methods

1 Complete the steps in the section "Create Profile Information," selecting **Payment Method List** in step **3**.

2 Type a name for the payment method.

3 Click ▾ and select a payment type.

4 Click **OK**.

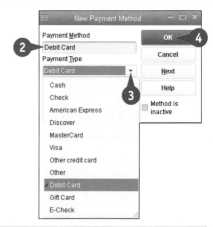

Ⓐ The new payment method appears in the Payment Method List window.

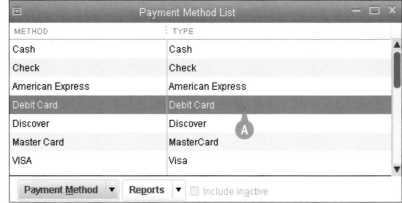

Create Customer Messages

Occasionally, you may want or need to include a message to a customer on a sales transaction. Customer messages appear on sales transactions on-screen and on the printed sales transaction form. You assign a message to a sales transaction from the transaction window. For help completing a sales transaction, see Chapter 8.

QuickBooks automatically creates some standard messages, but you may need to create a message of your own. For example, during the holiday season, you might want to include a "Happy Holidays" message on customer invoices and sales receipts.

Create Customer Messages

1 Complete the steps in the section "Create Profile Information," selecting **Customer Message List** in step **3**.

2 Type the customer message.

3 Click **OK**.

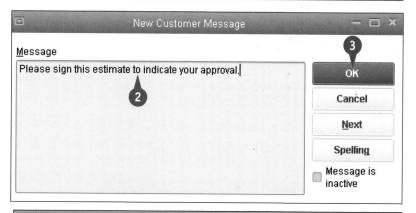

A The new customer message appears in the Customer Message List window.

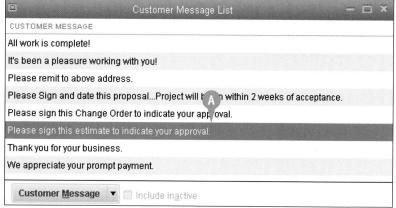

Create a New Price Level

Using *price levels* in QuickBooks, you can assign special pricing to customers and jobs or apply one-time markups or markdowns to sales transactions. QuickBooks calculates the new pricing you specify based on the current price of service, inventory, non-inventory, and inventory assembly items.

All versions of QuickBooks support fixed-percentage price level increases or decreases, which enable you to increase or decrease all item prices by a percentage you specify. QuickBooks Premier and QuickBooks Enterprise support per-item price levels that enable you to assign special pricing to selected items.

Create a New Price Level

1 Click **Lists**.

2 Click **Price Level List**.

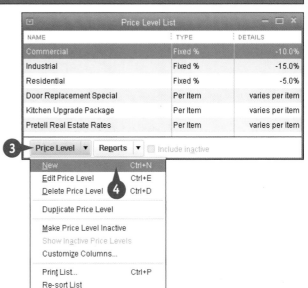

The Price Level List window appears.

3 Click **Price Level**.

4 Click **New**.

The New Price Level dialog box appears.

5 Type a name.

6 Click ▾ to select a price level type.

Note: This example uses Fixed %.

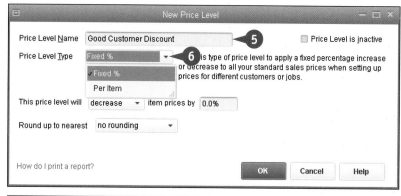

QuickBooks redisplays the New Price Level dialog box with options that you selected in step **6**.

7 Click ▾ to select **increase** or **decrease**.

8 Type a percentage.

9 Click **OK**.

The new price level appears in the Price Level List window.

What reports are available on the Reports menu in the Price Level List window?

You can print an Item Price List that shows all the selling prices you established when you created items; see Chapter 3 for details on creating items. Print this report by clicking **Reports** in the Price Level List window and clicking **Item Price List**. You also can print the Selected Price Level Report. Click a price level in the Price Level List window to select it. Then click **Reports** and click **Selected Price Level Report**. The report displays item prices based on the price level you selected.

Create Shipping Methods

Shipping methods represent the different ways you ship products to your customers, and you can select a shipping method as you fill out product-based sales transaction windows, as described in Chapter 8. QuickBooks automatically populates the Ship Via List with common shipping methods, but you might need to add a shipping method for your own trucks or a local delivery service.

QuickBooks also supports shipping using accounts you have previously established with shippers such as FedEX, UPS, and USPS, but covering these services is beyond the scope of this book; see QuickBooks Help for details.

Create Shipping Methods

1. Complete the steps in the section "Create Profile Information," selecting **Ship Via List** in step **3**.

2. Type a name for the shipping method.

3. Click **OK**.

A. The new shipping method appears in the Ship Via List window.

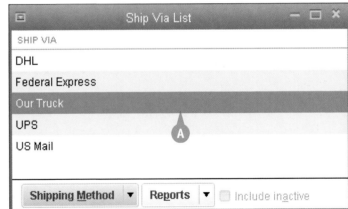

Create a New Customer Record

You can create customers in QuickBooks for any person or organization with whom you plan to do business on a long-term basis. In particular, you must create customers for those entities to whom you plan to send invoices and statements. When you create a customer, QuickBooks saves all the pertinent information about the customer that you need to prepare and mail or email invoices and statements.

You enter the customer's company name and general background information. You also establish payment settings, sales tax settings, and any additional information or job-related information.

Create a New Customer Record

1 Click **Customers** to open the Customer Center.

2 Click **New Customer & Job**.

3 Click **New Customer**.

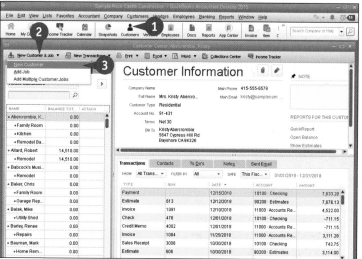

The New Customer dialog box appears.

4 Type a name for the new customer.

5 Type a company name.

6 Type first and last names, address information, and contact information.

Ⓐ You can click **Copy** to copy the invoice address to the shipping address; click **OK** in the dialog box that QuickBooks displays.

7 Click **Payment Settings**.

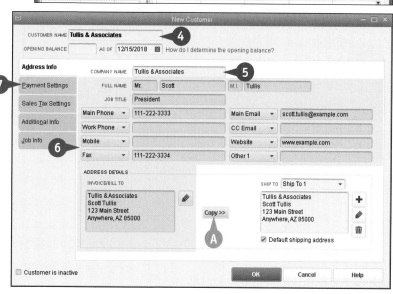

continued ▶

On the Additional Info tab, you can select a customer type and a sales rep. You also can supply information for custom fields; to define custom fields, see Chapter 14.

You use the Job Info tab while creating a customer if you plan to perform only one job for the customer. If you plan to perform several jobs for the customer, set up jobs separately. In transaction windows and on some reports, QuickBooks separates the job name from the customer name using a colon.

Create a New Customer Record (continued)

Ⓐ You can type an account number, credit limit, and select a price level.

⑧ Click ▾ to select payment terms.

Ⓑ You can click ▾ to select Email or Mail as a contact method.

⑨ Click ▾ and select a preferred payment method.

Ⓒ If appropriate, supply credit card information.

If you type a credit card number, press **Tab** and QuickBooks fills in other information from the Address Info tab.

⑩ Click **Sales Tax Settings**.

⑪ Click ▾ to select a sales tax code.

⑫ Click ▾ to select a sales tax item.

Ⓓ If appropriate, type a resale number.

⑬ Click **Additional Info**.

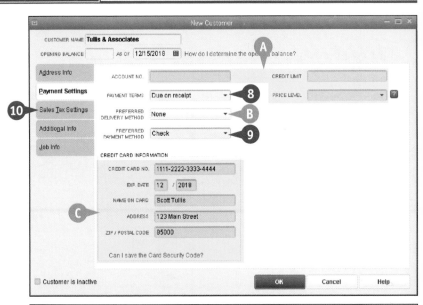

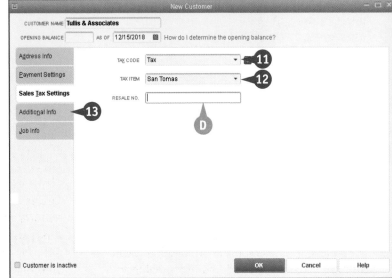

14 Click ▾ to select a customer type.

15 Click ▾ to select a sales rep.

E You can fill in custom field information.

Note: See Chapter 14 for details on creating custom fields.

16 Click **Job Info**.

Note: Fill in this tab if you plan to perform only one job for this customer.

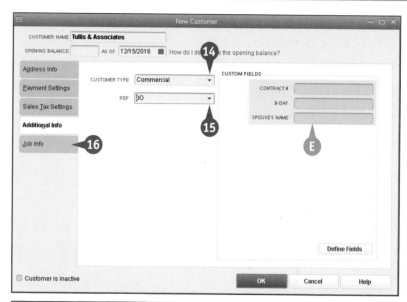

17 Type a job description.

18 Click ▾ to select a job type.

19 Click ▾ to select a job status.

20 Click ▦ for these options to select start, projected end, and end dates as appropriate.

21 Click **OK**; the new customer appears in the Active Customers list in the Customer Center list.

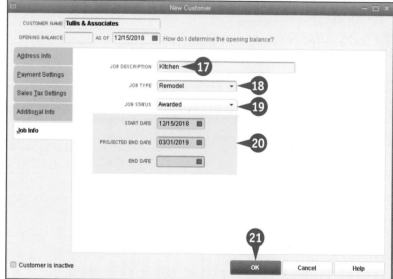

Should I enter my customer's currently outstanding balance as the Opening Balance?

No. Instead, enter each outstanding invoice using the Create Invoices window. To create beginning balance invoices, create an item called Beginning Balance, making it a non-taxable Other Charge item. Then, enter invoices; assign the total outstanding invoice amount using the item called Beginning Balance.

If I plan to perform multiple jobs for a customer, how do I set them up?

First, set up the customer. Then, in the Customer Center, select the customer for whom you want to create a job, click the **New Customer & Job** button, and then click **Add Job**. Type a Job Name and complete the Job Info tab and the Payment Settings tab.

Create Vendor Types

You create vendor types to help you organize vendors by whatever means makes most sense in your business. For example, suppose that you regularly obtain price quotes for materials and services from your suppliers. You can create a vendor type called "Supplier" and assign it to vendors who are suppliers. When you need to obtain quotes, you can print a Contact List of only those vendors who are suppliers.

After you create vendor types, you can assign a vendor type to each vendor you create. See the section "Create a New Vendor Record" for more information.

Create Vendor Types

1 Complete the steps in the section "Create Profile Information," selecting **Vendor Type List** in step **3**.

2 Type a name for the vendor type.

Ⓐ You can click this option (☐ changes to ☑) to create a subtype of an existing vendor type and then click ▾ to select the existing vendor type.

3 Click **OK**.

Ⓑ The new vendor type appears in the Vendor Type List.

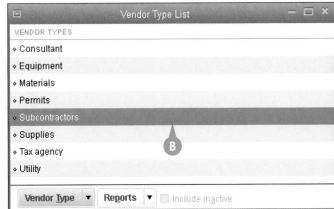

Create a New Vendor Record

Vendors are the companies from which you buy goods or services. In general, vendors fall into two categories. You buy goods or services from some vendors to make products that you sell to customers or to simply resell to customers. Other vendors supply you with goods and services such as telephone service, office space, and electricity that you need to run your business; these vendors are often referred to as *overhead vendors*.

Regardless of what you purchase from a vendor, you need to set up the vendor in QuickBooks. You supply contact, payment, tax, and account information.

Create a New Vendor Record

1 Click **Vendors** to open the Vendor Center.

2 Click **New Vendor**.

3 Click **New Vendor**.

The New Vendor dialog box appears.

4 Type a name for the new vendor.

5 Type a company name.

6 Type first and last names, address information, and contact information.

Ⓐ You can click here to copy the Billed From address to the Shipped From address; click **OK** in the dialog box that QuickBooks displays.

7 Click **Payment Settings**.

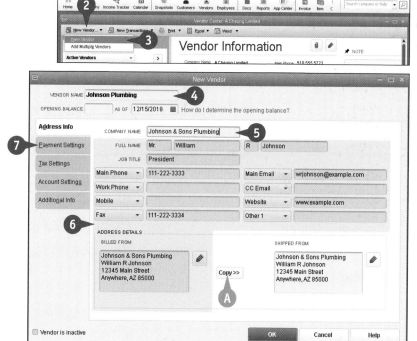

continued ▶

For payment settings, you can identify terms and your credit limit with the vendor. For tax settings, you identify if a vendor is a subcontractor and eligible for a Form 1099 and, if so, you supply a Tax ID number that QuickBooks prints on the Form 1099.

For account settings, you specify the accounts to which you most often assign bills from the vendor. And, the Additional Info tab gives you the option of assigning a vendor type and filling in custom field information. For details on creating custom fields, see Chapter 14.

Create a New Vendor Record (continued)

Ⓐ You can type an account number and a credit limit.

⑧ Click ▼ to select payment terms.

Ⓑ You can click ▼ to select a billing rate level.

⑨ Click **Tax Settings**.

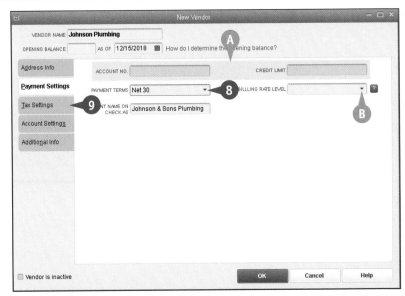

⑩ If you must produce a 1099 for the vendor, type a vendor tax ID number and click the check box (☐ changes to ☑).

⑪ Click **Account Settings**.

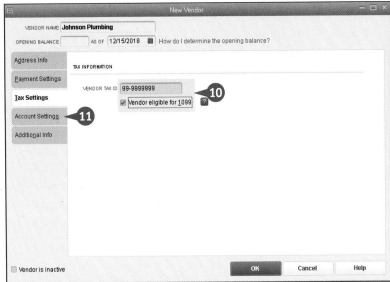

12 Click ▾ and select the account you use most often to record bills from the vendor.

13 Click **Additional Info**.

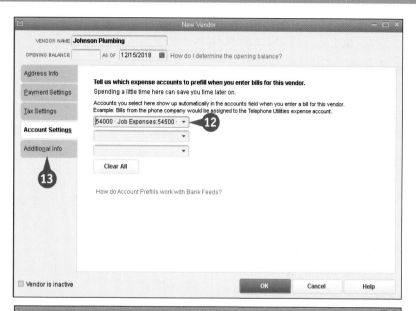

14 Click ▾ and select a vendor type.

C You can type custom field information here.

Note: See Chapter 14 for details on creating custom fields.

15 Click **OK**.

QuickBooks saves the vendor's information and displays the vendor's name in the Active Vendors list in the Vendor Center.

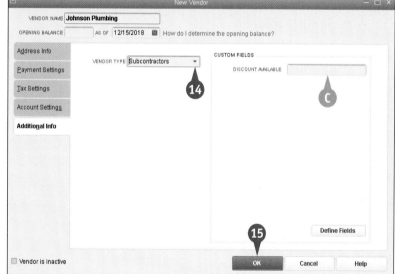

TIP

Should I enter my currently outstanding balance with a vendor as the Opening Balance?
No. Instead, you should enter each outstanding bill using the Enter Bills window, as described in Chapter 10. To create beginning balance bills, enter the one-line item on the bill for the total amount of the bill and assign the bill to the Beginning Bal Equity account. Make sure that you set the date for each outstanding bill correctly so that QuickBooks ages the bill properly.

Set Up Payroll Background Information

Before you start using payroll, you set up its features, including state or local items, schedules, and employee records. Accurate payroll reports hinge on a complete year's information. To minimize data entry, start your payroll January 1. If you start mid-year, plan to start on the nearest quarter: March 1, June 1, or September 1.

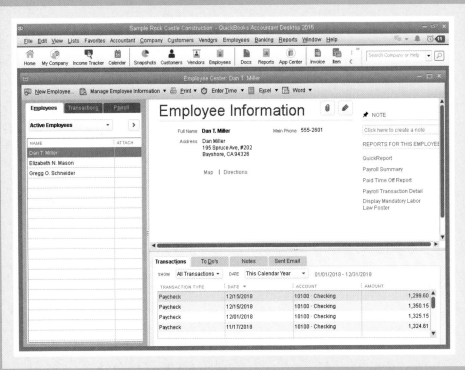

Set Up Payroll

To set up payroll, you must select a payroll service option, and then establish basic payroll-related information with the Payroll Setup wizard.

Your payroll service options are available at payroll.intuit.com. Most users select the fee-based Intuit Enhanced Payroll service, which enables you to prepare and print paychecks, federal payroll tax returns, W-2s, and 1099s from QuickBooks. After selecting a payroll service, QuickBooks establishes federal payroll tax items through the Payroll Setup wizard, which you learn about in this section. Later in the chapter, you see how to complete payroll setup.

Set Up Payroll

1 Click **Employees.**

2 Click **Payroll Setup.**

The QuickBooks Payroll Setup wizard starts.

3 On the first screen, click the **The company has never issued paychecks** option (◯ changes to ◉).

4 Click **Continue** in the lower right corner of the screen.

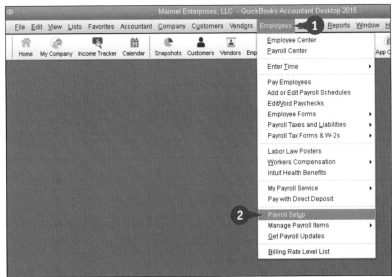

The Company Setup page appears.

5 Click the **Typical new employer setup** option (◯ changes to ◉).

6 Click **Finish Later.**

QuickBooks displays a message explaining that you can return to the QuickBooks Payroll Setup wizard interview at any time by clicking the **Employees** menu and then clicking **Payroll Setup.**

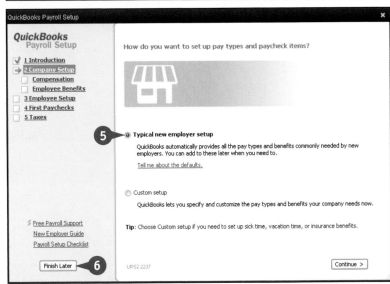

Create a Payroll Schedule

To pay a group of employees, you can create *payroll schedules* for each pay frequency that your company uses. After you define schedules, you can assign them to employees; see the section "Create an Employee Record" for details.

Each payroll schedule defines how often an employee group is paid, the next date on which paychecks are due, and the date on which you should prepare paychecks for the payroll schedule. QuickBooks uses this information to calculate future payroll dates and automatically adds typical payroll items for wages, additions, and deductions. See the section "Create a Payroll Item" for details.

Create a Payroll Schedule

1 Click **Employees**.

2 Click **Add or Edit Payroll Schedules**.

The Payroll Schedule List window appears.

3 Click **Payroll Schedule**.

4 Click **New**.

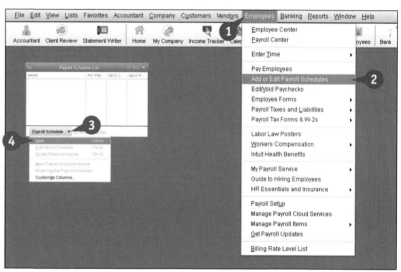

5 Type a name for the Payroll Schedule.

6 Click ▼ to select how often to pay employees.

7 Click 📅 to display a calendar and select a pay period end date.

8 Clicking 📅 displays a calendar for selecting a pay period date.

9 Click **OK**, and then **OK** again to dismiss a message telling you how to assign employees to the schedule.

You can repeat steps **3** to **9** for other payroll schedules.

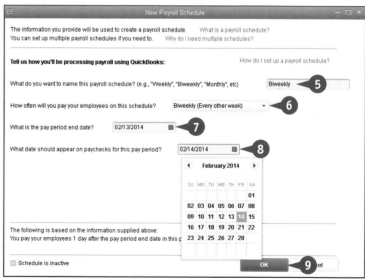

Create a Payroll Item

QuickBooks uses *payroll items* to describe elements on paychecks, and automatically sets up some of them for you: federal income tax, federal unemployment tax, Social Security, and Medicare, as well as typical wage, addition, and deduction payroll items. You set up payroll items for the various state and local taxes, deductions, and benefits your company uses. QuickBooks stores everything in the Payroll Item List.

The basic steps in this section show how to create any payroll item. Future sections focus on setting up state and local taxes.

Create a Payroll Item

① Click **Lists**.

② Click **Payroll Item List**.

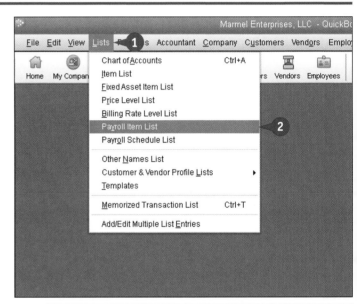

The Payroll Item List appears.

③ Click **Payroll Item**.

④ Click **New**.

The Add New Payroll Item
wizard appears.

5 Click the **EZ Setup** option
(◉ changes to ◉).

6 Click **Next**.

The Payroll Item Type screen
appears.

7 Click the **Custom Setup**
option (◉ changes to ◉).

8 Click **Next**.

Note: The selections you make on
subsequent Add New Payroll Item
wizard screens depend on the
type of item you want to create.

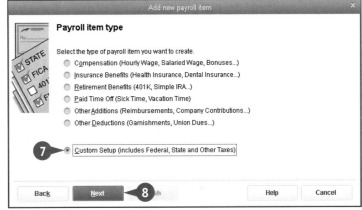

TIP

Should I set up employees before I set up payroll items?
You can, but setting up payroll items first means you then have all the information you need to set up
employees. For example, you can assign the correct benefits and deductions to employees if you create
those payroll items before creating employees. If you set up employees before setting up taxes, QuickBooks
automatically walks you through setting up taxes for each new state and locality as you assign it to an
employee, which can otherwise seem confusing.

Create a State or Local Tax Item

I f your state has an income, unemployment, or other tax, you create state tax payroll items to account for them. First, though, create a vendor to whom you pay the tax, and a liability account and an expense account in which to store the collected tax amount until you pay it. See Chapter 4 to create a vendor record and Chapter 2 to create accounts.

Remember to include the state-assigned identification number on the payroll tax item to ensure that it appears on your state remittance checks.

Create a State or Local Tax Item

Create a State Withholding Item

① Follow the steps in the section "Create a Payroll Item" to display the options for Custom Setup.

② Click the **State Tax** option (◯ changes to ◉) on the Payroll Item Type screen.

③ Click **Next**.

The State Tax screen appears.

④ Click ▾ and select a state.

⑤ Click the **State Withholding** option (◯ changes to ◉).

⑥ Click **Next**.

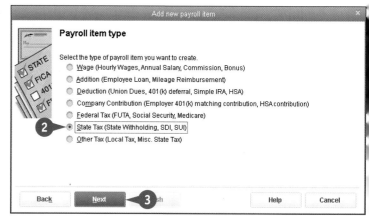

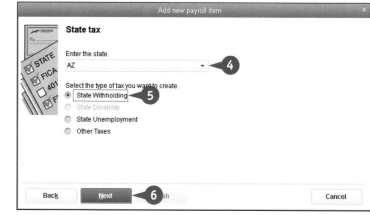

The Name Used in Paychecks
and Payroll Reports screen
appears.

Ⓐ QuickBooks suggests a name
that you can change if you
want.

7 Click **Next**.

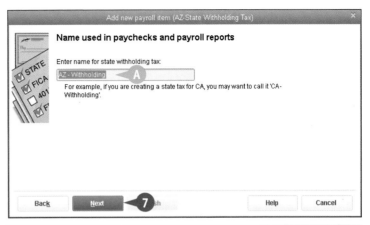

The Agency for Employee-
Paid Liability screen appears.

8 Click ▾ and select the name
of the vendor to whom you
pay the liability.

Ⓑ You can type the ID number
your state assigned to you.

9 Click ▾ and select your
payroll liability account.

10 Click **Next**.

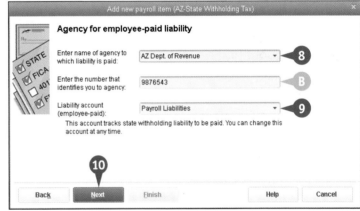

TIPS

**As I created my state withholding tax
item, why did the Pre-Tax Deductions
screen appear?**
If you set up payroll deductions before you
set up taxes, QuickBooks also displays the
Pre-Tax Deductions screen. Use this screen
to click each deduction that reduces gross
wages for the tax you are creating.

How do I know which state taxes to set up?
When you select a state, QuickBooks displays the only
options available to you. For example, Florida has no state
income tax or state disability tax, so those options are not
available. Florida does have an unemployment tax, so that
option is available. Similarly, California and New Jersey both
have state income tax, state disability tax, state
unemployment tax, and other taxes.

continued ▶

M ost states collect unemployment insurance from employers to pay unemployment compensation to eligible workers who lose their jobs. You set up unemployment payroll tax items for each state to which you pay state unemployment taxes.

Many states collect additional taxes from businesses on behalf of a municipality within the state or for other reasons imposed by state and local legislators. For example, Arizona collects a job training tax, similar to the California Employment Training tax. Michigan and Indiana both collect payroll taxes based on where employees work and reside.

Create a State or Local Tax Item (continued)

The Taxable Compensation screen appears, displaying the items most often subject to the tax you are creating.

⑪ Ensure that the selected items are subject to state withholding tax, deselecting any that are not (☑ changes to ☐).

⑫ Click **Finish**.

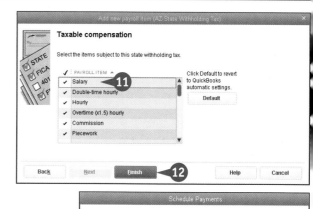

A message appears, explaining that you can set up a scheduled payment for this payroll tax item.

⑬ Click **OK** and the new state withholding tax item appears.

Create a State Unemployment Item

① Follow the steps in the section "Create a Payroll Item" to display the options for Custom Setup.

② Complete steps **2** to **7** in the subsection "Create a State Withholding Item." In step **5**, select **State Unemployment** and select your state.

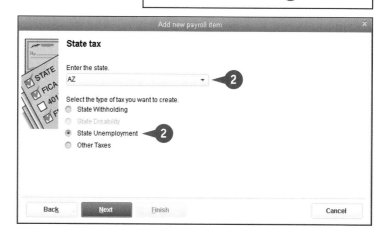

The Agency for Company-Paid Liability screen appears.

3 Click ▼ and select the name of the vendor to whom you pay the liability.

Ⓐ You can type the ID number your state assigned to you.

4 Click ▼ and select your payroll liability account.

5 Click ▼ and select your payroll expense account.

6 Click **Next**.

The Company Tax Rates screen appears.

7 As needed, change the rates QuickBooks suggests for any quarter.

8 Complete steps **11** to **13** in the subsection "Create a State Withholding Item."

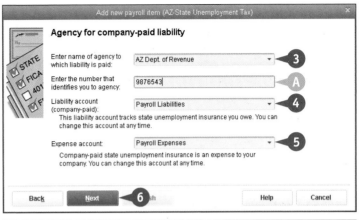

TIP

How do I create a local or other state tax item?

Follow the steps in the section "Create a Payroll Item" to display the options for Custom Setup. On the next screen, select **Other Taxes** and click **Next** to display the Other Tax screen. Then, click the drop-down list and select a tax to set up. Complete steps **7** to **10** in the subsection "Create a State Withholding Item," supplying both your payroll liability and expense accounts on the Agency for Company-Paid Liability screen. On the Company Tax Rate screen, click the drop-down list and select your company's rate. Finally, click **Next** and complete steps **11** to **12** in the subsection "Create a State Withholding Item."

Set Payroll & Employee Preferences

You can set preferences that affect the way QuickBooks handles certain payroll issues. The powerful Payroll & Employee preference enables you to identify and save the payroll items most commonly assigned to employees, which saves time as you create new employees. You also can establish the most common rates for those items. QuickBooks assigns these default payroll items and their settings to each new employee that you create.

Set Payroll & Employee Preferences

① Click **Edit**.

② Click **Preferences**.

The Preferences dialog box appears.

③ Click **Payroll & Employees**.

④ Click the **Company Preferences** tab.

⑤ Click an option (⊙ changes to ⦿) to display employees by first or last name.

Note: If you intend to track workers' compensation, click the **Workers Compensation** button, click **Track Workers Comp**, and click **OK.**

⑥ Click **Employee Defaults**.

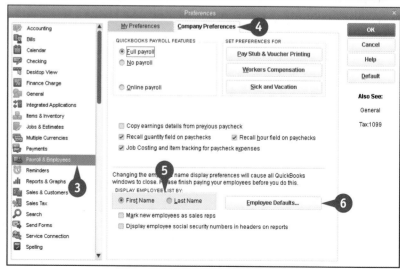

The Employee Defaults window appears.

7 Click ▾ to select the most commonly used payroll schedule or pay period.

8 Click here to select commonly used wage payroll items.

9 Click this area to select commonly used additions, deductions, and company contributions.

10 Click these buttons to set up defaults for taxes and sick and vacation leave.

11 Click **OK**.

The Preferences dialog box reappears.

12 Click **Pay Stub & Voucher Printing**.

The Payroll Printing Preferences dialog box appears.

13 Click any check boxes (☑ changes to ☐) to avoid printing elements on paycheck vouchers or paystubs.

14 Click **OK** twice to save your choices.

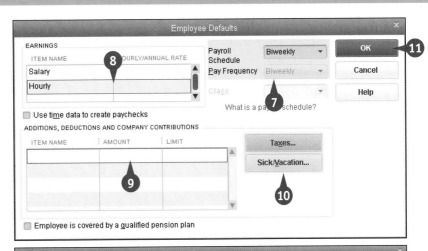

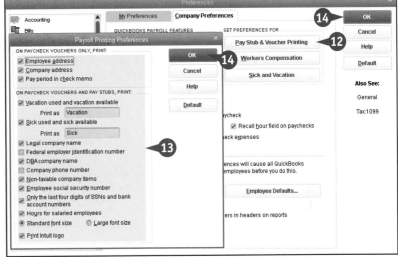

TIPS

What does the Job Costing and Item Tracking for Paycheck Expenses option do?

This option tracks payroll costs by job, class — if you use class tracking — or service item. QuickBooks prorates company-paid taxes to jobs and service items based on how you allocate pay between wage items. You can also prorate payroll item additions or company contributions on employee paychecks based on your allocation.

What does the Mark New Employees as Sales Reps option do?

It automatically creates sales reps whenever you create an employee. You then can assign the sales reps to customers and invoices to track sales by rep. To create sales rep records, see Chapter 4.

Create an Employee Record

You are ready to create new employees after you set payroll options and create necessary payroll items.

The New Employee dialog box contains several sets of payroll information including: personal, address and contact, payroll, employment, and, if you enabled the Workers Compensation feature, workers' compensation information. Most of the information you supply as you create an employee record appears on paychecks and reports, helping you quickly and easily complete everyday payroll tasks.

Create an Employee Record

1 Click **Employees**.

The Employee Center appears.

2 Click **New Employee**.

The Personal tab of the New Employee window appears.

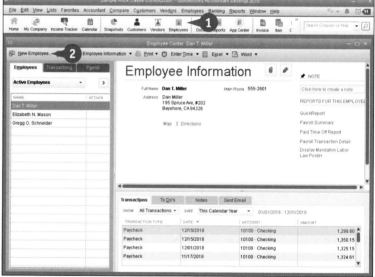

3 Type the employee's name here.

A QuickBooks fills in this box.

4 Type the Social Security number.

5 Select the employee's gender and date of birth, marital status, U.S. citizen status, and, optionally, ethnicity.

B You can supply disability, I-9 Form, and military status information.

6 Click the **Address & Contact** tab.

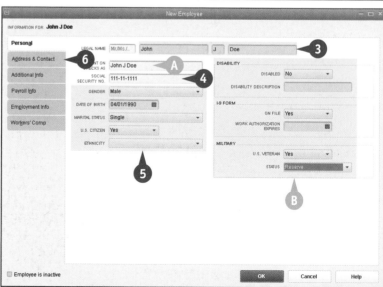

7 Type the employee's address information here.

8 Type phone numbers here.

9 Type email and other contact information here.

C You can supply emergency contact information here.

10 Click the **Additional Info** tab.

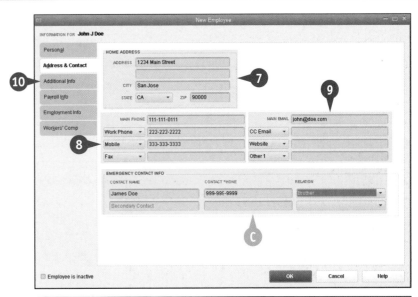

11 Fill in the employee's ID number.

D You can fill in any custom field information here.

Note: See Chapter 2 for details on custom fields.

12 Click the **Payroll Info** tab.

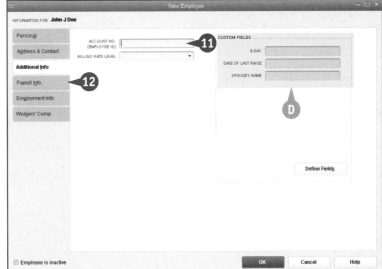

continued ▶

TIPS

If I start using payroll on March 1, how do I enter payroll information since January 1?
Use historical payroll information as practice for entering upcoming payrolls. Chapter 6 shows how to enter a payroll; for historical payrolls, make one change: Select the **Assign Check Numbers to Handwritten Checks** option (☐ changes to ◉) in the Review and Create Paychecks dialog box and enter the original check number.

What does the Use Time Data to Create Paychecks option do?
Clicking this option (☐ changes to ☑), found on the Payroll Info tab below the Earnings section, prefills the employee's paychecks either with data entered on the weekly timesheet or with individual time entries. For more information, see Chapter 7.

Create an Employee Record (continued)

On the Payroll Info tab, you identify the employee's pay period, add or delete payroll items as necessary, and fill in rates for wage, addition, deduction, and company contribution payroll items applicable to the employee record you are creating. From this tab, you also can assign taxes to the employee and access tax, sick, and vacation leave settings for the employee.

Create an Employee Record (continued)

13 Click ▼ and select a payroll schedule.

14 Click to select payroll earnings items that apply to the new employee.

15 Type an annual salary amount or an hourly rate here.

16 Click to select additions, deductions, and company contributions and type pay period amounts.

17 Click **Taxes**.

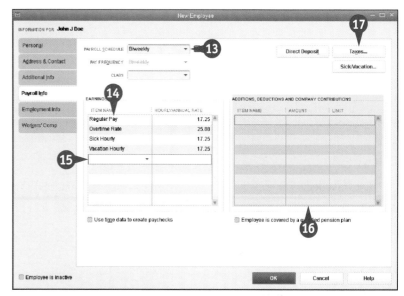

The Federal tab of the Taxes dialog box appears.

Ⓐ You can click ▼ to select a new filing status.

Ⓑ You can type numbers for allowances and extra withholding here.

Ⓒ You can click these options to change the taxes to which an employee is subject.

18 Click the **State** tab.

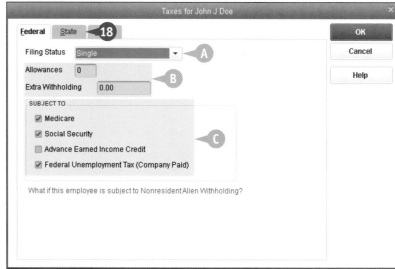

19 Click ▾ to select the employee's work state.

20 Click ▾ to select the employee's state for withholding purposes.

ⓓ You can supply state withholding status, amounts, and allowances here.

21 Click the **Other** tab.

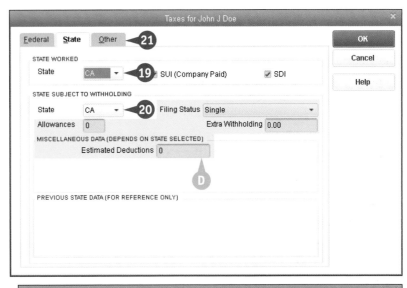

The Other tab appears.

22 Click here and click ▾ to add any other state and local taxes needed.

23 Click **OK**.

The Payroll Info tab of the New Employee dialog box reappears.

24 Click the **Sick/Vacation** button.

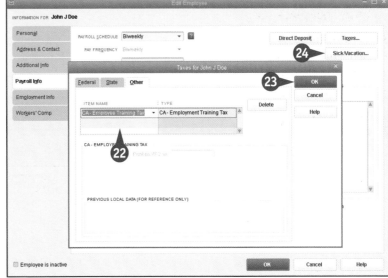

TIPS

How do I enter amounts for commission wage items and deductions?

You enter it as a percentage, making sure that you type a percent sign (%) so QuickBooks treats it as a percentage. For deductions, entering positive or negative numbers makes no difference; QuickBooks automatically subtracts them.

Why must I click the Taxes button if I already set up state and local tax payroll items?

To calculate payroll accurately, you must assign the correct payroll tax items to each employee, and QuickBooks monitors whether you review tax settings for each employee. If you do not review the settings and you try to save the employee, QuickBooks prompts you to review the tax settings.

continued ▶

You can set vacation and sick leave options for the employee. For both, you enter the hours available as of the date you set up the employee, the hours used in the current year, how much and how often each type of leave accrues, and the maximum number of hours for each type of leave. You also can specify whether unused leave rolls over to a new year.

The Employment Info tab stores the employee's hire date, termination date, and the employee's type, as described in the Tips section.

Create an Employee Record (continued)

The Sick and Vacation dialog box appears.

25 Type sick hours available and used here.

26 Set sick leave accrual options here.

27 Type vacation hours available and used here.

28 Set vacation leave accrual options here.

29 Click **OK**.

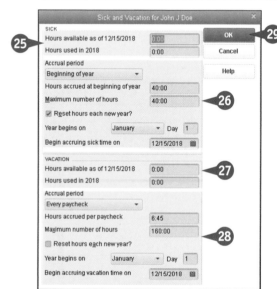

The New Employee dialog box reappears.

30 Click the **Employment Info** tab.

31 Fill in employment date information here.

32 Fill in employment details in this area.

33 Fill in job details here.

34 Click the **Workers' Comp** tab.

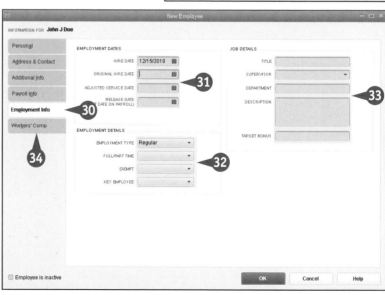

35 Click ⏷ to select a workers' compensation code.

Note: For details on creating workers' compensation codes, see the section "Set Up Workers' Compensation."

36 Click **OK**.

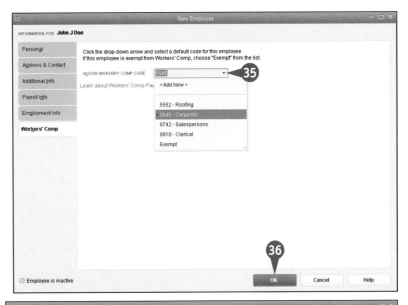

A The new employee appears in the Employees list.

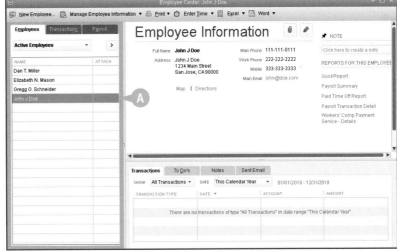

What do the employee types on the Employment Info tab mean?

Regular employees perform services that you control. You have officers if you are incorporated. IRS Publication 15, Circular E defines statutory employees very specifically; read this document for information on all employee types. If you are not certain of an employee's type, check with your accountant.

How should I set up business owners?

Use the Other Names list unless the owners already appear in your Employees list; then, on the Employment Info tab, designate them as owners. Because of tax laws, QuickBooks does not allow you to pay owners or partners through payroll. Instead, you use the Write Checks window, as described in Chapter 10.

Set Up Workers' Compensation

You can set up payroll to track and accrue your workers' compensation insurance liability. *Workers' compensation* is a payment that companies make, usually to insurance companies, to provide benefits to workers injured on the job.

The Workers' Compensation Setup wizard assigns default workers' compensation codes to employees, decides whether to exclude overtime premiums from workers' compensation premium calculations, and enters an experience modification factor, if you have one. The wizard requires you to first set up your workers' compensation insurance carrier as a vendor; see Chapter 4.

Set Up Workers' Compensation

Note: To turn on the Workers Compensation feature, see the section "Set Payroll & Employee Preferences."

1 Click **Employees**.

2 Click **Workers Compensation**.

3 Click **Manually Track Existing Workers' Comp Policy**.

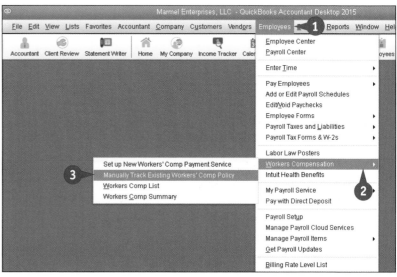

The Workers Compensation Setup wizard begins.

4 Click **Next** on the Welcome screen.

The next wizard screen appears.

5 Click ▼ to select your Workers Comp insurance carrier.

Ⓐ You can type your account number here.

6 Click **Next**.

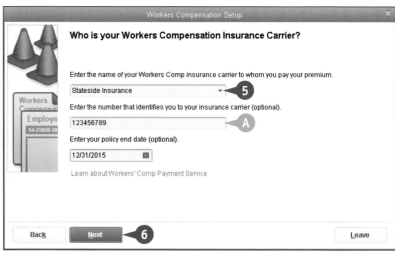

The next wizard screen appears.

7 Click ▾ and select a workers comp code.

B If the code you need does not appear, click **Add New**, type the code number, description, and rate per $100.00 of gross wages, click 🗓 to select the starting date for the rate, and click **OK**.

8 Repeat step **7** to add more codes and assign a code to each employee.

9 Click **Next**.

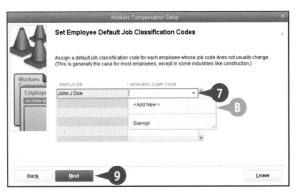

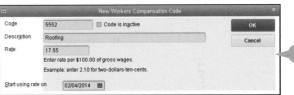

The next wizard screen appears.

10 Click an Experience Modification Factor option (◯ changes to ◉).

C If you click **Yes**, type a factor here as a whole number, which QuickBooks converts to a percentage; then click 🗓 to select a starting date for the experience factor.

11 Click **Next**.

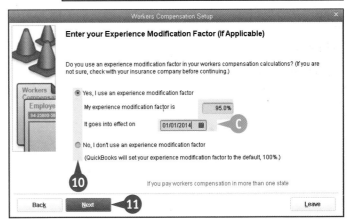

continued ▶

TIPS

What are new workers' comp codes and how do I add a new one after completing the wizard?
Each state establishes workers' compensation codes and rates based on the danger level of the work. Premiums are based on the amount of gross pay each employee receives. Click **Lists** and then click **Workers Comp List**. Next, click the **Workers Comp Code** button and click **New**. QuickBooks displays the same dialog box shown in these steps.

What is an experience factor?
A rate your insurance carrier assigns based on your company's workers' compensation claims and uses to calculate your premium. Typically, fewer claims receive lower rates. To change your experience factor, click the **Experience Modification** button in the Workers Comp Code List window.

Workers' compensation insurance liability accrues automatically as you pay your employees. To use the Workers' Compensation feature in QuickBooks effectively, you must set up workers' compensation before writing paychecks; otherwise, the workers' compensation reports and liability amount will not be accurate. So, plan to start using workers' compensation in QuickBooks on January 1.

Most companies pay an overtime premium when an employee works more than the specified number of hours in a pay period. But, in many states, you calculate your workers' compensation liability only on regular wages. Check the rules in your state before completing the wizard.

Set Up Workers' Compensation (continued)

The next wizard screen appears.

⑫ Click **Yes** or **No** to specify whether you pay overtime wages (⬤ changes to ⬤).

If you click **No**, you do not see the screen where you describe handling overtime premiums; for this example, click **Yes**.

⑬ Click **Next**.

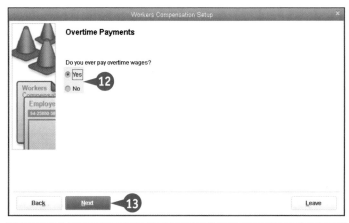

The next wizard screen appears.

⑭ Click an option to handle overtime premiums (⬤ changes to ⬤).

⑮ Click **Next**.

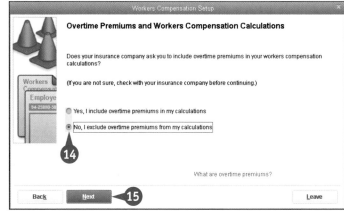

The next screen appears.

16 Type a name for the Workers'
Compensation payroll item.

17 Click **Next**.

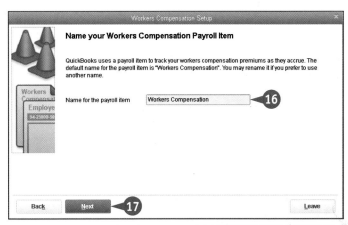

The last wizard screen
appears.

18 Review the summary
information.

Ⓐ You can deselect this option
if you do not want to view
help information on workers'
compensation (☑ changes
to ☐).

19 Click **Finish**.

QuickBooks saves the setup
information.

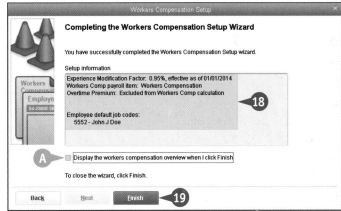

TIP

Can the QuickBooks Workers' Compensation feature handle workers' compensation calculations for more than one state?
Not entirely, but you can use a portion of the feature. Set up separate workers' compensation codes for the same job in different states. The Workers' Compensation feature supports only one experience factor at a time; if you have different experience factors in different states, set your experience factor to 100 percent. At this rate, QuickBooks does not adjust your workers' compensation liability, and you can accurately calculate it manually using workers' compensation reports.

CHAPTER 6

Handling Payroll and Tax Reporting

In this chapter, you learn to pay employees and payroll tax liabilities. You also learn to produce federal payroll tax returns such as the Federal Form 941 and to process W-2s, and you learn to summarize payroll data in Microsoft Excel.

Pay Employees

After you complete all the sections in Chapter 5, you can pay your employees in QuickBooks. You select a pay schedule, employees to pay, the paycheck date, and, if necessary, the pay period ending date.

To generate accurate payroll reports and W-2s, you must enter payroll information for the entire year. If you start payroll on any date other than January 1, you can enter historical payrolls using the steps in this section with just a few changes. See the Tip section for details.

Pay Employees

1 Click **Employees**.

2 Click the **Payroll** tab.

3 Select a payroll schedule.

4 Click **Start Scheduled Payroll**.

The Enter Payroll Information window appears.

A If necessary, change the Pay Period Ends date and the Check Date (📅).

B To avoid paying an employee, you can click in this column (☑ changes to ☐).

5 Enter or modify paycheck hours as needed.

6 Click **Open Paycheck Detail**.

The Preview Paycheck window appears.

C You can view the details that payroll calculated in these boxes.

D If necessary, you can make changes in these sections.

7 Click **Save & Next** to review the next paycheck.

E Click **Save & Close** if you do not want to review additional paychecks or when you finish reviewing paychecks.

The Enter Payroll Information window reappears.

8 Click **Continue**.

The Review and Create Paychecks window appears.

9 Review the information and make changes if needed.

F You can set paycheck options here.

G To make paycheck changes, click **Open Paycheck Detail** to redisplay the Preview Paycheck window.

10 Click **Create Paychecks**.

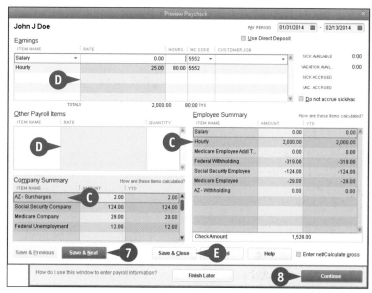

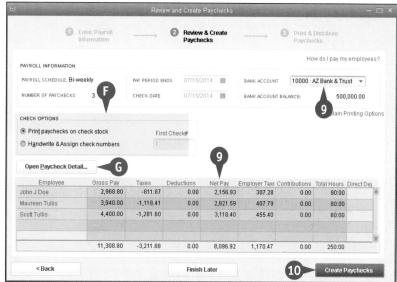

TIP

What changes should I make to these steps if I am entering historical payrolls?
In step 4, click **Start Unscheduled Payroll**. You might see a message about a paycheck already existing; click **Continue**. If your opening bank balance already includes these paychecks, set up a dummy bank account for these paychecks, and after you complete historical payroll, have your accountant help you zero out the dummy bank account. In the Review and Create Paychecks window, select the **Assign check numbers to handwritten checks** option (◎ changes to ◉) in the Paycheck Options section and assign the original check numbers.

continued ▶

Pay Employees (continued)

For historical payrolls or if you prepare handwritten paychecks, you can assign check numbers. Alternatively, you can let QuickBooks print paychecks for you; you can order check forms online from Intuit as well as outside sources. And, if you pay employees using direct deposit, QuickBooks can print pay stubs that you give to your direct deposit employees. If you print pay stubs, you can preview them before printing them. This section demonstrates printing payroll checks, as well as previewing pay stubs before printing them.

Pay Employees (continued)

The Confirmation and Next Steps window appears from which you can print paychecks or pay stubs.

11 For this example, click **Print Paychecks**.

The Select Paychecks to Print window appears.

A You can opt not to print a particular paycheck by clicking here (☑ changes to ☐).

B You can change the bank account and starting check number here.

C You can use these options (◉ changes to ◉) to display only paychecks, only direct deposit checks, or both.

12 Click **OK** to print the selected checks or click **Cancel**.

Note: For this example, click **Cancel** to redisplay the Confirmation and Next Steps window.

13 Click **Print Pay Stubs**.

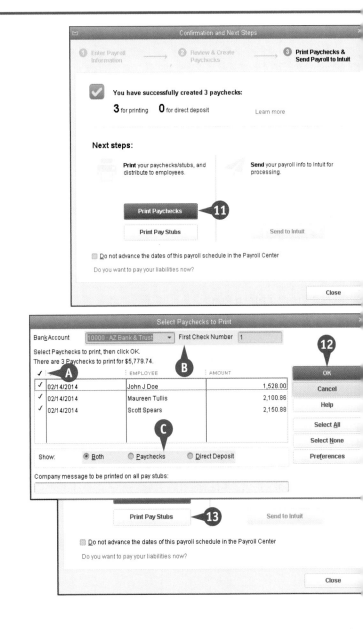

The Select Pay Stubs window appears.

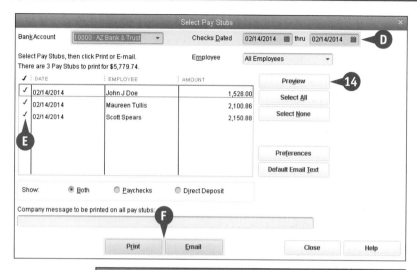

D You can change the bank account and selected check dates in these areas.

E You can opt not to print a particular pay stub by clicking here (☑ changes to ☐).

F You can use these buttons to print or email the stubs.

14 Click **Preview** to preview the pay stubs.

QuickBooks displays a preview of the check stub.

15 Click **Print** to print the selected stubs.

6 Click **Close** to redisplay the Select Pay Stubs window.

7 Click **Close** to redisplay the Confirmation and Next Steps window.

8 Click **Close** to finish your payroll and redisplay the Payroll Center.

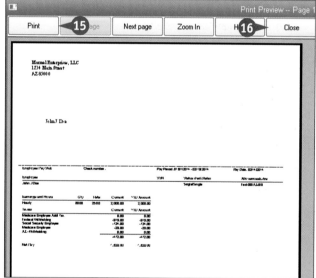

Print a Paycheck Stub

You are not limited to printing paycheck stubs when you complete a payroll; you can print them after the fact. This feature is particularly useful if you forget to print pay stubs after completing payroll, or if an employee loses a pay stub and wants a duplicate. Printing pay stubs is also useful if you use an outside payroll service and enter payroll information into QuickBooks to keep your company data accurate; in this case, you can produce a paycheck stub for each employee.

Print a Paycheck Stub

1 Click **Employees**.

2 Click the **Transactions** tab.

3 Double-click the transaction for which you want to print a stub.

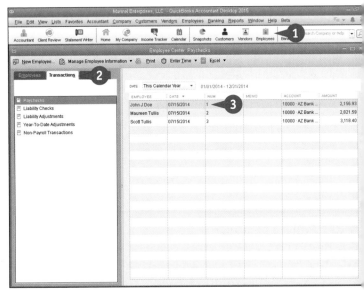

The transaction appears on-screen.

4 Click **File**.

5 Click **Print Forms**.

6 Click **Pay Stubs**.

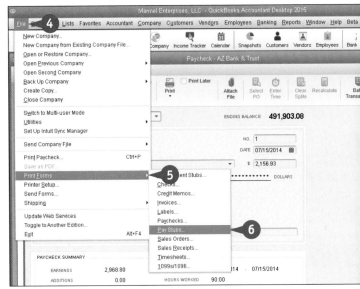

The Select Pay Stubs window appears, with all available pay stubs selected.

⑦ Click in this column to deselect a pay stub (☑ changes to ☐).

Ⓐ You can change the checks you view by changing the bank account and check dates here.

Ⓑ You can use these buttons to print or email the stubs.

⑧ Click **Preview** to preview the pay stubs.

QuickBooks displays a preview of the check stub.

Note: You can click the image to zoom in.

⑨ Click **Print** to print the selected stubs.

QuickBooks closes the Preview window and redisplays the transaction window you opened when you double-clicked in step **3**.

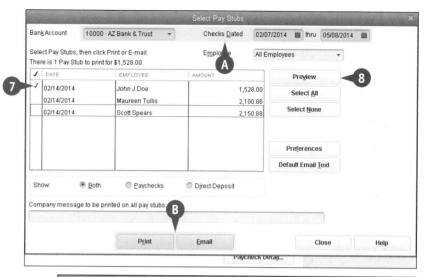

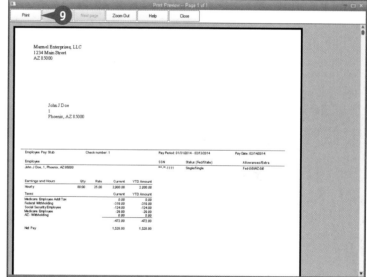

TIP

How can I control the information that appears when I print paycheck stubs?

While viewing the Select Paystubs dialog box, click **Preferences**. QuickBooks displays the Payroll Printing Preferences dialog box. On paystubs, QuickBooks usually prints employee and company addresses, the pay period, vacation and sick time used and available information, nontaxable company payroll items, and the employee's social security number. You can opt to print only the last four digits of social security numbers and bank account numbers, and you can opt to print hours for salaried employees.

Edit or Void Paychecks

If you create an incorrect paycheck, you need to either edit or void the paycheck. For example, after creating paychecks, suppose that you discover that an employee went home sick two hours early on the last day of the pay period. If you have not yet printed the paycheck, you can edit it. If you have printed the paycheck but it is still in your possession, you can void it. Remember to avoid changing net pay on paychecks already in an employee's possession.

Edit or Void Paychecks

Void a Paycheck

1 Click **Employees**.

2 Click **Edit/Void Paychecks**.

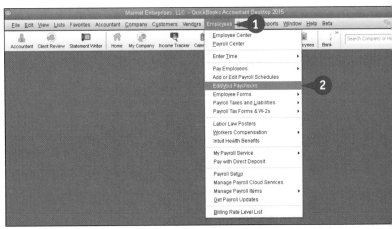

The Edit/Void Paychecks window appears.

3 Click the calendar (📅) to select a date range for paychecks.

4 Click ▾ and select a sorting method.

5 Click the check transaction to void.

6 Click **Void**.

QuickBooks voids the check and redisplays the Edit/Void Paychecks window.

Ⓐ VOID: appears in the Memo column next to the voided check, and a message for the selected check appears below the list of paychecks and indicates the check is void.

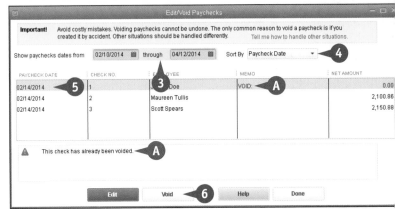

Edit a Paycheck

1 Complete steps **1** to **6** on the previous page, but for step **6**, click **Edit**.

The Paycheck window appears.

2 Click **Paycheck Detail**.

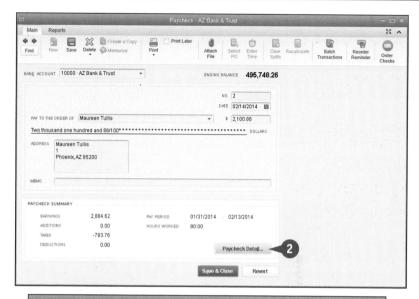

The Review Paycheck window appears.

3 Make changes.

Note: If you have already given the paycheck to the employee, be careful to not make changes that affect the check amount.

4 Click **OK** to save your edits.

5 Click **Save & Close** in the Paycheck window.

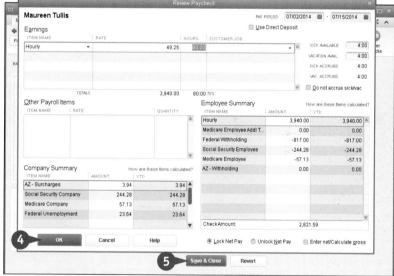

Print a Termination Check

When an employee leaves your company, you can print a final paycheck called a *termination check*. During the process, you supply the employee's release date, which is the last day that the employee works for you. Supplying a release date notifies QuickBooks to no longer display the employee's record when you pay employees.

You also have the option to set the employee's status as inactive so that he or she no longer appears in the Active Employees list.

Print a Termination Check

1 Click **Employees** in the icon bar.

2 Click **Employees**.

3 Double-click the employee whose check you want to write.

The Edit Employee dialog box appears.

4 Click the **Employment Info** tab.

5 Click 📅 to select a release date.

6 Click **OK**.

QuickBooks displays an information message explaining how QuickBooks uses the release date. Click **OK** to dismiss the message and **OK** to close the Edit Employee dialog box.

The Employee Center reappears.

7 Click the **Payroll** tab.

8 Click **Create Termination Check**.

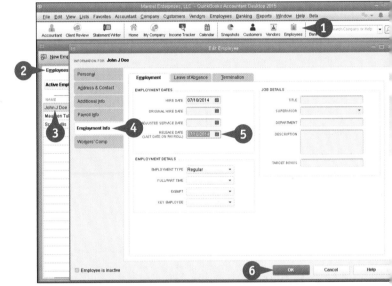

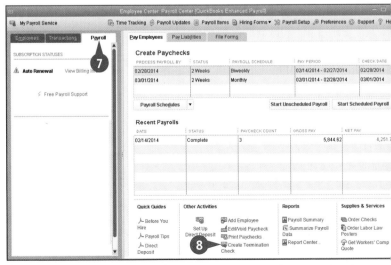

The Enter Payroll Information window appears.

9 Select the employee (☐ changes to ☑).

10 Click **Continue**.

The Make Employees Inactive dialog box appears.

11 Choose to keep the employee active or make him inactive; for this example, click **Make Inactive**.

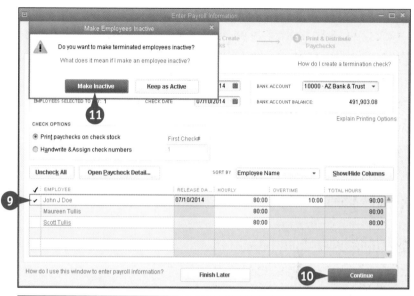

The Review and Create Paychecks window appears.

12 Double-check the termination check information.

A You can click **Open Paycheck Detail** to view the details of the paycheck and make changes if necessary.

13 Click **Create Paychecks**.

The Confirmation and Next Steps window appears; you can print the paycheck or a stub. See the section "Pay Employees" for details.

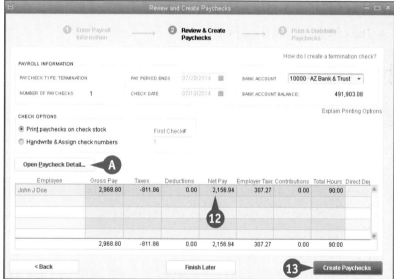

TIP

What is the difference between an active and an inactive employee?

Active employees appear in the Active Employees and the Released Employees lists in the Employee Center for six months after their release date. They do not, however, appear in the Scheduled Payroll or Unscheduled Payroll windows. Inactive employees no longer appear in any of the Enter Payroll Information windows or on the Active Employees list. They do appear on the All Employees list and the Released Employees list with an X beside their names. Regardless of status, employees who receive a paycheck during the year receive a W-2 form.

Pay Payroll Liabilities

You must deposit the federal taxes you withhold each payroll by a date specified by the IRS. Every business follows one of two tax deposit schedules: monthly or semiweekly, and you can identify your schedule using IRS Publication 15, Circular E. The way you pay state taxes varies by state.

To pay federal payroll taxes, you can use the *Electronic Federal Tax Payment System* (EFTPS), or you can take your liability check to your local bank and let them make the deposit for you.

Pay Payroll Liabilities

1 Click **Employees**.

2 Click the **Payroll** tab.

3 Click the **Pay Liabilities** tab.

4 Select one or more liabilities to pay.

Note: QuickBooks creates separate checks for each liability.

5 Click **View/Pay**.

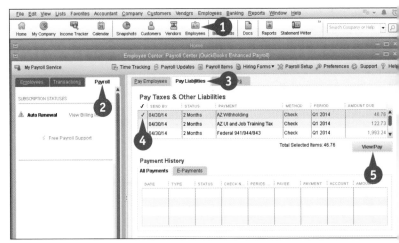

The Liability Payment window appears.

6 Click **Print** to print the check.

QuickBooks records the check and displays the Print Check dialog box where you can confirm or change the check number and then click **OK**.

QuickBooks walks you through the process of selecting a printer and settings to print the check.

7 Click **Save & Close** in the Liability Payment window when it reappears.

Review the Payroll Liability Payment Summary window that appears and click **Close**.

Adjust Payroll Liabilities

On occasion, you may need to adjust the amount in your Payroll Liabilities account as it appears on the Balance Sheet. For example, suppose that your state unemployment rate changes, but you forget about the change until you see the preprinted rate on your state unemployment tax return. As a result, during the quarter, QuickBooks calculates and accrues state unemployment at the wrong rate.

You enter the liability adjustment amount as a positive number to increase your liability or a negative number to decrease it.

Adjust Payroll Liabilities

1 Click **Employees**.

2 Click the **Payroll** tab.

3 Click the **Pay Liabilities** tab,

4 Click **Adjust Payroll Liabilities**.

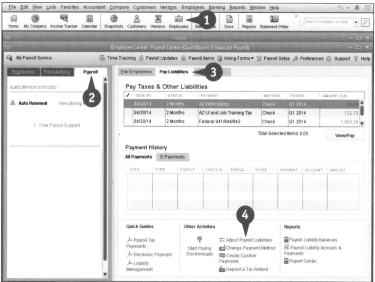

5 Click 🖩 to select transaction and adjustment dates.

6 Click an option to adjust the company's or an employee's balance (◯ changes to ◉).

7 Click here and select an item to adjust.

8 Type an amount and describe the reason for the adjustment here.

9 Click **Accounts Affected**.

10 Click **Affect liability and expense accounts** (◯ changes to ◉).

11 Click **OK** twice to save the adjustment.

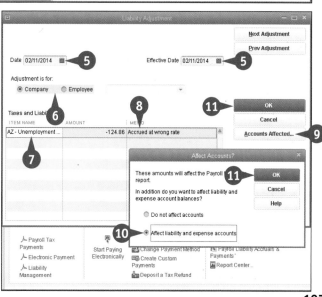

Create Federal Payroll Tax Returns

Every calendar quarter, you must file the *Federal Form 941 Payroll Tax Return* to report on employee wages, taxes withheld, and tax deposits made. QuickBooks enables you to complete the form and print it, producing a form that has been approved by the IRS. Both monthly and semiweekly depositors can prepare Federal Form 941 from QuickBooks.

To prepare Federal Form 941, you use a wizard that interviews you and shows you the information currently recorded for your company. You can and should correct any inaccuracies before filing the return.

Create Federal Payroll Tax Returns

1. Click **Employees**.

2. Click the **Payroll** tab.

3. Click the **File Forms** tab.

4. Click a tax return; for this example, choose Quarterly Form 941/Sch. B, Employer's Quarterly Federal Tax Return.

5. Click **Create Form**.

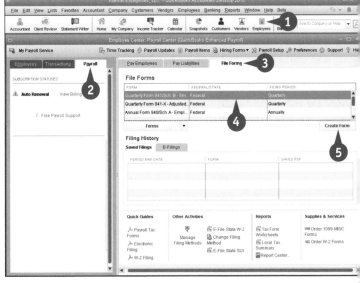

The File Form dialog box appears.

6. Adjust the Filing Period selections by clicking ▾ to select a quarter and then 📅 to select an end date.

7. Click **OK**.

The Payroll Tax Form window appears, prefilled with your company's information.

Review the questions, clicking in boxes to select them as appropriate.

Note: Scroll down to complete the interview page.

Click **Next**.

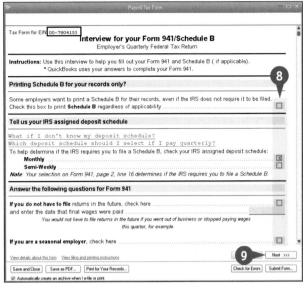

The first page of the Form 941 appears.

Review the information on the page and make changes if necessary.

Click **Next**.

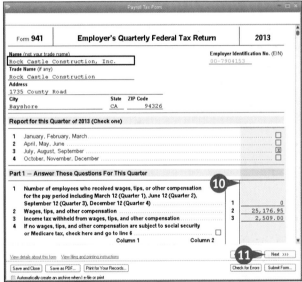

How does QuickBooks know how much I deposited as my payroll tax liability?

When you pay your liabilities using the steps in the section "Pay Payroll Liabilities," you supply a date through which you want to pay your liabilities. QuickBooks uses that date on liability checks in the quarter for which you prepare a Federal Form 941 to calculate amounts paid and amounts due.

How do I prepare a Federal Form 940?

You use the steps shown in this section, but in step 4, you choose Annual Form 940/Schedule A – Employer's Annual Federal Unemployment (FUTA) Tax Return.

continued ▶

Create Federal Payroll Tax Returns (continued)

If you are a monthly depositor, you do not need to complete Schedule B; instead, you verify total deposits for each of the three months in the quarter for which you are reporting on Form 941 and make changes as needed. If you are a semiweekly depositor, you complete Lines A, B, and C of Schedule B of Federal Form 941, reporting your payroll tax liability for each day of the first, second, and third months of the quarter and adjusting values as needed.

Create Federal Payroll Tax Returns (continued)

Parts 2 to 5 of the tax form appear.

12 Review the information on the page and make changes if necessary.

13 Click **Next**.

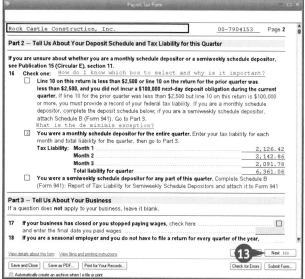

Note: If you owe money, the Payment Voucher page may appear; click **Next**.

The Filing and Printing Instructions page appears.

Note: Schedule B appears if you indicated on the Interview page that you need a Schedule B.

14 Click **Check for Errors**.

A If the form contains errors, they appear here. Click **Close Errors** and then click **Previous** until you find the errors and correct them.

B Click either of these buttons to print your copy of the tax form or save a PDF copy.

15 Click **Submit Form**.

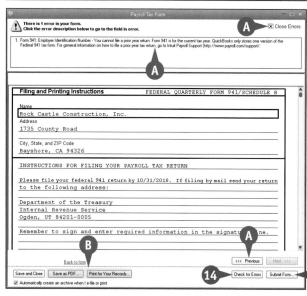

The Submit Form dialog box appears, where you can opt to print or efile the form in the Submit Form window.

⑤ For this example, click **Print**.

The Printing dialog box appears.

⑦ Select an item to print (⬤ changes to ⦿).

⑧ Click **Print**.

QuickBooks prints the form and redisplays the Payroll Tax Form window.

⑨ Click **Save and Close**.

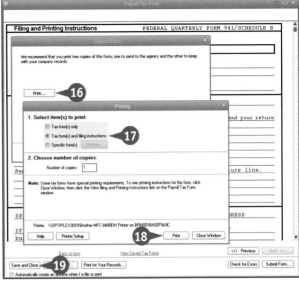

The Next Steps dialog box appears, telling you to update QuickBooks with any changes you made to the 941.

⑩ Click **OK** to dismiss it.

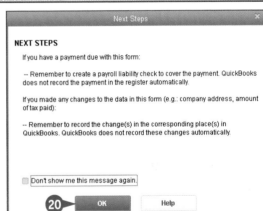

TIPS

What do I do if, on the tax form, net taxes and the total liability for the quarter are different by just a few cents?
Typically, these amounts do not match because of rounding errors. You do not need to take any action, however, because QuickBooks automatically records the difference for you on Line 7 of the tax form, the Fraction of Cents line.

Why is the State form option not available in the Select Form Type dialog box?
The State form option is available only when you subscribe to the Enhanced Payroll Service.

Process W-2s

At the beginning of each calendar year, your business must prepare W-2s that report wages, Social Security wages, Medicare wages, and federal, Social Security, and Medicare taxes withheld for each employee for the preceding calendar year. In some cases, the W-2 also reports certain state information. If you subscribe to the Enhanced Payroll service, you can use a wizard to print W-2s and the W-3 transmittal form using the payroll data in your company. You should not need to make changes as you complete the wizard.

Process W-2s

1 Complete steps **1** to **5** in the section "Create Federal Payroll Tax Returns," selecting Annual Form W-2/W-3 – Wage and Tax Statement/Transmittal in step **4**.

The File Form dialog box appears.

2 As needed, adjust the Filing Period selections.

3 Click **OK**.

The Select Employees for Form W-2/W-3 window appears.

4 Review the selected employees and click the check box to deselect employees as needed (☑ changes to ☐).

5 Click **Review/Edit**.

The Payroll Tax Form window appears, prefilled with your company's information.

⑥ Review the instructions, scrolling down to complete the interview page.

⑦ Click **Next**.

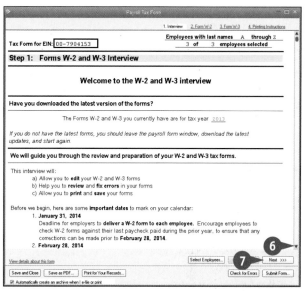

The next page of the Forms W-2 and W-3 Interview appears.

⑧ Review the information, scrolling down and making changes if necessary.

⑨ Click **Next**.

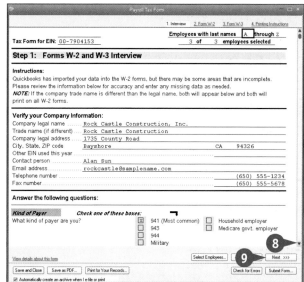

TIP

Can I change any field on the W-2?

You can change any field containing information. To change information in some fields, such as Boxes B to F, you must close the W-2 wizard and make the changes in your QuickBooks company, because the wizard collects the information from your company information. To change the information in Boxes B and C, use the Company Information window, which you open by clicking **Company** and then **Company Information**. To change information in Boxes D, E, and F, open the employee's record and make the changes.

continued ▶

Process W-2s (continued)

When you use the wizard, you select employees for whom you want to print W-2s, and then you review the W-2s on-screen. You can use the Employee Earnings Summary to help you verify that the amounts on the W-2 are accurate; see Chapter 14 for details on printing reports.

Any changes you make as you use the W-2 wizard do not affect the employee's payroll data or paychecks in your company. If you have questions about if or how to report particular benefits, talk to your accountant.

Process W-2s (continued)

The Form W-2 Worksheet page for the first employee appears.

10 Review the information, scrolling down and making changes if necessary.

11 Repeat steps **9** to **10** for each employee.

12 Click **Next**.

The step 2 page of the interview appears, displaying summary information for your employees.

13 Review the information, scrolling down and making changes if needed.

14 Click **Next**.

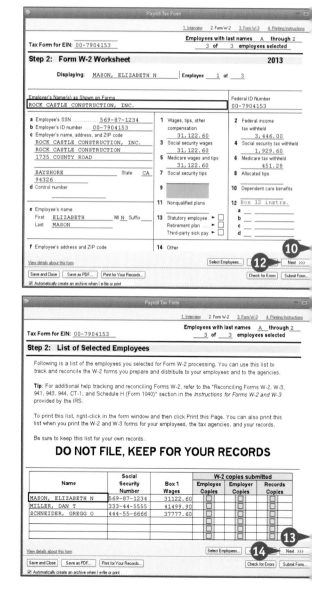

The W-3 Transmittal form appears.

⑤ Review the information, scrolling down and making changes if needed.

⑥ Click **Next**.

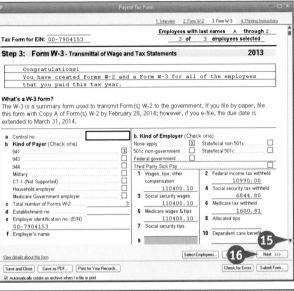

The Filing and Printing Instructions page appears.

⑦ Review the information.

⑧ Click **Submit Form**.

⑨ Complete steps **16** to **18** in the section "Create Federal Payroll Tax Returns."

⑩ Click **Close Window**.

The Payroll Tax Form window reappears.

⑪ Complete steps **19** to **20** in the section "Create Federal Payroll Tax Returns."

TIP

Are there different options for printing W-2s than for printing the Federal 941?
Yes. Because multiple copies of W-2s and W-3s are needed, QuickBooks gives you the option to print employee, employer, and government copies. In addition to selecting the items to print, you also can opt to print W-2s and W-3s on plain paper or on preprinted forms. If you print on preprinted forms, you need to deal with aligning the forms. Be aware that the forms that QuickBooks prints on blank paper are accepted by the federal government.

Summarize Payroll Data in Excel

Y ou can summarize QuickBooks payroll wage information in a preformatted Excel workbook. To use this feature, you must use Excel 97 or higher and you must set security in Excel to permit macros to run.

The workbook contains nine preformatted worksheets, and each contains different payroll information. Some worksheets are formatted using *PivotTables*, which are interactive tables that you can use to quickly and easily swap rows and columns to summarize data in different ways. You also can use PivotTables to filter the data to display only information that interests you.

Summarize Payroll Data in Excel

1. Click **Reports**.

2. Click **Employees & Payroll**.

3. Click **Summarize Payroll Data in Excel**.

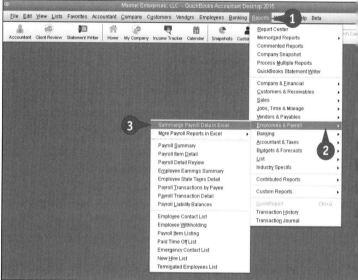

Note: You may see a screen explaining that macros have been disabled; click the yellow **Enable Content** button.

An Excel workbook opens and the QuickBooks Payroll Reports Workbook window appears.

4. Select a date range for data you want QuickBooks to use to summarize information.

5. Click **Get QuickBooks Data**.

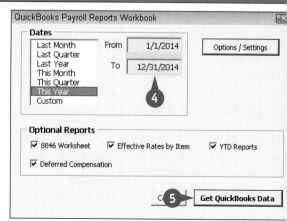

QuickBooks exports your company data to the workbook and displays a message explaining how to use the workbook.

6 Click **OK**.

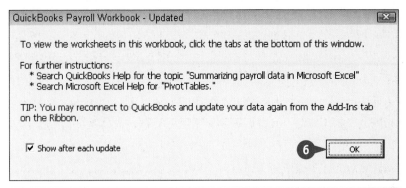

QuickBooks Payroll Workbook - Updated

To view the worksheets in this workbook, click the tabs at the bottom of this window.

For further instructions:
* Search QuickBooks Help for the topic "Summarizing payroll data in Microsoft Excel".
* Search Microsoft Excel Help for "PivotTables."

TIP: You may reconnect to QuickBooks and update your data again from the Add-Ins tab on the Ribbon.

☑ Show after each update

6 OK

A Excel displays the information on the YTD Summary 1 tab.

B You can click the various tabs to review the information on them.

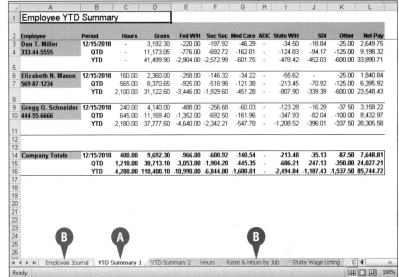

TIP

Do I have to start over if I want to look at a different range of payroll data?

No. You can click the **Add-Ins** tab on the Ribbon and then click **QB Payroll Summary Reports**. From the drop-down list that appears, click **Get QuickBooks Data**. Excel displays the QuickBooks Payroll Reports Workbook window shown in this section. After you supply the date range, click **Get QuickBooks Data,** and Excel imports your company data into the workbook again, replacing existing information. In earlier versions of Excel, the Get QuickBooks Data button is available on the toolbars at the top of the screen.

CHAPTER 7

Tracking Time and Mileage

If you sell services, time is money because you get paid based on the time you spend. If you sell products, time can be money if you want to increase productivity — and the first step to increasing productivity is tracking the time spent on various work activities. Take advantage of the time tracking features in QuickBooks.

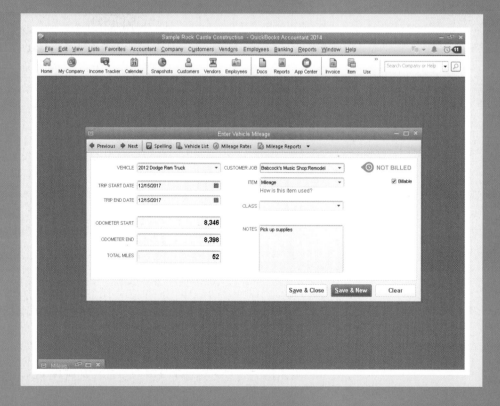

Set Time Tracking Preferences

You can track time that you, your employees, and your vendors work for customers by turning on the Time Tracking feature. You can bill back time spent to customers, and you can pay employees, vendors, owners, and partners based on the hours they enter.

You can create invoices for time entries using a list or from the Create Invoices window. You can use separate accounts to track your expenses and your customer's reimbursement. And you can set a default markup percentage and the account to which you want to assign the markup.

Set Time Tracking Preferences

1. Click **Edit**.

2. Click **Preferences**.

3. In the Preferences dialog box that appears, click **Time & Expenses**.

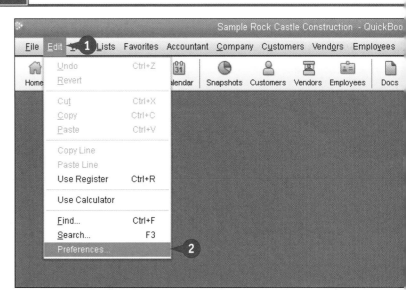

4. Click the **Company Preferences** tab.

5. Click **Yes** (◯ changes to ⦿).

6. Click ▼ to select the first day of the work week.

Note: QuickBooks adjusts your timesheets so that each weekly period begins with the day you select.

7. Click these options (◻ changes to ☑) to control invoicing behavior related to time entries.

8. Click **OK**.

    QuickBooks saves your preferences.

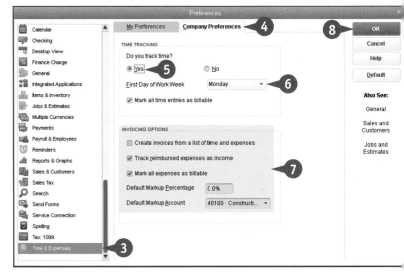

Record Time Single Activity

To record time spent by one person on one task for one customer on one date, you can use the Time/Enter Single Activity window.

You select a service item to identify the work performed, and QuickBooks records the income associated with the time entry to the income account associated with the selected service item. Any information you type in the Notes box can appear on a customer invoice. You can enter the duration of the task or use the stopwatch to time the activity. If you use the stopwatch, the window must remain open while the timer runs.

Record Time Single Activity

1 Click **Employees**.

2 Click **Enter Time**.

3 Click **Time/Enter Single Activity**.

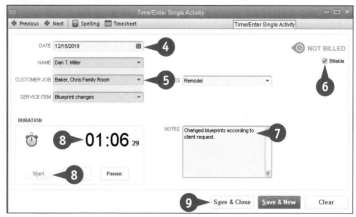

The Time/Enter Single Activity window appears.

4 Click 🗓 to select a date.

5 Click ▼ and select the name of the person recording the time, a Customer:Job, and a service item.

6 Click the check box (☐ changes to ☑) to make the activity billable.

7 Type a description of the work here.

8 Type a duration here, or click **Start** and let QuickBooks time the activity for you.

9 Click **Save & Close** to save the entry.

Record Time Weekly

Using the Weekly Timesheet window, you can record all entries for a particular employee, vendor, owner, or partner during a given week. Entries you record in the Time/Enter Single Activity window also appear in the Weekly Timesheet window; the window you use to enter time is a matter o personal preference. Use the Time/Enter Single Activity window if you need to use the stop watch.

To make data entry easy, you can print blank timesheets and distribute them. Because the form matches the Weekly Timesheet window, data entry is easy.

Record Time Weekly

1 Click **Employees**.

2 Click **Enter Time**.

3 Click **Use Weekly Timesheet**.

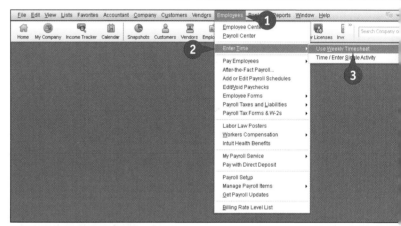

The Weekly Timesheet window appears.

4 Click ▾ and select the name of the person recording time.

5 Click 📅 to select the week for which you want to record time.

Ⓐ You can click **Next** or **Previous** to view the timesheet of the next or previous week.

The Set Date dialog box appears.

6 Click a date.

You can select any day in the week for which you want to record time.

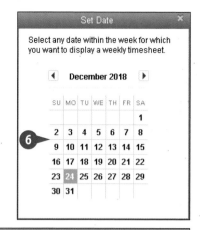

The Weekly Timesheet window for the week you selected appears.

7 Click ▼ to select a customer for whom work was performed.

8 Type here to describe the work done.

9 Click in a day column and type the time worked.

Ⓑ QuickBooks totals the time for the day.

10 Repeat steps **8** and **9** as needed, or steps **4** to **9** for another person.

11 Click **Save & Close** to save the entries.

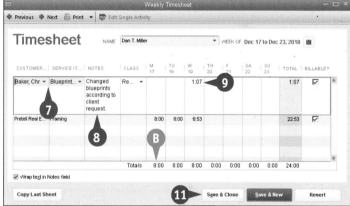

TIP

How can I print a blank timesheet form?

Perform steps **1** to **3** to display the Weekly Timesheet window. Then, click ▼ beside the **Print** button. QuickBooks displays a menu; click **Print Blank Timesheet**

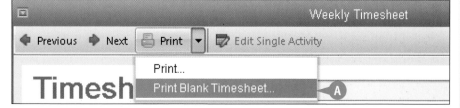

Ⓐ. The Print Timesheet window appears, where you can select a printer. Click **Print**.

Pay Employees for Recorded Time

I f you track the time that employees work, you can pay employees for the hours recorded on time entries, if you set up the employee so that QuickBooks knows to use time entries when calculating paychecks.

You still pay employees as described in Chapter 6. QuickBooks supplies the hours recorded on time entries for the pay period but calculates the employee's pay based on the rates stored in the employee' record. Hourly employees are paid for the hours recorded as time entries. Salaried employees are paid based on their salary, but QuickBooks allocates their salary based on the time entries.

Pay Employees for Recorded Time

1 Click **Employees**.

2 Click **Employee Center**.

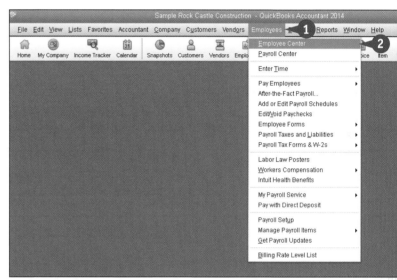

The Employee Center appears.

3 Right-click an employee.

4 Click **Edit Employee**.

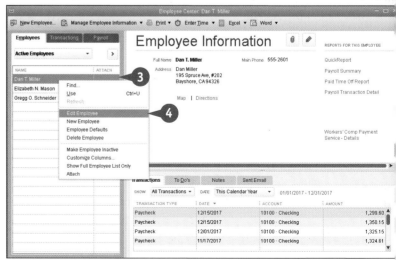

The Edit Employee window appears.

5 Click the **Payroll Info** tab.

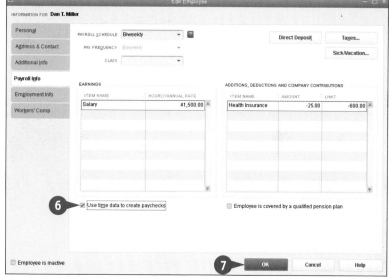

The Payroll Info tab appears.

6 Click **Use time data to create paychecks** (☐ changes to ☑).

7 Click **OK**.

QuickBooks saves the change.

Note: When you pay the employee, QuickBooks automatically displays hours recorded for the pay period.

I understand how paying employees based on time entries affects hourly employees, but how does it affect salaried employees?

When you pay based on time entries, QuickBooks prefills the hours worked on the paycheck. For salaried employees, QuickBooks allocates their salary to jobs based on the customer for whom they worked and the service item stored on the time entry. When you pay a salaried employee without using time entries, only one line appears for gross wages in the Earnings section of the paycheck. When you pay a salaried employee using time entries, multiple lines appear, but the pay remains the same.

Add Vehicles to the Vehicle List

You can use the *Vehicle Tracking feature* to track the mileage you use on your vehicles, assign a cost to the mileage and, if you want, bill your customers for the mileage. The mileage incurred on your vehicles may be tax deductible; you are permitted to deduct either the actual vehicle expenses or a standard mileage rate, but you cannot deduct both. With the vehicle mileage tracking information you collect in QuickBooks, your accountant can help you decide which deduction most benefits you.

After you add vehicles to the Vehicle List, vehicle drivers need to record the vehicles' odometer readings per trip.

Add Vehicles to the Vehicle List

1 Click **Lists**.

2 Click **Customer & Vendor Profile Lists**.

3 Click **Vehicle List**.

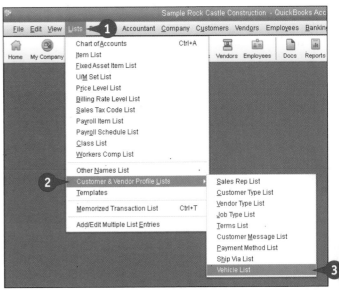

The Vehicle List window appears.

4 Click **Vehicle**.

5 Click **New**.

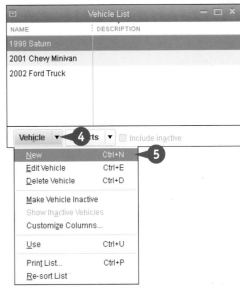

The New Vehicle dialog box appears.

6 Type the name of the vehicle here.

7 Type a description of the vehicle here.

8 Click **OK**.

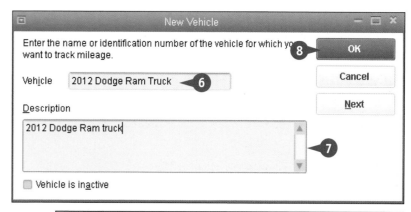

A QuickBooks saves the vehicle in the Vehicle List.

TIP

If my employees use their own cars for business purposes, should I set up their cars in the Vehicle List?
Yes, because your employees are entitled to mileage reimbursement for business use of a personal vehicle. Because the vehicles you set up in the list do not affect your company data, you can set up vehicles you do not own so that you can record and track mileage. At the end of the year, you can use vehicle mileage reports to help determine the amount of reimbursement, and include it on the employee's last paycheck of the year. See the section "Reimburse Employees for Mileage Expense" for details on creating the reimbursement.

Track Vehicle Mileage

To track mileage for a vehicle, you enter mileage slips. If you intend to bill your customers for mileage, set up a Service or an Other Charge item to establish an account and a billing rate for the mileage. See Chapter 3 for details on creating a Service item and an Other Charge item.

You can adjust the rates QuickBooks uses to calculate vehicle expenses. Typically, you use the IRS-issued rates for vehicle expense, which usually change at the beginning of each year. Check with your accountant for the latest IRS rates. You also can print reports for vehicle mileage.

Track Vehicle Mileage

Enter Vehicle Mileage

1 Click **Company**.

2 Click **Enter Vehicle Mileage**.

The Enter Vehicle Mileage window appears.

3 Click ▾ and select a vehicle.

4 Click 📅 to select trip starting and ending dates.

Ⓐ You can type starting and ending odometer values, and QuickBooks calculates total miles.

5 Type the miles traveled here.

6 Click the **Billable** option (☐ changes to ☑) to bill the mileage to a customer and then click ▾ to select the customer and the item.

Ⓑ You can type a description of the trip here.

7 Click **Save & Close**.

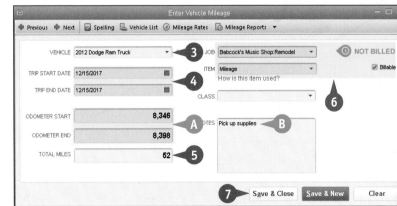

Change Mileage Rates

1 Perform steps **1** and **2** in the section "Enter Vehicle Mileage."

2 Click **Mileage Rates**.

3 In the Mileage Rates window, click 🔳 to select an effective date.

4 Type the mileage rate.

5 Click **Close**.

QuickBooks redisplays the Enter Vehicle Mileage window.

6 Click the Close button (❎) to close the window.

View Vehicle Mileage Summary

1 Perform steps **1** to **2** on the previous page.

2 Click **Mileage Reports**.

QuickBooks displays the Mileage by Vehicle Summary report.

C You can double-click any value to see the details behind it.

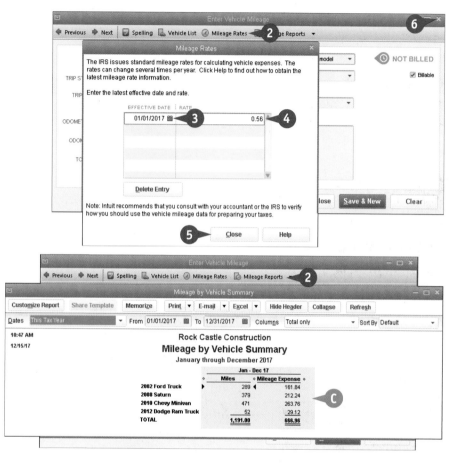

TIP

What is the difference between the mileage rates I enter from the Enter Vehicle Mileage window and the mileage rate I establish on the Service or Other Charge item?

The mileage rates you enter through the Enter Vehicle Mileage window help establish the cost of mileage that can be tax deductible. To correctly calculate tax-deductible values for mileage expenses, you should use the most current IRS-established rates when you establish mileage rates in the Mileage Rates window. QuickBooks uses the rate you establish on the Service or Other Charge item to assign a billing value to mileage, and that rate appears when you include mileage on an invoice to a customer.

Create Billing Rate Levels

You can use fixed or custom billing rate levels to override standard rates assigned to service items on customer invoices.

You create billing rate levels and then edit employees, vendors, or names on the Other Names List to assign billing rate levels. These people perform services and record associated time or expenses using the Weekly Timesheet window or the Time/Enter Single Activity window. Then, when you prepare an invoice for a customer that includes time or expenses (see the section "Invoice for Time, Expense, and Mileage Charges"), QuickBooks uses associated billing rate levels to bill based on who performed the work.

Create Billing Rate Levels

Open the Billing Rate Level List

① Click **Lists**.

② Click **Billing Rate Level List**.

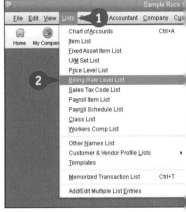

The Billing Rate Level List appears.

③ Click **Billing Rate Level**.

④ Click **New**.

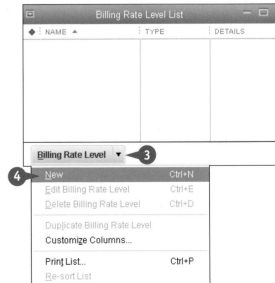

Create a Fixed Hourly Billing Rate Level

1 Complete steps **1** to **4** on the previous page, typing a name for the billing rate level here.

2 Click **Fixed Hourly Rate** (◯ changes to ◉).

3 Type an hourly rate.

4 Click **OK** to save the billing rate level. QuickBooks displays a reminder to assign the billing rate to appropriate people; click **OK**.

Create a Custom Billing Rate Level

1 Complete steps **1** to **4** in the subsection "Open the Billing Rate Level List," typing a name for the billing rate level here.

2 Click **Custom Hourly Rate Per Service Item** (◯ changes to ◉).

3 Click these columns to select service items the billing rate level should cover, and type a billing rate.

4 Click **OK** to save changes.

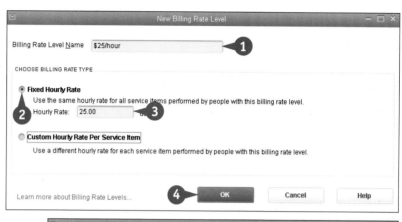

TIP

Can I set a billing rate level that adjusts a service item's price by a percentage?

1 Follow steps **1** to **4** in the subsection "Create a Custom Billing Rate Level," but click the **Adjust Selected Rates** button to display the Adjust Selected Prices/Rates window.

2 Type a percentage.

3 Click ▾ to adjust the price higher or lower than its standard or current custom rate.

4 Click **OK** to save your changes.

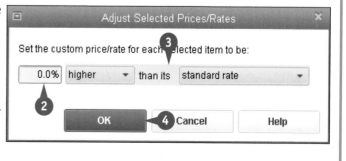

Invoice for Time, Expense, and Mileage Charges

You can invoice customers for time spent, mileage, or other expenses incurred while performing work. This section shows examples for mileage and expense entries, but you can include time and items using the same steps. The entries appear as line items on an invoice; if you have many entries, you can combine the entries onto one line. You can mark up the expenses by a percentage or a flat amount. Markups appear on invoices unless you choose to print one entry for all expenses.

After you place items on an invoice, you can change their descriptions.

Invoice for Time, Expense, and Mileage Charges

① Click **Customers**.

② Click **Create Invoices**.

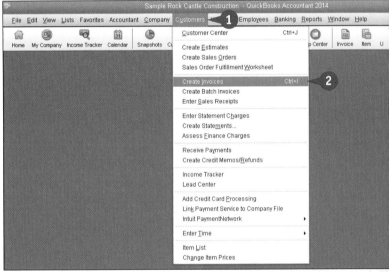

The Create Invoices window appears.

③ Click to select the Customer:Job.

A message appears, indicating billable costs exist.

④ Click **OK** to display the Choose Billable Time and Costs dialog box.

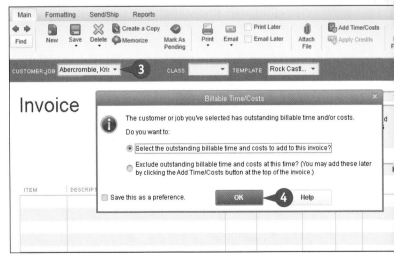

A QuickBooks organizes billable time and costs on these four tabs.

5 Click a tab, in this example, the **Mileage** tab; this example also demonstrates the Expenses tabs.

6 Click beside each entry you want to include on the invoice.

B You can click the check box (☐ changes to ☑) to combine the items onto one line on the invoice.

Note: On-screen, the items appear separately, but on the invoice, one entry appears.

7 Click the **Expenses** tab.

8 Click beside entries to include on the invoice.

C You can type a markup amount or percentage here.

D You can click the check box (☐ changes to ☑) to mark the expenses as taxable.

9 Repeat steps **5** and **6** as needed, clicking **OK** to save your changes.

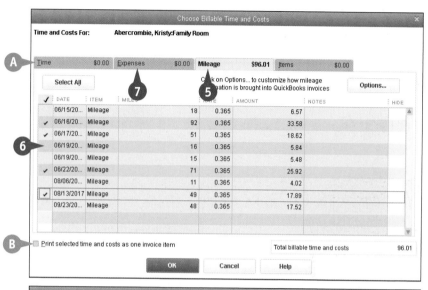

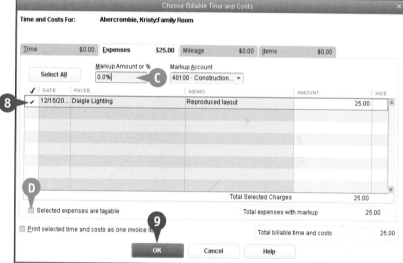

TIP

What happens if I click Options on the Mileage tab?
This dialog box appears. Here, you can print each entry separately on the invoice **A**, or you can print one line for all entries with the same service item **B**. If you print one line, the service item description prints on the invoice. If you include separate lines, you can print either the information stored in the Notes field of the entry, the service item description, or both.

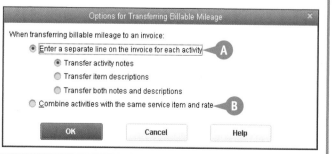

Reimburse Employees for Mileage Expense

Employees who use their personal vehicles for business are entitled to reimbursement for the mileage expense, and you can include the reimbursement when you pay the employee, or you can write a check using the Write Checks window and a non-taxable Service item. This section shows how to reimburse for mileage during payroll using a non-taxable payroll addition.

When you receive the employee's mileage report, you use the current year's IRS guidelines for the mileage reimbursement rate to calculate the reimbursement. The employee's mileage report should become an important part of the papers you keep as supporting documentation.

Reimburse Employees for Mileage Expense

1 Click **Employees**.

2 Click **Pay Employees**.

3 Click **Scheduled Payroll**.

The Employee Center: Payroll Center window appears, showing the Pay Employees tab; select a payroll schedule and click **Start Scheduled Payroll**.

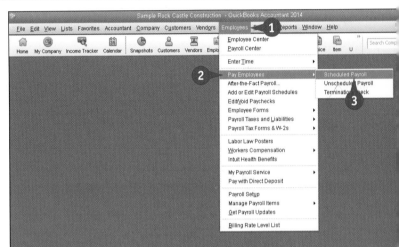

The Enter Payroll Information window appears.

4 Click ▼ to select a bank account.

5 Click this option to mark checks for printing (◉ changes to ◉).

6 Click next to each employee you intend to pay (☐ changes to ☑).

7 Click **Open Paycheck Detail**.

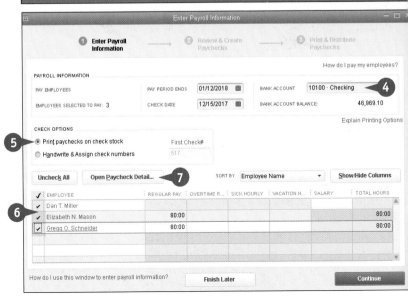

The Preview Paycheck window appears.

Ⓐ If you are creating a mileage reimbursement check only, delete items in these sections by highlighting them and pressing Delete .

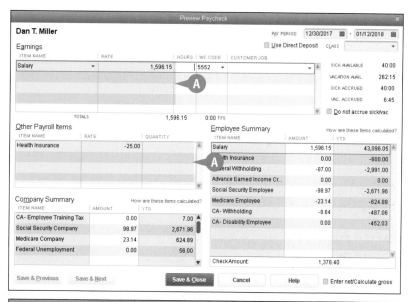

8 Click ▾ to select the mileage reimbursement item.

Ⓑ QuickBooks supplies the rate.

9 Type the number of miles to reimburse.

Ⓒ QuickBooks adds the mileage reimbursement total to the paycheck.

10 Click **Save & Next**.

QuickBooks creates the paycheck and displays the next employee's paycheck.

11 Repeat steps **8** to **10** for each employee you selected in step **6**, and see Chapter 6 to complete printing paychecks.

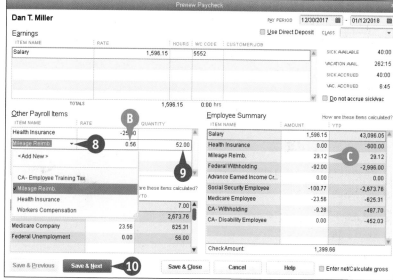

TIP

Can I use the Vehicle Mileage Tracking feature in QuickBooks to calculate and reimburse employee mileage?
If an employee uses his own car predominantly for business, you can set up the employee's vehicle in the Vehicle List — use the employee's name as the name of the car — and track mileage for the car. To reimburse the employee, print the Mileage by Vehicle Summary or Detail report to view the mileage associated with the employee's car for the reimbursement time period. Then, reimburse the employee on a paycheck as described in this section, or use the Write Checks window. To print either report, click **Reports**, then click **Jobs, Time & Mileage**, and then click the report.

CHAPTER 8

Invoicing and Recording Payments

To survive in business, you need to tell your customers how much they owe you and when payment is due. This chapter describes how to bill customers and record customer credits, assess finance charges, receive payments, and manage customer leads.

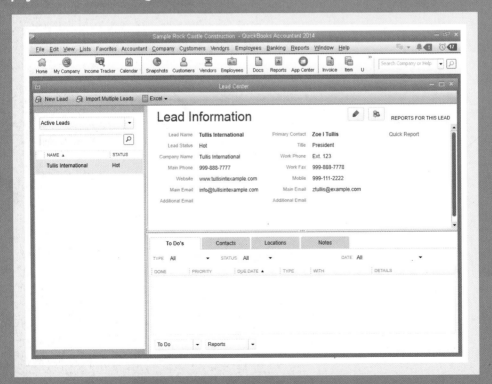

Create an Invoice

When customers purchase items or services from you and do not pay immediately, you record an invoice to account for the income and record the customer's debt to you.

If you include an out-of-stock item on an invoice, QuickBooks warns you; you can use sales orders to track orders for out-of-stock items. See the section "Create a Sales Order" for details. You can preview and print the invoice immediately, or you can print a group of invoices as described in the section "Print Invoices in a Batch." You also can email invoices, with or without file attachments.

Create an Invoice

Set Up the Invoice

1 Click **Customers**.

2 Click **Create Invoices** to display the Create Invoices window.

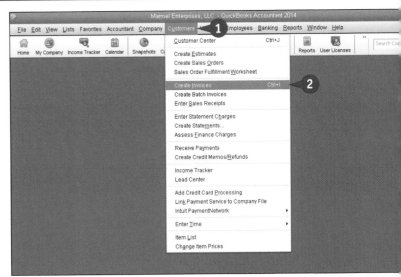

3 Click ▼ and select a Customer:Job.

Ⓐ QuickBooks fills in the customer's address here.

Ⓑ You can click ▼ to select a different invoice form.

Ⓒ You can click ▼ to change the invoice terms.

Ⓓ This area shows summary customer and transaction information.

4 Click ▼ to select an item, and QuickBooks fills in the description and rate.

5 Type a quantity, and QuickBooks fills in the amount.

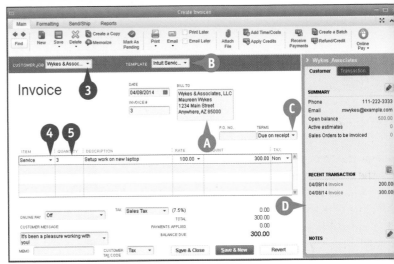

6 Repeat steps **4** and **5** for additional items.

E If necessary, click ▾ to change the sales tax code.

F If necessary, click ▾ to change the sales tax item.

G You can click ▾ to assign a customer message.

H You can click the check box (☐ changes to ☑) to print the invoice later, in batch.

7 Click **Save & New**.

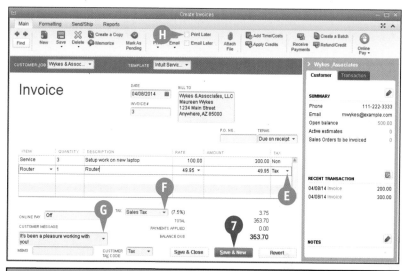

Preview the Invoice

1 Complete steps **1** to **6** of "Set Up the Invoice."

2 Click ▾ on the **Print** button, and from the menu that appears, click **Preview**.

I You can click **Zoom In** to enlarge the preview.

J You can click **Print** to print the invoice now.

3 Click **Close**.

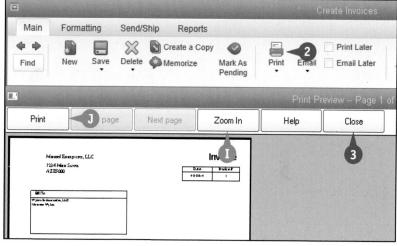

TIPS

Can I email invoices?

Yes, you can, using a variety of email services, including several web-based services. First, set up email preferences as described in Chapter 14. Then, in the Create Invoices window, click ▾ below the Email button on the window's toolbar. In the window that appears, select **Invoice** to send just the invoice or **Invoice and Files** to include all files attached to the invoice.

How do I attach files to an invoice?

On the Create Invoices window toolbar, click the **Attach File** button in the window that appears, and drag and drop files or click **Computer** to navigate to the file you want to attach. You can also attach files from the Document Center, described in Chapter 13.

Using Statement Charges to Invoice

If you accumulate non-taxable transactions for a customer before preparing an invoice — the way lawyers, accountants, and consultants work — you might prefer to record statement charges as you work rather than creating invoices. Then, on some regular basis such as once each month, you can prepare a customer statement that includes the statement charges you enter. For details on creating statements to bill your customer, see the section "Create Customer Statements."

QuickBooks keeps track of each customer's balance in an accounts-receivable register for the customer. When you enter statement charges, you record an entry to a customer's accounts-receivable register.

Using Statement Charges to Invoice

1. Click **Customers**.

2. Click **Enter Statement Charges**.

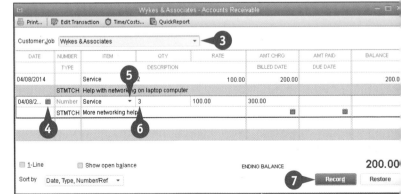

The Accounts Receivable window appears.

3. Click ▾ to select a Customer:Job.

4. Click 🗎 to select a date.

5. Click ▾ to select an item, and QuickBooks fills in the description and rate.

Note: You can replace the description by typing over it.

6. Type a quantity.

7. Click **Record**.

8. Repeat steps 4 to 7 for additional items.

QuickBooks calculates the customer's balance.

Create a Sales Order

QuickBooks Premier or above users can use sales orders to track out-of-stock items that customers order. Suppose that a customer places an order, and you have everything the customer needs except one item. You can create an invoice for the in-stock items and enter a sales order for the out-of-stock item. When you receive it, you can convert the sales order to an invoice and ship it to the customer. See the section "Create an Invoice from a Sales Order" for details on converting a sales order to an invoice. QuickBooks Pro users see Chapter 12 to track back orders.

Create a Sales Order

1 Click **Customers**.

2 Click **Create Sales Orders**.

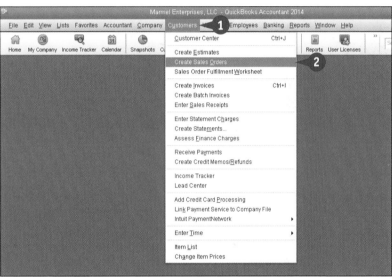

The Create Sales Orders window appears.

3 Click ▾ to select a Customer:Job.

A You can click ▾ to select a different sales order form.

4 Click ▾ to select an item, and QuickBooks fills in the description and rate.

5 Type a quantity.

6 Repeat steps **4** to **5** for additional items.

7 Click **Save & New**.

QuickBooks saves the sales order.

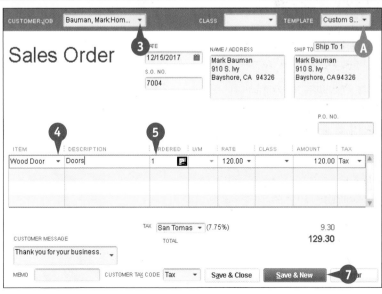

Create an Invoice from a Sales Order

If you use QuickBooks Premier or above and you have enabled sales orders, you can create invoices from sales orders as back-ordered merchandise arrives.

You can invoice for all or selected items on a sales order starting from either the Create Invoices window, as demonstrated in this section, or from the Create Sales Order window. If you start from the Create Invoices window, QuickBooks displays a dialog box that lets you know sales orders exist when you select the customer, and lets you select the sales order that you want to fill.

Create an Invoice from a Sales Order

1 Click **Customers**.

2 Click **Create Invoices**.

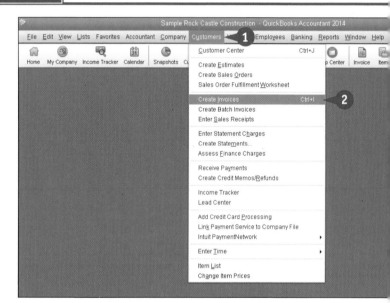

The Create Invoices window appears.

3 Click ▼ to select the Customer:Job.

The Available Sales Orders dialog box appears.

4 Click the order you want to fill.

5 Click **OK**.

The Create Invoice Based On Sales Order(s) dialog box appears.

6 Click an option for creating the invoice (◉ changes to ◉).

7 Click **OK**.

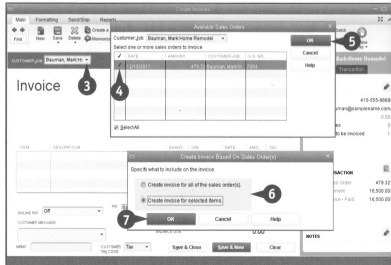

If you invoice the entire sales order, the Create Invoices window appears; otherwise, the Specify Invoice Quantities for Items on Sales Order(s) dialog box appears.

8 Type the number of items to invoice.

9 Repeat step **8** as needed.

10 Click **OK**.

QuickBooks places the items on the invoice.

11 Click **Save & Close**.

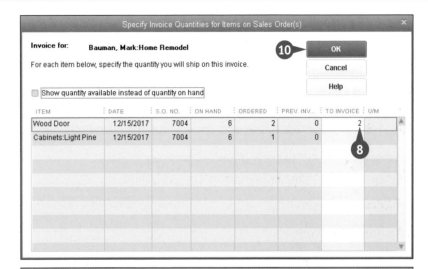

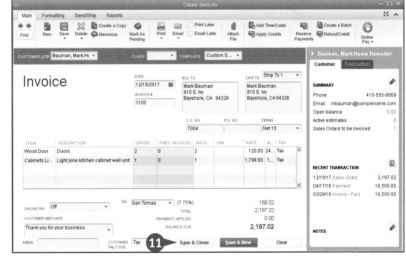

TIPS

How can I create an invoice while viewing the sales order?

Open the Create Sales Order window (see the section "Create a Sales Order"), and then click the Find arrows until the appropriate sales order appears. Then, click the **Create Invoice** button on the toolbar of the Create Sales Order window and follow steps **6** to **11** in this section.

How can I figure out what sales orders to fill?

Use the Stock Status by Item report. Click **Reports**, **Inventory**, and then **Stock Status by Item**. You can double-click the item to display an Inventory Item QuickReport, which lists sales orders for the item. Double-click any entry in that list, and QuickBooks displays the sales order in the Create Sales Orders window.

Create Credit Memos and Refund Checks

You can issue a *credit memo* that reverses a sale on your books. You can apply the credit to the customer's outstanding balance or to a future invoice, or you can issue a refund check.

If your customer returns the merchandise, select the items on the credit memo to return them to inventory. If the customer does not return the merchandise — it might have been defective — use a taxable item called Returns and Allowances on the credit memo. Making the Returns and Allowances item taxable adjusts your sales tax liability, sales, and receivables.

Create Credit Memos and Refund Checks

Create a Credit Memo

1 Click **Customers**.

2 Click **Create Credit Memos/ Refunds**.

The Create Credit Memos/ Refunds window appears.

3 Click ▼ to select a Customer:Job.

A You can click ▼ to select a different credit memo form.

B This area shows summary customer and transaction information.

4 Click ▼ to select an item, and QuickBooks fills in the description and rate.

5 Type a quantity.

6 Repeat steps **4** and **5** for additional items.

7 Click **Save & Close**.

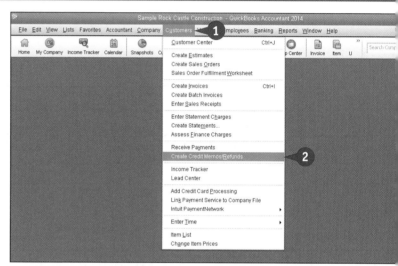

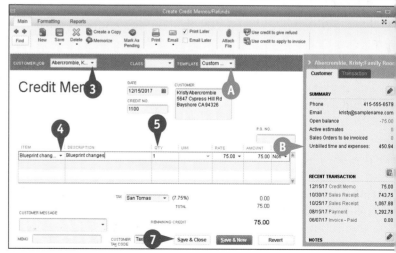

QuickBooks saves the credit memo and displays the Available Credit dialog box.

8 Click an option (⊙ changes to ⦿).

9 Click **OK**.

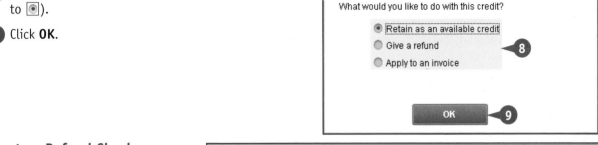

Create a Refund Check

1 Complete steps **1** to **7** in the preceding section.

2 In step **8**, click **Give a refund**.

QuickBooks saves the credit and displays the Issue a Refund window.

3 Confirm the information in the window.

4 To print the check, select the **To be printed** check box (☐ changes to ☑).

5 Click **OK**.

6 Click **Save & Close** to create the credit memo and the refund check.

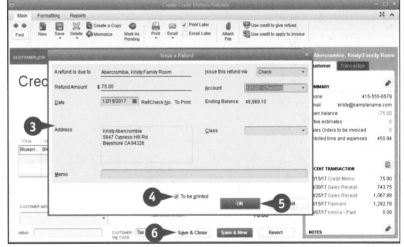

What should I do if the customer wants me to apply the overpayment to the next invoice?

Record a credit memo as described in the subsection "Create a Credit Memo." In the Available Credit dialog box, click the **Use credit to apply to invoice** option, or if no open invoices exist, click **Retain as an available credit** (☐ changes to ⦿). When you next enter an invoice for the customer, save it, and the Apply Credits button in the Create Invoices window will be available. Click it to display the Apply Credits dialog box. Select the credit you want to apply and click **Done**.

Print Invoices in a Batch

You may find it most efficient to print all invoices at the same time — in a batch — rather than printing them as you create them. This approach works particularly well if you take orders over th phone; toward the end of the day, you can print and mail all the day's invoices.

To print a batch of invoices, make sure that you select the Print Later option as you create your invoices; see the section "Create an Invoice" for details. QuickBooks marks these invoices for printing and displays them as available for printing when you print the batch.

Print Invoices in a Batch

1 Click **File**.

2 Click **Print Forms**.

3 Click **Invoices**.

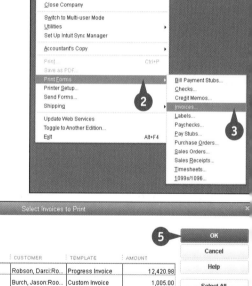

The Select Invoices to Print dialog box appears.

4 Click next to each invoice you want to print (☐ changes to ☑).

5 Click **OK**.

The Print Invoices dialog box appears.

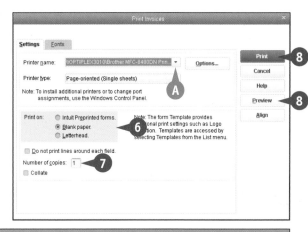

A You can click ▼ to select a printer.

6 Click a form option (◯ changes to ◉).

7 Type the number of copies you want to print of each invoice.

8 Click **Print** or **Preview**.

If you click **Print**, QuickBooks prints the invoices.

If you click **Preview**, QuickBooks displays the invoices on-screen.

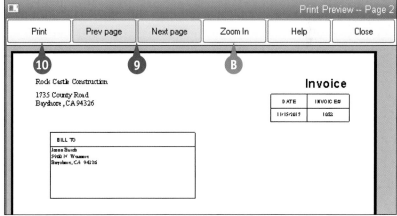

B You can click **Zoom In** to enlarge the print and read the invoice.

9 Click **Prev page** or **Next page** to navigate between invoices.

10 Click **Print**.

QuickBooks prints the invoices.

TIP

What happens if I click the Do Not Print Lines Around Each Field option in the Print Invoices dialog box?
The lines that separate the fields on the form shown in this section do not appear if you click this option. You should click this option (☐ changes to ☑) if you select Intuit Preprinted Forms as the type of form you are using. If, however, you print invoices on blank paper or letterhead, the lines make the invoice easier to read.

Assess Finance Charges

You may want to charge a *late fee* when customers do not pay on time. If your customers pay slowly for goods or services you already provided, you may not have the cash you need to purchase inventory or pay your operating expenses. See Chapter 14 for details on setting finance charge preferences, where you specify the finance charge rate and how QuickBooks should calculate the amount.

You can assess finance charges as you create statements or separately, as described in this section. See the section "Create Customer Statements" for details on assessing finance charges as you create statements.

Assess Finance Charges

1. Click **Customers**.
2. Click **Assess Finance Charges**.

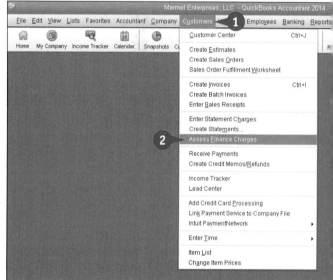

The Assess Finance Charges window appears.

3. Click 📅 to select a date for the finance charge.

4. Click next to each Customer:Job (🔲 changes to ☑) for whom you want to assess finance charges.

Ⓐ You can change the amount of the finance charge by typing here.

Note: If an asterisk appears beside a customer name, the customer has unapplied credits.

5. Click a customer.
6. Click **Collection History**.

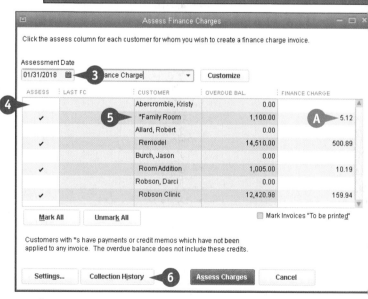

The Collections Report for the selected customer appears.

B You can double-click a transaction to view it in the window where it was created.

7 Click ☒ to close the report.

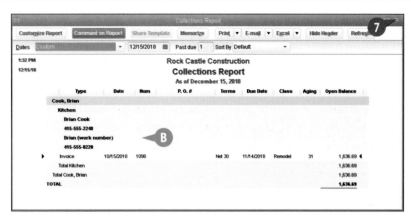

The Assess Finance Charges window reappears.

8 Click **Assess Charges**.

QuickBooks assigns the charges to the customers.

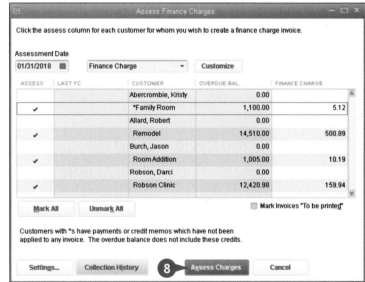

TIPS

What does the Mark Invoices "To Be Printed" option do?

This option (☐ changes to ☑) creates invoices containing only finance charges; you can print and send them to customers. If you intend to send statements as described in the section "Create Customer Statements," deselecting this option includes the finance charge on the statement.

How should I handle unapplied credits?

Complete steps **5** and **6** in this section, and on the Collection History report, double-click an unapplied credit to display it. On the Memos/Refunds window's toolbar, click the **Use credit to apply to invoice** button to display available invoices; select an invoice, click **Done,** and click **Save & Close**. The Collections Report redisplays without the credit and the customer's balance adjusted.

Create Customer Statements

If you issue many invoices to customers, you may find it useful to periodically send a *statement*, which lists all the invoices issued during the specified statement period. Most businesses send statements monthly to recap the invoice activity during the preceding month.

You also can print statements if your company uses statement charges to track work performed. For details on entering statement charges, see the section "Using Statement Charges to Invoice." When you print statements, you can select customers by name, by type, or by preferred send method.

Create Customer Statements

1 Click **Customers**.

2 Click **Create Statements**.

The Create Statements window appears.

3 Click 🔳 to select a statement date.

4 Click 🔳 to select the period the statement covers.

5 Click these options to select customers (🔘 changes to ⦿).

Ⓐ You can click **View Selected Customers** to view a list of customers for whom QuickBooks will print statements.

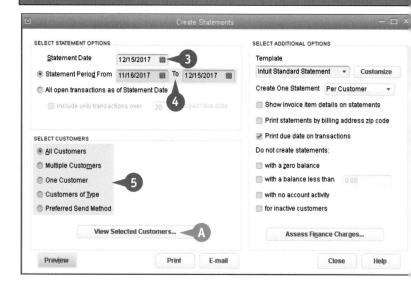

B You can click ⏷ to select a statement form.

6 Click ⏷ to create statements per customer or per job.

7 Click options in this area (☐ changes to ☑) to control the information that appears on statements and the order in which statements print.

8 Click **Preview** to display statements.

C You can click **Zoom In** to enlarge the print and read the statement.

9 Click **Prev page** or **Next page** to navigate between statements.

10 Click **Print**.

QuickBooks prints the statements and displays a message box asking if they printed properly.

11 Click **Yes** or **No**.

If you click **Yes**, QuickBooks sets the beginning date for the next set of statements to the day after the ending date of the statements you just printed.

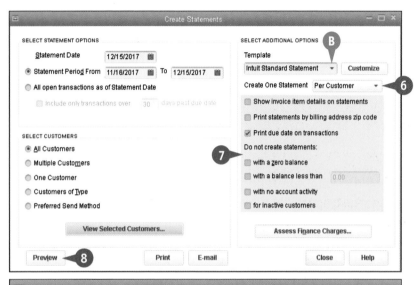

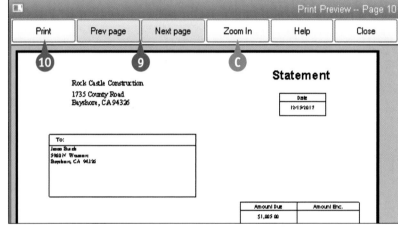

TIP

What happens if I click the All Open Transactions As of Statement Date option?
Using the Statement Period From and To dates includes all transactions the customer made between those dates — whether paid or unpaid. Some people feel that showing all activity, both paid and unpaid, is confusing and prefer to show only open transactions on a statement. You can print a statement that shows only open transactions as of the date of the statement if you click the **All open transactions as of Statement Date** option (◉ changes to ◉).

Manage Customer Leads

If your tracking needs are simple, you can use the QuickBooks Lead Center to track potential customers. You meet a new prospective client while having lunch or while attending a conference. To turn those leads into new customers, you need to, at a minimum, follow up on the questions that prospects asked and send out more information about your products and services.

The Lead Center can help you track prospects while you try to turn them into customers. Then, if you succeed, you can transform leads into customers in QuickBooks as described in the section "Convert a Lead to a Customer."

Manage Customer Leads

1 Click **Company**.

2 Click **Lead Center**.

The Lead Center appears.

3 Click **New Lead**.

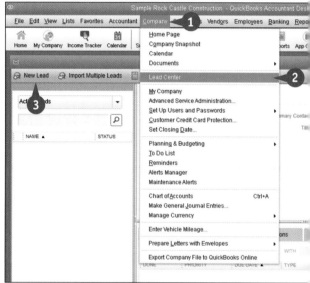

The Company tab of the Add Lead window appears.

4 Type the name of the lead.

5 Click ⯆ to select a lead status.

6 Fill in the company information for the lead.

Ⓐ You can click **Add Another Location** to add more than one location for the lead.

7 Click the **Contacts** tab.

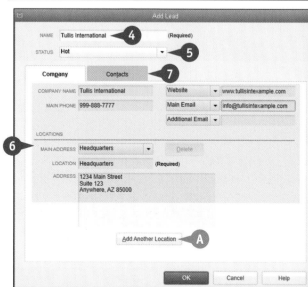

8 Provide contact details here.

B You can click **Add Another Contact** to store more than one contact for the company.

9 Click **OK**.

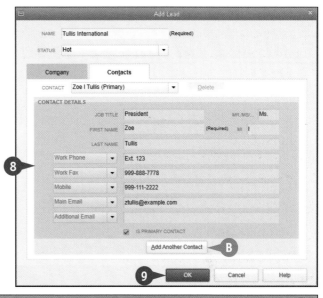

QuickBooks saves the lead and redisplays the Lead Center window.

C The lead appears in this list.

D Information about the lead appears in this area.

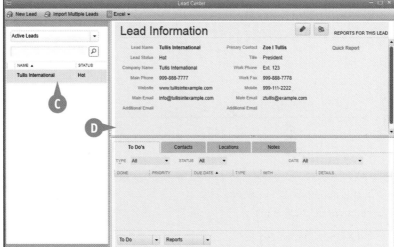

TIP

Can I send an email from the Lead Center?

No. The Lead Center's features are not as powerful as the ones you find in customer relationship management (CRM) programs. You also cannot create an estimate for a lead. But without any extra cost to you, the QuickBooks Lead Center can help you organize leads and eliminate tracking in a notebook or a spreadsheet. If you need more sophisticated tracking tools, consider Sales Force and other CRM programs that integrate with QuickBooks. You can find CRM programs that integrate with QuickBooks at the Intuit Marketplace (http://marketplace.intuit.com/).

Import Leads

If you have *leads* stored in an Excel spreadsheet, you can import them into the QuickBooks Lead Center by copying and pasting. Although you can copy multiple columns simultaneously, for best results, copy one column of Excel data at a time. You switch between Excel and QuickBooks using the Windows taskbar.

In QuickBooks, you paste Excel information into the Import Leads window, which contains all the fields you complete when you manually set up a lead as described in the section "Manage Customer Leads." The Import Leads window lays out the fields in row/column format.

Import Leads

1. Open your list of leads in Excel.

2. Click a column letter to select that column.

3. Click **Copy** or press **Ctrl**+**C**.

4. Click the QuickBooks icon (⬚) on the Windows taskbar.

5. Complete steps **1** and **2** in the section "Manage Customer Leads" to open the QuickBooks Lead Center.

6. Click **Import Multiple Leads**.

7. Right-click in the column where you want data to appear.

8. Click **Paste**.

   The information you copied from Excel appears in the Import Leads window.

9. Click the Excel icon (⬚) on the Windows taskbar to switch back to Excel.

10. Repeat steps **2** to **9** for each set of lead information.

11. Click **Continue**.

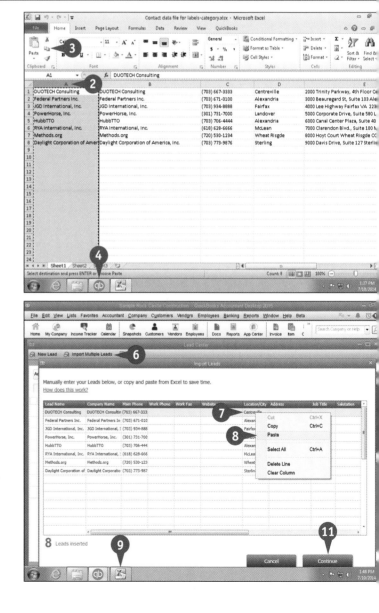

This screen appears, telling you the number of leads that QuickBooks will import.

Ⓐ You can click **Fix** if you need to make changes.

⑫ Click **Continue**.

A message appears, telling you that the import completed successfully; click **OK**.

The Lead Center reappears.

Ⓑ The leads you added appear in the Active Leads list.

Are any fields required when importing leads from Excel to the Lead Center?
Yes. To successfully import a lead from Excel to QuickBooks, your Excel workbook must contain information for two fields in the Import Lead window: the Lead Name field and the Location/City field. All the other fields in the Import Leads window are optional, but the more information you have on a lead, the more likely you are to succeed in transforming that lead to a customer.

Create a To Do for a Lead

You can establish *To Do* items for each lead. Having a lead is great, but having a way to remember the things you want to do for a lead is even better. You can categorize each To Do item by establishing its type; you can opt to set up To Do's to call, fax, or email the lead as well as establishing To Do's for meetings, appointments, or tasks you want to accomplish. You also can establish the date on which you want to do the item and, if appropriate, the time.

Create a To Do for a Lead

1 Complete steps **1** and **2** in the section "Manage Customer Leads" to open the QuickBooks Lead Center.

2 Click the lead in the Active Leads list.

3 Click the **To Do's** tab.

4 Click the To Do box [▾].

5 Click **New To Do**.

The Add To Do window appears.

6 Click [▾] and select a To Do type.

7 Click [▾] and select a priority.

8 Click [▦] and select a due date.

A You can click here ([▢] changes to [☑]) to set a time for the To Do.

9 Type any details here.

10 Click **OK**.

QuickBooks adds the entry on the To Do's tab.

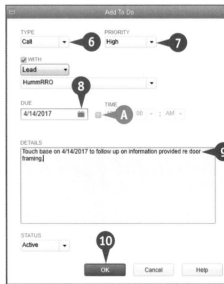

Convert a Lead to a Customer

When a lead becomes a customer, you can easily convert the lead to a customer in QuickBooks. Be aware that you cannot undo the action and change the customer back to a lead.

After the conversion, you can view a list of leads you have converted to customers in the Lead Center by changing the Active Leads list to the Converted Leads list. But, you cannot edit the lead in the Lead Center after you convert it. Instead, the converted lead appears in the Customer Center, where you can edit it.

Convert a Lead to a Customer

1 Complete steps **1** and **2** in the section, "Manage Customer Leads" to open the QuickBooks Lead Center.

2 Click the lead you want to convert to a customer.

3 Click **Convert this Lead to a Customer** (🔳).

QuickBooks asks you to confirm your action.

4 Click **Yes**.

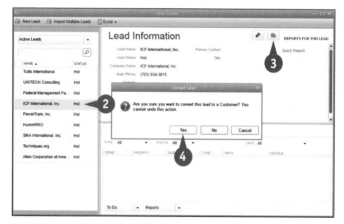

A QuickBooks displays the Customer Center, and the lead appears in the Active Customers list.

B To edit a customer, right-click it in the Active Customers list and then click **Edit Customer:Job**.

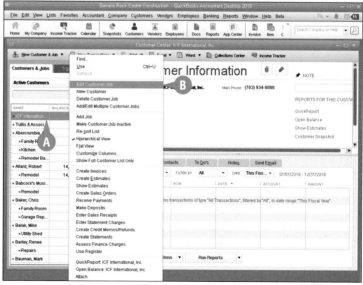

Record a Cash Sale

A customer may make a purchase and pay for the items immediately. To record this transaction, you enter a Sales Receipt.

When you record a sales receipt, you can have QuickBooks deposit the money directly to a bank account, or you can group cash receipts into an Undeposited Funds account. This account acts as a suspense account where QuickBooks holds your money until you make your bank deposit, as described in the section "Make Bank Deposits." You can use the Undeposited Funds account to make your deposits match your bank statement, which makes bank statement reconciliation much easier.

Record a Cash Sale

1. Click **Customers**.

2. Click **Enter Sales Receipts**.

   The Enter Sales Receipts window appears.

3. Click ▼ to select a Customer:Job.

   You can record noncustomer cash sales to a customer called Cash Sale, or leave the Customer:Job field blank.

4. Click ▼ to select a deposit account.

5. Click ▼ to select an item, and QuickBooks fills in the description and rate.

6. Type a quantity, and QuickBooks fills in the amount.

7. Repeat steps **5** and **6** for additional items.

8. Click **Save & Close**.

   QuickBooks saves the cash receipt and closes the window.

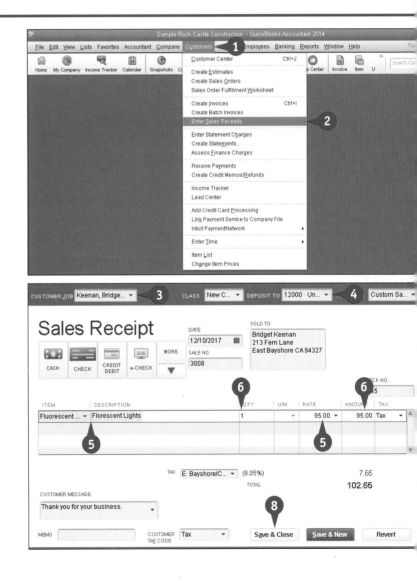

Receive a Payment

When a customer sends you a payment for an invoice you issued, you record it and QuickBooks places it in the Undeposited Funds account.

QuickBooks automatically applies amounts to the oldest open invoice. If the amount paid is greater than the invoice amount, QuickBooks applies the remainder to the next oldest invoice, repeating this process until the entire payment amount is applied. However, if an open invoice exists for the exact amount of the payment, QuickBooks applies the payment to that invoice, even if it is not the oldest. If a customer overpays, QuickBooks automatically creates a credit.

Receive a Payment

1 Click **Customers**.

2 Click **Receive Payments** to display the Receive Payments window.

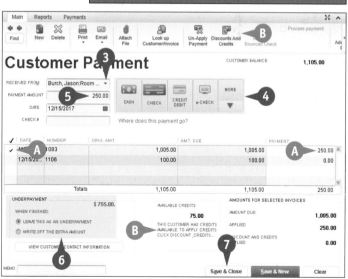

3 Click ▼ to select a Customer:Job.

4 Click this area to select a payment method.

5 Type the amount of the payment here.

A QuickBooks marks invoices paid and displays the paid portion of the invoice here; you can change the payment distribution by changing this number.

6 Click an option (◉ changes to ◉) to select a method to handle under- or overpayments.

B Available credit information appears here. You can click **Discounts And Credits** to apply them.

7 Click **Save & Close** to save the payment and close the window.

Make Bank Deposits

When customers pay you, you record transactions in QuickBooks that deposit the payments into the Undeposited Funds account, then you deposit the checks or cash in the bank. Using the bank deposit feature in QuickBooks, you can group the cash or checks in the Undeposited Funds account to match the deposits as they will appear on your bank statement, making the bank statement reconciliation process much easier. For details on reconciling a bank statement, see Chapter 11.

You can include payments that did not come from customers in a deposit, and you also can receive cash back from the deposit.

Make Bank Deposits

① Click **Banking**.

② Click **Make Deposits**.

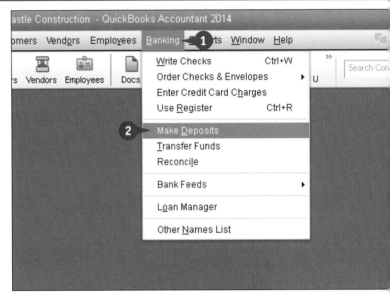

The Payments to Deposit window appears. Behind it, the Make Deposits window appears.

③ Click next to each payment you want to include in the deposit (☐ changes to ☑).

Ⓐ QuickBooks displays the subtotal for the deposit here.

④ Click **OK**.

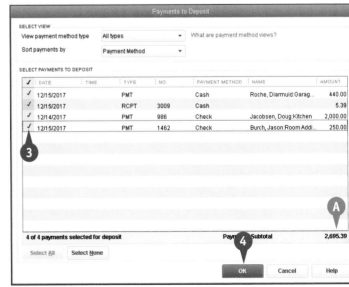

The Make Deposits window appears.

⑤ Click ▼ to select the account into which you are depositing.

⑥ Click 📅 to select the deposit date.

Ⓑ You can type a memo here.

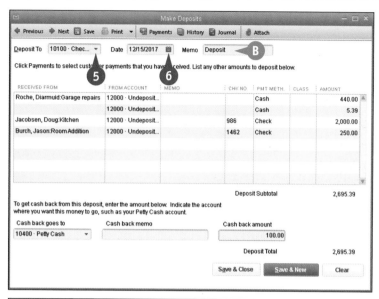

⑦ Review the list of payments to be deposited.

Ⓒ You can type an amount of cash you want back from the deposit here; you must also click ▼ to select an account.

⑧ Click **Save & Close**.

QuickBooks moves the deposit amount from the Undeposited Funds account to the account you selected in step **5**.

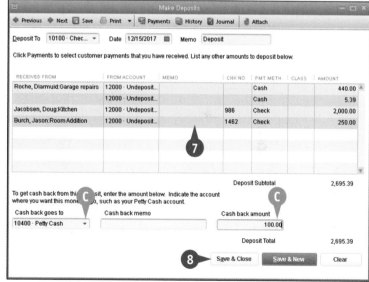

TIPS

Can I print a deposit ticket that my bank will use?
Yes, as long as the deposit contains transactions with a Payment Method of cash, checks, or a combination of them. Click ▼ on the **Print** button in the Make Deposits window and then click **Deposit Slip** to save the bank deposit; a dialog box asks you to set printer options. Click **Print** to print your selection.

Can I change the deposits I selected after I click OK in the Payments to Deposit window as I view the Make Deposits window?
Yes. Click the **Payments** button at the top of the Make Deposits window. QuickBooks redisplays the Payments to Deposit window, where you can change your selection. Then, continue with steps **5** to **8**.

CHAPTER 9

Working with Estimates

Many businesses need to produce a description of proposed work or products before customers make a purchase. In QuickBooks, you can create estimates to handle these proposals. If the customer approves the estimate, you can convert it to an invoice when appropriate, or you can prepare invoices as a job progresses.

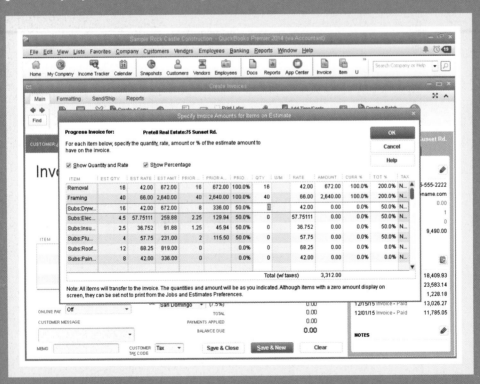

Create a Job Estimate

If your business requires that you produce a description of proposed work or products before you sell them, you can create *estimates*. Estimates do not actually update the account or item values in your company because no accounting transactions have occurred. If a customer accepts your estimate, you can convert the estimate to an invoice in a couple of different ways; see the sections "Convert an Estimate to an Invoice" and "Create a Progress Invoice" for more details.

If you make relatively the same bids over and over, consider using the Memorize feature to record an estimate.

Create a Job Estimate

1 Click **Customers**.

2 Click **Create Estimates**.

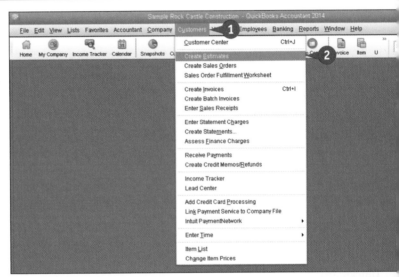

The Create Estimates window appears.

3 Click ▼ to select a Customer:Job.

A You can click ▼ to select a different estimate form.

4 Click 🔳 to select a date for the estimate.

B You can click here to change the estimate number.

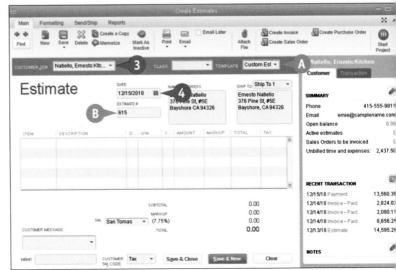

5 Click ⏷ to select an item.

C QuickBooks fills in any description and rate you provided when you defined the item.

6 Type a quantity.

D You can type a markup percentage or amount for the line here.

7 Repeat steps **5** and **6** for additional items.

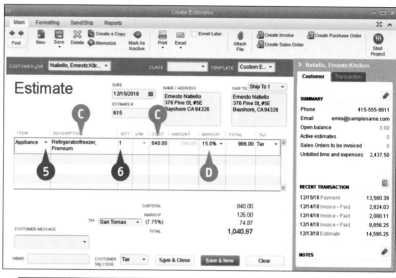

8 Click ⏷ to select a customer message.

E You can click ⏷ to change the sales tax authority.

F You can click ⏷ to change the customer tax code.

G You can type a memo here.

9 Click **Save & Close**.

QuickBooks saves the estimate and closes the window.

TIPS

How do I memorize an estimate for multiple use?
Fill out the estimate as described in this section, but do not save it. Instead, after step **8**, click **Edit** and click **Memorize Estimate**. QuickBooks removes the Customer:Job for the estimate, making it usable for any Customer:Job. To use the memorized estimate, double-click it in the Memorized Transaction List. For details, see Chapter 12.

Can I create a change order in QuickBooks?
Only if you use the Contractor's Edition of QuickBooks. Users of other versions can change estimates, but they cannot track change orders. If you plan to change an estimate, print the estimate and then make changes. Your printed copy is the only record of the original estimate.

Convert an Estimate to an Invoice

To save time and avoid entering data twice, you can convert an estimate to an invoice, a purchase order, or, if you use QuickBooks Premier or higher, a sales order. You convert an estimate to an invoice when you want to prepare an invoice for a customer.

Once you convert an estimate to an invoice, you can add items to the invoice or change amounts. If you invoice for more than the amount shown on the estimate, Transaction History indicates that the estimate has been billed for more than 100%. To avoid confusion, you may want to edit the estimate or create an additional estimate.

Convert an Estimate to an Invoice

1 Click **Customers**.

2 Click **Create Invoices**.

The Create Invoices window appears.

3 Click ▾ to select a Customer:Job.

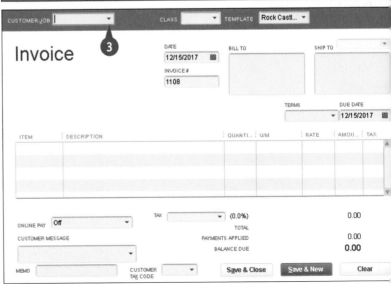

The Available Estimates window appears.

4 Click an estimate.

5 Click **OK**.

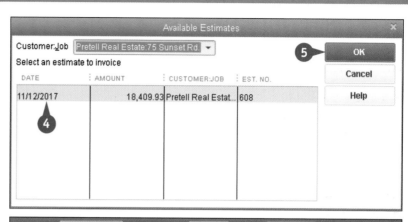

Note: If you selected to do progress invoicing in the Preferences dialog box in Chapter 4, the Create Progress Invoice Based On Estimate box appears.

6 Click an option (○ changes to ◉).

(A) You can create an invoice for part of the estimate if you click this option and type a percentage.

Note: For details on the last option, see "Create a Progress Invoice" later in this chapter.

7 Click **OK**.

QuickBooks redisplays the Create Invoices window.

8 Click **Save & Close** to save the invoice.

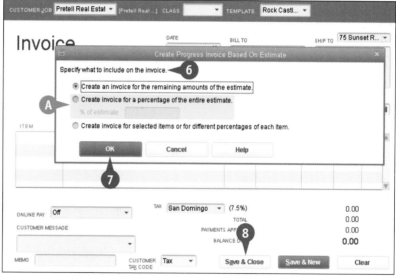

TIPS

If I opted not to do progress invoicing, what happens?

If outstanding billable time, expense, or mileage charges exist for the Customer:Job, QuickBooks displays the Billable Time/Costs dialog box, where you can opt to include any or all of these charges on the invoice you are creating from an estimate. See Chapter 7 for details.

When would I convert an estimate to a sales order or purchase order?

You convert an estimate to an invoice, as shown in this section, when you want to prepare an invoice for a customer. Convert an estimate to a sales order or a purchase order when a customer accepts the estimate, but you do not have everything in stock and you need to order items to fulfill the estimate.

Duplicate an Estimate

If you create an estimate for one customer, and another customer comes along needing very similar or the same work performed, you can *duplicate* that estimate to use it for the new customer, thus saving yourself the work of re-creating it. You can also duplicate an estimate and use it to create several similar but not identical estimates for a single customer.

During duplication, QuickBooks makes an exact copy of the estimate, with one exception: The estimate number changes. You can make changes on the duplicate as appropriate.

Duplicate an Estimate

1. Click **Customers**.

2. Click **Create Estimates**.

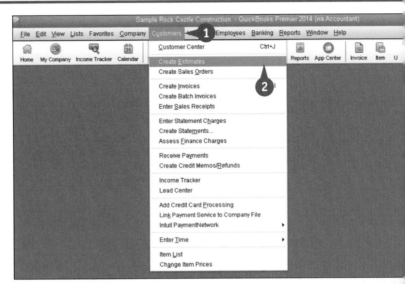

The Create Estimates window appears.

3. Click the Previous button (◄) to display the estimate you want to convert.

Ⓐ You can click **Find** to open the Find Estimates window.

Note: Finding a transaction is described in Chapter 12.

Ⓑ The estimate appears in the window.

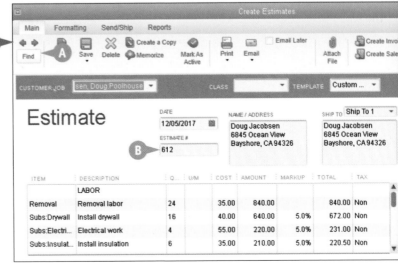

④ Click **Edit**.

⑤ Click **Duplicate Estimate**.

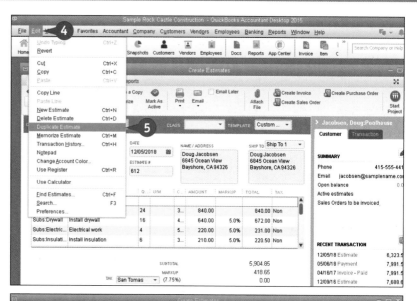

Ⓒ QuickBooks creates a new estimate and displays a message to that effect.

Ⓓ The new estimate looks exactly like the original except for the estimate number.

⑥ Click **OK**.

⑦ Click **Save & Close** to save the estimate and close the window.

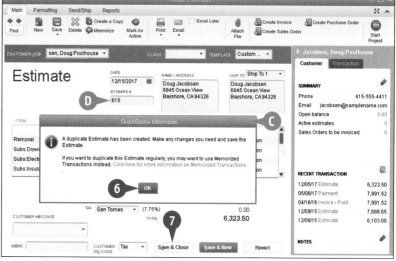

When should I memorize an estimate, and when should I duplicate an estimate?

You memorize an estimate when you include the same information again and again for many different customers. You duplicate an estimate when you have already created an estimate, and another job comes along that is so similar to the first that you can simply make a few changes to the duplicate for it to suit your needs. For more information on memorizing an estimate, see the section "Create a Job Estimate."

Create a Progress Invoice

You can create a progress invoice when you need to invoice a customer for part of a job; many companies have agreements with their customers to present an invoice for a portion of a job even though the job is not yet complete. You can invoice for a percentage of the job or for specific portions of the job that are complete.

The section "Convert an Estimate to an Invoice" showed how to convert an entire estimate into an invoice. This section shows how to convert only portions of an estimate to an invoice.

Create a Progress Invoice

1 Click **Customers**.

2 Click **Create Invoices**.

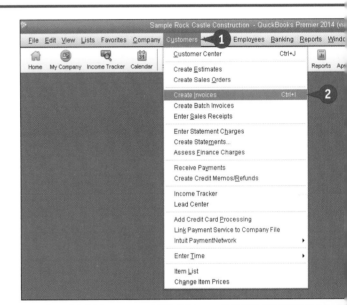

The Create Invoices window appears.

3 Click ⬇ and select a Customer:Job.

The Available Estimates window appears.

4 Click the estimate you want to use to create a progress invoice.

5 Click **OK**.

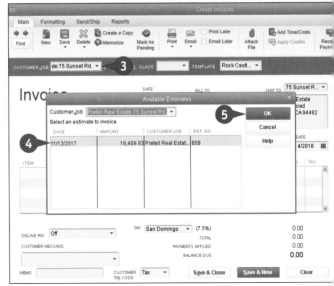

The Create Progress Invoice
Based On Estimate dialog box
appears.

⑥ Click here (◉ changes to ◉).

Ⓐ You can create a progress
invoice based on a percentage
of the entire invoice by
clicking here and supplying a
percentage.

⑦ Click **OK**.

The Specify Invoice Amounts
for Items on Estimate dialog
box appears.

⑧ Click a line and type the
quantity for which you want
to invoice.

Ⓑ You can type an estimated
percent complete here.

Ⓒ The invoice amount appears
here.

⑨ Repeat step **8** as needed.

⑩ Click **OK**.

The lines and amounts you
selected appear on the
invoice.

⑪ Click **Save & Close**.

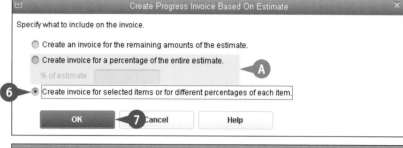

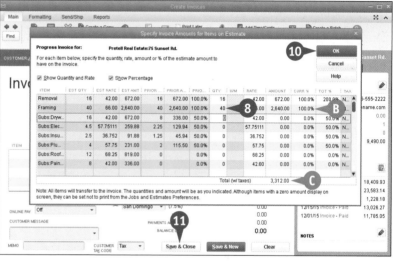

TIPS

**Can I delete lines that I do not want to bill
yet from the invoice?**

$0 lines appear on the invoice on-screen, but
they print based on preference settings. Click
Edit and then click **Preferences** to display the
Preferences dialog box. Click **Jobs & Estimates**,
and select the "Don't print items that have zero
amount" option.

**When I follow steps 1 to 5, why does the Create
Progress Invoice Based On Estimate dialog box not
appear?**

You did not enable preparing progress invoices. Click
Edit and then click **Preferences** to display the
Preferences dialog box. Click **Jobs & Estimates**, and
then click the **Company Preferences** tab. Select **Yes** in
the Do You Do Progress Invoicing section and click **OK**.

CHAPTER 10

Managing Vendor Bills

To maintain accurate financial records, you need to enter transactions that describe the expenses you incur. In this chapter, you learn to pay bills immediately when they arrive or later, at a predetermined time. You also learn how to record transactions to buy goods and manage inventory, pay sales taxes, print 1099s, and handle other related bill-paying activities.

Create Purchase Orders

You can use *purchase orders* to identify goods you want to order and to track ordered goods before the vendor bills you. When you receive goods against a purchase order, QuickBooks uses the purchase order information to create a bill, a check, or a credit card charge for the vendor. You also can use a purchase order to create a drop shipment — that is, order goods from a vendor and have the goods shipped directly to a customer.

To use purchase orders, you must enable them; see Chapter 4 for details on setting preferences to enable purchase orders.

Create Purchase Orders

1 Click **Vendors**.

2 Click **Create Purchase Orders**.

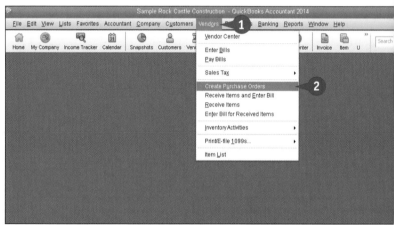

The Create Purchase Orders window appears.

3 Click ▾ to select a vendor; QuickBooks fills in the vendor's address.

Ⓐ You can click ▾ to select a drop-ship customer.

Ⓑ You can click ▾ to select a template.

Ⓒ Information about the vendor appears here.

4 Click 📅 to change the date.

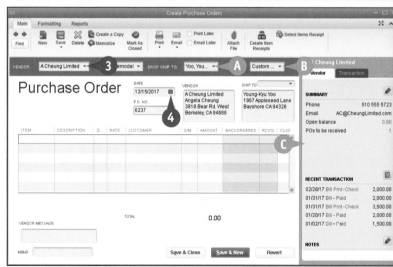

5 Click ▼ to select an item.

D QuickBooks fills in the description and rate.

6 Type a quantity.

E QuickBooks calculates the line amount.

F Click ▼ to assign the line to a customer.

Note: If you selected a customer in step **3**, QuickBooks automatically fills in the customer name.

7 Repeat steps **5** and **6** for additional items.

G You can click the **Print Later** option to mark the purchase order for batch printing (☐ changes to ☑).

H You can click the **Email Later** option to mark the purchase order for emailing (☐ changes to ☑).

I You can type a message to the vendor that prints on the purchase order.

J You can type a memo that does not print on the purchase order.

8 Click **Save & Close** to save your changes

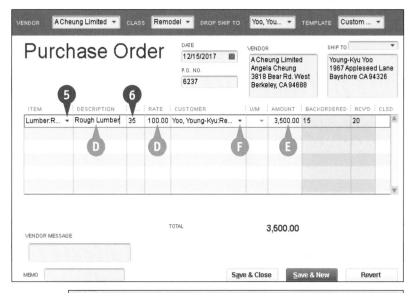

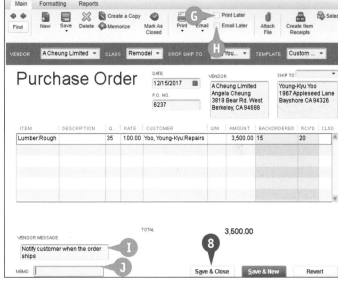

TIPS

How can I identify both the items I have on hand and the items I ordered on purchase orders?

Print the Inventory Stock Status by Item report or the Inventory Stock Status by Vendor report. Both reports show both the quantity on hand and the quantity on purchase orders. For more on printing reports, see Chapter 13.

What is the purpose of the Clsd column?

If you do not receive items on a purchase order, it remains open. When you receive all items on a purchase order, QuickBooks automatically closes the purchase order. If you receive items for some lines, you can click in the Clsd column (☐ changes to ☑) to close those lines on the purchase order but leave other lines open.

Enter Bills

Y ou can enter bills from vendors to track them and pay them on time. This section describes how to record a bill for both an expense, such as a telephone bill, and for inventory items. When you record a bill that involves inventory items, you record both the bill, which updates Accounts Payable, and the receipt of the items, which updates inventory.

You can assign one or more lines of the bill or item receipt to a customer to create a reimbursable expense that you can bill back to a customer on an invoice, as described in Chapter 7.

Enter Bills

Record an Expense

1 Click **Vendors**.

2 Click **Enter Bills**.

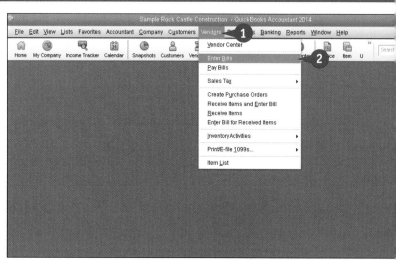

The Enter Bills window appears.

A You can click the Credit option to record a credit from a vendor (○ changes to ◉).

3 Click 🛲 to select the bill date.

4 Click ▾ to select a vendor.

B QuickBooks fills in the vendor terms and Bill Due date.

C You can type the vendor's bill number here.

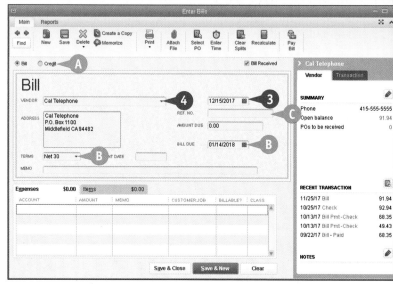

5 Click the **Expenses** tab.

6 Click ⏷ to select an account.

7 Type an amount to charge the account; the amount updates.

D You can click ⏷ and assign the expense to a Customer:Job.

E You can click here to create a reimbursable expense.

8 Repeat steps **6** and **7** to assign the bill to additional accounts.

9 Click **Save & Close**.

Enter a Bill for Items

1 Perform steps **1** to **4** on the previous page.

2 Click the **Items** tab.

3 Click ⏷ to select an item.

F QuickBooks fills in the description and cost.

4 Type a quantity.

G QuickBooks calculates the line amount and updates the bill.

H This area assigns the line to a customer and creates a reimbursable expense (☐ changes to ☑).

5 Repeat steps **3** and **4** for additional items.

6 Click **Save & Close**.

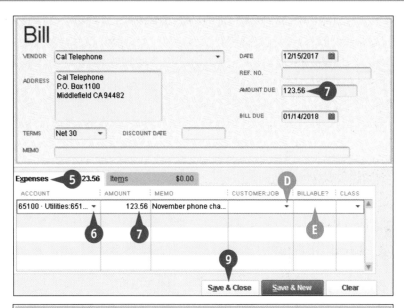

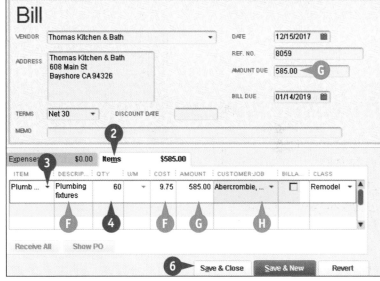

What should I do if I receive items I ordered before I receive the bill?

Record the receipt of the items using the Create Item Receipts window, which updates inventory quantities without affecting Accounts Payable.

What if I created a purchase order for the items?

When you select the vendor to record the bill or item receipt, a message box tells you that open purchase orders exist for the vendor. To use one of these orders, click **Yes**. QuickBooks then displays the Open Purchase Orders dialog box, from which you can select the appropriate purchase order.

Manage Recurring Bills

I̲f you pay the same amount to the same vendor on a regular basis, you can use the Memorize feature to make QuickBooks *remember* the bill and help reduce the amount of time it takes you to meet repetitive obligations. You also can memorize a bill in QuickBooks even if the amount changes each month; for these types of transactions, you memorize the bill for $0 and supply the amount at the time you enter the memorized bill. QuickBooks affects the accounts associated with a memorized transaction at the time you enter the transaction.

Manage Recurring Bills

Memorize a Bill

1 Perform the steps in the section "Enter Bills" to record a cost or to enter a bill for items, but do not click **Save & Close**.

Note: You also can memorize other types of transactions, such as customer invoices.

2 Click **Edit**.

3 Click **Memorize Bill**.

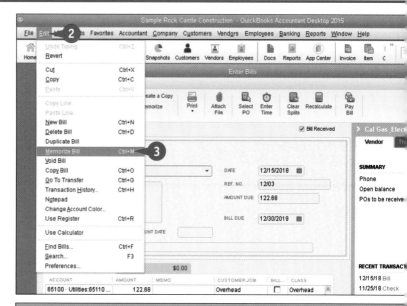

The Memorize Transaction dialog box appears.

4 Click the **Add to my Reminders List** option (⊙ changes to ⊚).

5 Click ▾ to select a frequency.

6 Click 📅 to select the next date for the transaction.

7 Click **OK**.

QuickBooks memorizes the transaction and redisplays the bill.

8 Click **Save & Close**.

Enter a Memorized Transaction

1. Click **Lists**.

2. Click **Memorized Transaction List**.

   The Memorized Transaction List window appears.

3. Click the transaction you want to enter.

4. Click **Enter Transaction**.

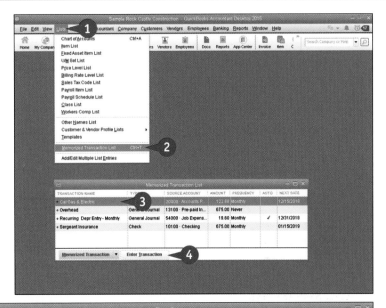

The transaction appears in the window where you created it.

5. Make changes as needed.

6. Click **Save & Close** to record the transaction.

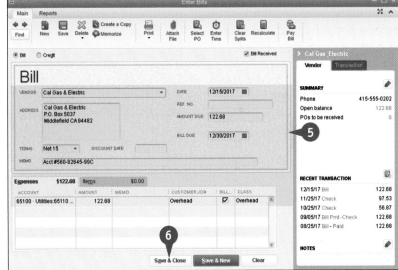

TIP

What do the options in the Memorize Transaction dialog box mean?
If you select **Add to my Reminders List** (⊙ changes to ⊙), QuickBooks displays a reminder on the date that you should enter the bill; see Chapter 14 for more on Reminders. If you select **Do Not Remind Me** (⊙ changes to ⊙), you must remember to open the Memorized Transaction List and enter the bill. If you select **Automate Transaction Entry** (⊙ changes to ⊙), QuickBooks automatically enters the bill on the selected date and displays a message to that effect when you open QuickBooks on or after the scheduled date of the transaction.

Enter Credit Card Charges

You can enter credit card slips into QuickBooks so that you know, at any point in time, exactly how much is outstanding on your credit card. You can record credit card charges for expenses an for items. You set up credit card accounts for each credit card; see Chapter 2 for details on setting up accounts.

If your credit card financial institution supports QuickBooks, you can download credit card transactions directly into QuickBooks without manually entering credit card slips. Downloading credit card transactions is typically a free service at most financial institutions.

Enter Credit Card Charges

Record an Expense

1. Click **Banking**.
2. Click **Enter Credit Card Charges**.

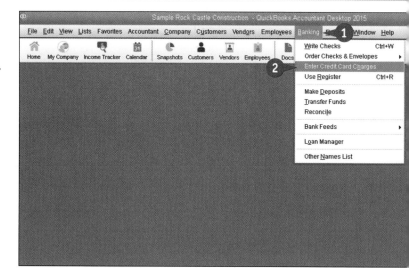

The Enter Credit Card Charges window appears.

3. Click ▼ to select a credit card.

Ⓐ The balance on the card appears here.

4. Click an option to record either a charge or a credit (◯ changes to ◉).

5. Click ▼ to select a vendor for the charge.

6. Click 📅 to select the charge date.

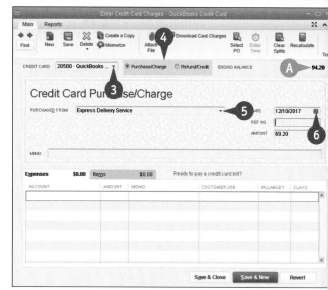

7 Click the **Expenses** tab.

8 Click ▾ to select an account.

9 Type the amount of the charge.

B You can type a memo here.

C You can click ▾ to assign the expense to a Customer:Job and, if appropriate, identify the expense as reimbursable.

10 Repeat steps **8** and **9** to assign the charge to additional accounts.

11 Click **Save & Close** to save the expense.

Enter a Charge for Items

1 Perform steps **1** to **4** on the previous page.

2 Click the **Items** tab.

3 Click ▾ to select an item.

D QuickBooks fills in the description and, if appropriate, the cost.

4 Type a quantity.

E QuickBooks calculates the line amount.

F This area assigns the line to a customer and creates a reimbursable expense (▢ changes to ☑).

5 Repeat steps **3** and **4** for additional items.

G QuickBooks fills in the amount of the charge.

6 Click **Save & Close** to save the charge.

> ### TIP
>
> **How do I pay my credit card bill when it arrives?**
> Before you write your monthly check, reconcile the account; at the end of the reconciliation process — see Chapter 11 for more details — QuickBooks prompts you to write the check. You can make a partial or full payment.

Pay Bills

You can use the Pay Bills window to pay many bills at one time, saving you time and effort. You can sort unpaid bills by Discount Date to ensure that these bills are paid in time to take the offered discount. Available credits and discounts appear for each bill; QuickBooks applies credits and discounts to the selected bill.

QuickBooks prints one check per vendor, even if you pay multiple bills from the same vendor. You can print checks immediately or print them later, as a batch, as described in the section "Print Checks in a Batch."

Pay Bills

1 Click **Vendors**.

2 Click **Pay Bills**.

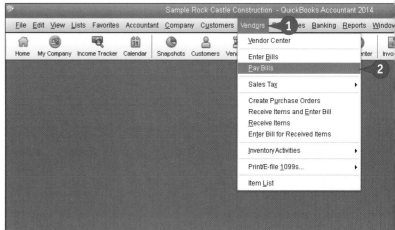

The Pay Bills window appears.

Ⓐ You can click this area to select bills due on or before a date (🔘 changes to 🔘) and click 📅 to select the date.

3 Click ▾ to sort the bills, remembering to click **Discount Date** to avoid losing discounts.

4 Click this column to select a bill to pay (🔲 changes to ☑).

Ⓑ As you select bills, QuickBooks updates your checking account ending balance and displays vendor credits and discounts.

5 Click a bill and then click **Set Credits**.

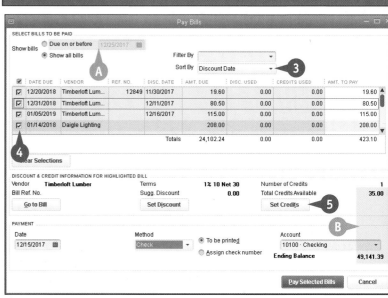

The Discount and Credits window appears.

⑥ On the Credits tab, click this column to select a credit to apply (☐ changes to ☑).

⑦ Repeat step **6** to apply additional credits.

Note: If discounts exist for a bill, click the Discount tab and select an account for the discount.

⑧ Click **Done**.

The Pay Bills window reappears; QuickBooks adjusts the amount to pay and the total credit amount available.

⑨ Click ▼ to select an account from which to pay.

⑩ Click ▼ to select a payment method.

⑪ Click an option to print the check immediately or later, in a batch.

⑫ Click 📅 to select a payment date.

⑬ Click **Pay Selected Bills**.

QuickBooks pays the bills and reduces your Accounts Payable.

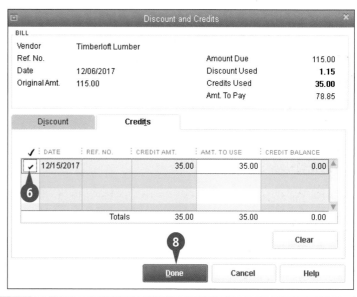

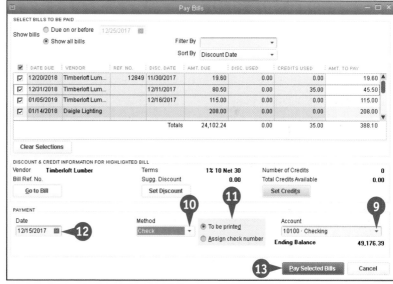

Is there a way that I can print the vendor's account number on the check?
Yes. You can print it in the Memo field on the check. First, make sure that you have entered the vendor's account number; click **Vendors** on the Icon Bar to open the Vendor Center, and in the Active Vendors list, double-click the vendor to edit information. Then, click the **Payment Settings** tab and make sure the vendor's account number appears in the Account No. field and click **OK**. Click **Edit** and then **Preferences**. In the Preferences dialog box that appears, click **Checking**. On the Company Preferences tab, select the **Autofill payee account number in the check memo box** (☐ changes to ☑).

Write Checks

You can use the Write Checks window to pay for an expense or a service, other charge, fixed asset, inventory, or non-inventory items. You should not use the Write Checks window to pay a bill that you entered or to write a paycheck, pay payroll liabilities, or pay sales tax liabilities. In all these cases, you need to use the QuickBooks feature specifically designed for the tasks. For details on paying bills and paying sales tax liabilities, see the sections "Pay Bills" and "Pay the Sales Tax Liability." For details on paying payroll liabilities, see Chapter 6.

Write Checks

Pay an Expense

1 Click **Banking**.

2 Click **Write Checks**.

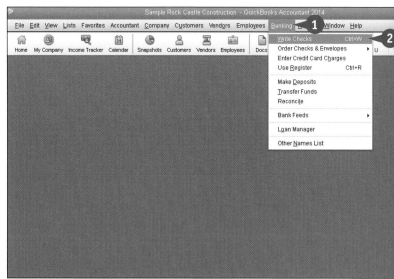

The Write Checks window appears.

3 Click ▦ to select the check date.

4 Click ▾ to select a vendor.

Ⓐ QuickBooks fills in the vendor's address information.

Ⓑ You can type a memo for the check face here.

5 Click the **Expenses** tab.

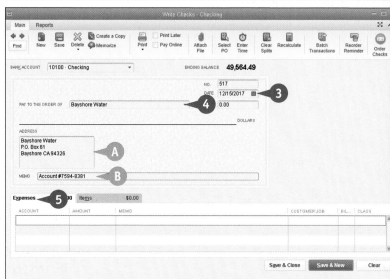

6 Click ▼ to select an account.

7 Type an amount.

8 Repeat steps **6** and **7** as needed to update the check amount.

9 Click **Print Later** (☐ changes to ☑) to print checks in a batch.

10 Click **Save & Close** to pay the expense.

Pay for Items

1 Perform steps **1** to **4** on the previous page.

2 Click the **Items** tab.

3 Click ▼ to select an item.

C QuickBooks fills in the description and cost.

4 Type a quantity.

D QuickBooks calculates the line amount.

E You can click ▼ and assign the expense to a Customer:Job and create a reimbursable expense.

5 Repeat steps **3** and **4** for additional items.

F QuickBooks fills in the amount of the check.

6 Perform steps **9** and **10** on the previous page.

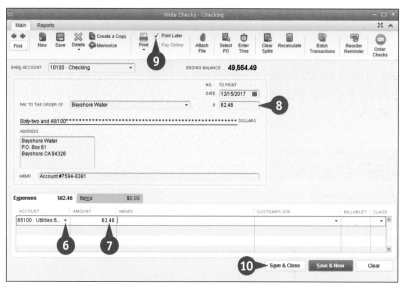

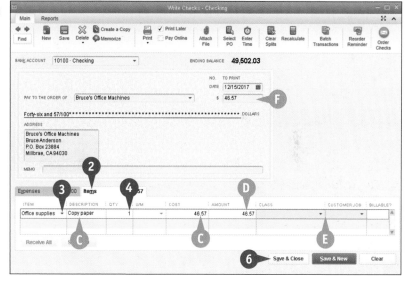

TIPS

How can I display a specific bank account each time I open the Write Checks window?
Click **Edit** and then **Preferences**. Click **Checking** on the left side of the dialog box, and on the My Preferences tab, select **Open the Write Checks form with**. Then, click ▼ to select the account you want to use.

Do I need to set up a vendor if I only purchase occasionally?
Set up a vendor only if you want to track purchasing history for that vendor. To write checks to an occasional vendor, set up the payee on the Other Names List or print the check with no vendor selected at all and handwrite the vendor's name on the printed check.

Print Checks in a Batch

You can print all checks at the same time in a batch instead of printing them as you create them. This approach works particularly well if you have a lot of checks to print; you can create the checks in either the Pay Bills window or the Write Checks window and then, toward the end of the day, you can print the day's checks and mail them. To print a batch of checks, you need to ensure that you select the Print Later option as you pay bills or create checks in the Write Checks window.

Print Checks in a Batch

1 Click **File**.

2 Click **Print Forms**.

3 Click **Checks**.

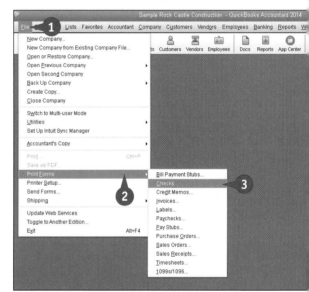

The Select Checks to Print dialog box appears, and QuickBooks selects all checks by default.

4 Click ▼ to select an account from which to print checks.

5 Confirm the first check number.

Ⓐ You can click in this area to deselect a check (☑ changes to ☐).

6 Click **OK**.

The Settings tab of the Print Checks window appears.

7 Click ⏷ to select a printer.

8 Click ⏷ to select the printer type.

9 Click a Check Style option (◯ changes to ◉).

10 Click **Print**.

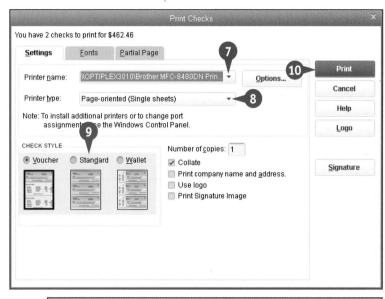

QuickBooks prints the checks and displays the Print Checks – Confirmation dialog box.

11 If any checks failed to print properly, you can click beside them (☐ changes to ☑).

12 Click **OK**.

QuickBooks reprints any selected checks.

For all checks that printed correctly, QuickBooks saves the check number.

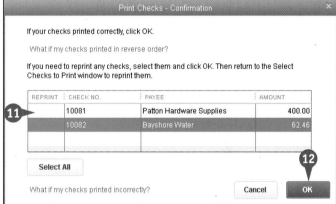

TIP

What is the difference between the style checks, and where can I get checks?

All three check styles come on 8½-x-11-inch paper. Standard check pages contain three checks, with no voucher or stub. Voucher check pages contain only one check; QuickBooks prints stub information twice on the remaining portion of the page, providing you with two vouchers. Wallet check pages contain three checks, but the pages are not 8½ inches wide because the left edge of each check contains the stub. You can purchase checks through your bank, directly from Intuit, or from a variety of form providers that you can locate on the Internet.

Pay the Sales Tax Liability

Periodically, you must remit sales tax you collect from customers to a state taxing authority. In many states, you collect sales tax not only for the state but also for cities, counties, and other localities.

Various states have different requirements concerning how often you must remit sales tax. In addition, many states offer you an allowance for handling the collection and record keeping associated with collecting sales tax; you are permitted to keep a small percentage to cover your expenses, so you must adjust the amount due as you create the sales tax liability check.

Pay the Sales Tax Liability

Pay the Liability

1. Click **Vendors**.

2. Click **Sales Tax**.

3. Click **Pay Sales Tax** to display the Pay Sales Tax window.

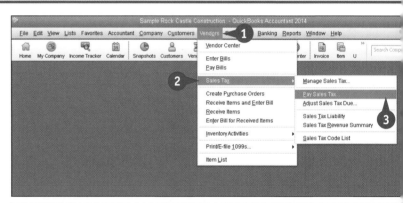

4. Click ▼ to select an account from which to pay sales tax.

5. Click 🛗 to select the check date.

6. Click 🛗 to select the date through which you want to pay the sales tax liability.

7. Click this column to select sales tax items to pay (☐ changes to ☑).

Ⓐ QuickBooks updates the Amt. Paid column.

8. Click the **To be printed** option (☐ changes to ☑) to create a check to print later.

Note: You typically create one check for each taxing authority.

9. Click **OK**.

QuickBooks creates the check.

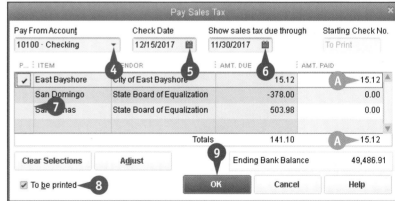

Adjust the Liability Before Paying

1 Complete steps **1** to **7** on the previous page.

2 Click **Adjust**.

3 In the Sales Tax Adjustment dialog box, click 📅 to select a date for the adjustment.

4 Click ▾ to select the sales tax vendor.

5 Click ▾ to select an account.

6 Click an option to increase or reduce sales tax (◯ changes to ◉).

7 Type the adjustment amount here.

8 Click **OK**.

The Pay Sales Tax window reappears, displaying a message indicating that QuickBooks has reset the amounts paid.

9 Click this column to select sales tax items and adjustments (☐ changes to ☑).

B QuickBooks updates the Amt. Paid column.

10 Click **OK**.

QuickBooks creates the check.

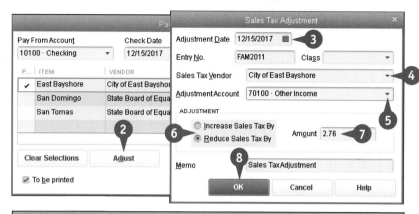

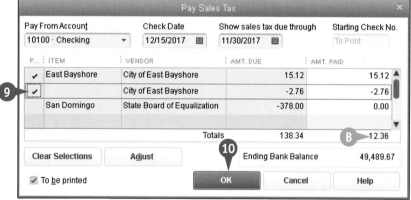

TIPS

How do I know what account to select for an adjustment?

QuickBooks records sales tax adjustments as journal entries. Select an income account if you are decreasing the amount of sales tax due; select an expense account if you are increasing the amount of sales tax due.

What happens if I click Vendors, click Sales Tax, and then click Sales Tax Liability?

QuickBooks displays the Sales Tax Liability report, which shows total sales for each taxing authority and divides them into taxable and non-taxable sales. The report shows each authority's tax rate, the tax you collected, and the sales tax due. This report can help you complete the Sales Tax Liability report required by most states.

Print 1099s and 1096s

Tax laws require that you provide *Form 1099* to all independent subcontractors with whom you did business during the previous year and to whom you paid by check more than the threshold amount of $600.00. QuickBooks can track payments to 1099 vendors for you and produce the 1099s you need.

To process 1099s in QuickBooks, you must turn on the feature and identify 1099 accounts. You also must identify 1099 vendors, provide their Tax ID numbers, and make sure that a ZIP code appears in the address. See Chapter 4 for details.

Print 1099s and 1096s

① Click **Vendors**.

② Click **Print/E-file 1099s**.

③ Click **1099 Wizard**.

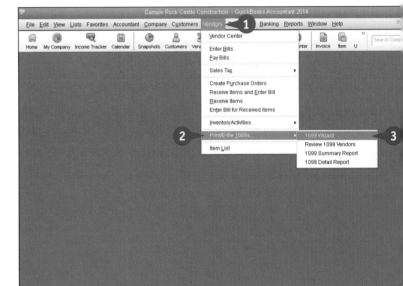

The first wizard screen describes the steps you take to prepare 1099s.

④ Click **Get Started**.

To prepare and file your 1099-MISC/1096 forms

1. Select your 1099 vendors
Select vendors to receive 1099-MISC forms.

2. Verify vendor information
Review and edit information for selected vendors.

3. Map your accounts
Choose which payments to report in each box on Form 1099-MISC.

4. Review vendor payments
Select debit, gift card and PayPal transactions to exclude from 1099-MISC forms.

5. Confirm 1099-MISC entries
Review the amounts to be reported on each vendor's Form 1099-MISC.

6. Choose a filing method
- **Print** 1099s and 1096 on preprinted forms to file by mail.
- **E-file** 1099s electronically with the IRS using the Intuit 1099 E-File Service. You can also print copies on plain paper.

ⓘ Learn more about these options

④ Get Started

The Select Your 1099 Vendors window appears.

5 Confirm that QuickBooks has selected all the vendors who need 1099s.

6 Click **Continue**.

The Verify Your Vendors' 1099 Information window appears.

7 Verify each vendor's information and make corrections as needed.

8 Click **Continue**.

TIPS

How do I edit vendor information while using the 1099 Wizard?
Double-click the field containing the information you want to edit and make changes as you would in a text editor; your typing replaces the existing information. To make small corrections, press any arrow key on the keyboard to cancel the selection and position the insertion point where you need to type; use the Backspace and Delete keys to remove information.

Is there an easy way to review vendor 1099 information before starting the printing process?
Yes. Print the Vendor 1099 Review report. Click **Vendors**, click **Print/ E-file 1099s**, and click **Review 1099 Vendors**.

continued ▶

You also should use the 1099 Summary Report in QuickBooks to verify that the information that appears on the 1099s is correct. The report shows only vendors set up as 1099 vendors to whom you made payments posted against designated 1099 accounts, and the payments exceeded the 1099 threshold requirement set by the IRS. Be aware that the default view of the report might not show everything you need to see.

The 1099 Wizard shows you 1099 thresholds on the Report 1099 Vendor Payments page. You can contact the IRS to confirm current threshold information.

Print 1099s and 1096s (continued)

The Map Vendor Payment Accounts window appears; QuickBooks displays the accounts you used when recording payments to 1099 vendors.

9 Click ▼ to select a 1099 box in which QuickBooks should report payments.

10 Click **Continue**.

The Check Payments for Exclusions window appears.

11 Click **View Excluded Payments** to view check payments QuickBooks excluded from 1099s.

The Check Payments Excluded from Forms 1099-MISC appears.

12 If appropriate, edit a payment to include it as a 1099 payment.

13 Click ▣ to close the report.

14 Click **View Included Payments** to view payments QuickBooks has included in reporting on 1099s.

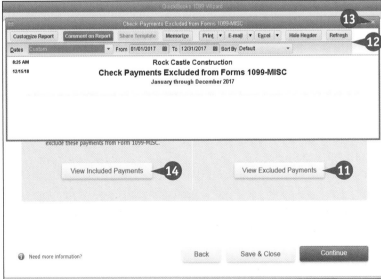

The Check Payments Included on Forms 1099-MISC window appears.

15 If appropriate, edit a payment to exclude it as a 1099 payment.

16 Click ☒ to close the report.

17 Click **Continue**.

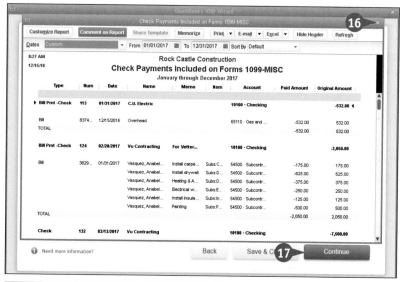

The Confirm Your 1099 Entries window appears.

18 Review the information QuickBooks will include on 1099s.

Note: You can double-click any amount to view the transactions included in it.

19 Click **Continue**.

continued ▶

TIPS

How can I modify the 1099 Summary Report to see everything I need?

Change the report to display all accounts and all vendor names; if new 1099 payments appear, you might have paid a 1099 vendor using an account you did not establish as a 1099 account, or you might have paid a vendor using a 1099 account, but the vendor does not qualify as a 1099 vendor. If nothing new appears, you can proceed with printing 1099s.

What if I see a message telling me that my 1099 settings do not match the IRS thresholds?

Click **Show IRS 1099-MISC filing thresholds**. QuickBooks displays the 1099-MISC IRS Thresholds dialog box; click **Reset to IRS thresholds**, and then **Save & Close**.

Print 1099s and 1096s (continued)

QuickBooks intends that you print Form 1099 and the cover sheet Form 1096 on preprinted forms that you can obtain from the IRS. Do not download the form from the IRS website; the web version cannot be scanned, and the IRS requires that you use the official IRS form that can be scanned. Call 1-800-TAX-FORM to order the form.

Alternatively, you can efile your 1099 and 1096 forms with the IRS and then print copies for your records and to mail to your vendors. This section shows you how to print forms 1099 and 1096.

Print 1099s and 1096s (continued)

The Choose a Filing Method window appears.

Ⓐ You can click **Go to Intuit 1099 E-File Service** and follow the instructions on-screen to file forms 1099 and 1096 electronically.

⑳ To print 1099s, click **Print 1099s**.

The Printing 1099-MISC and 1096 Forms dialog box appears.

Ⓑ You can click ▾ to select a date range.

Ⓒ Alternatively, you can click 🔲 to select a date range.

㉑ Click **OK**.

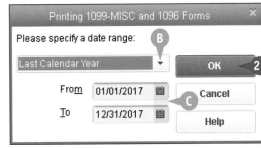

The Select 1099s to Print window appears.

㉒ Click this area to select (☐ changes to ☑) or deselect (☑ changes to ☐) 1099s to print or preview.

Ⓓ You can click **Print 1099**.

Ⓔ You can click **Print 1096**.

㉓ Click **Preview 1099**.

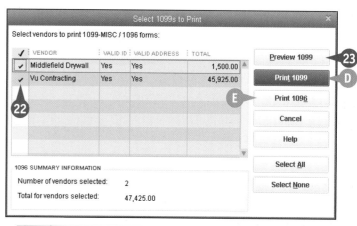

The Print Preview window appears.

Ⓕ You can click **Zoom Out** to enlarge or compress the view.

㉔ Click **Print** or click **Close**.

The Select 1099s to Print window reappears.

㉕ Click **Print 1099** or **Print 1096** or **Cancel**, on the Select 1009s to Print dialog box as appropriate.

TIPS

How do I designate payments that should be excluded from 1099s?

By law, you exclude any payments you made by credit card, debit card, gift card, or third-party payment network such as PayPal to vendors who qualify for 1099s. To exclude these payments, replace information in the Check Number field with Debit, Debitcar, DBT, DBT card, DCard, Debit cd, Masterc, MC, MCard, Visa, Chase, Discover, Diners, or PayPal.

How do I know which box on the 1099 to use for my vendor payments?

Many businesses use Box 7 to report payments for services performed by individuals not classified as employees. For a description of each box on Form 1099-MISC, visit www.irs.gov and search the site for "1099-MISC instructions."

Change Item Prices

You can change the price of Service, Inventory Part, Inventory Assembly, Non-Inventory Part, and Other Charge items. You change item prices either by manually modifying a price, or increasing or decreasing the price by a uniform amount or percentage. For example, you can increase the price of all service items by 10%.

When you change item prices, QuickBooks displays current prices for all items within the selected group of items. You can base dollar or percentage increases or decreases on the selected item's current price or unit cost.

Change Item Prices

Change Prices Individually

1 Click **Lists**.

2 Click **Item List**.

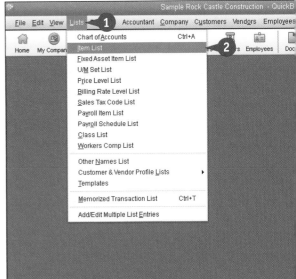

The Item List window appears.

3 Click **Activities**.

4 Click **Change Item Prices**.

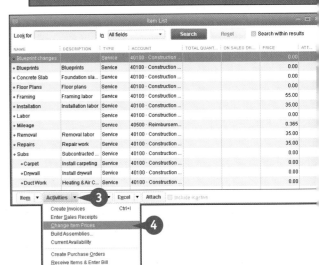

The Change Item Prices window appears.

5 Click ▼ and select an item type.

6 Click this column to select an item to change (☐ changes to ☑).

7 Type a new price in this column.

8 Repeat steps **6** and **7** to change additional prices.

9 Click **OK**.

QuickBooks updates the prices.

Change Prices Uniformly

1 Complete steps **1** to **6** on the previous page, repeating step **6** for each item price to change.

2 Click here to type a percentage or amount of price change.

Note: You can include a percent sign (%) to change price by a percentage.

Ⓐ You can click ▼ to select a basis for the new price.

3 Click **Adjust**.

Ⓑ QuickBooks displays the new prices here.

4 Click **OK**.

QuickBooks saves the new prices.

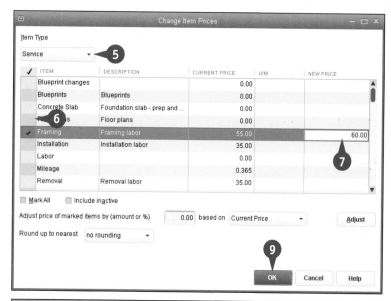

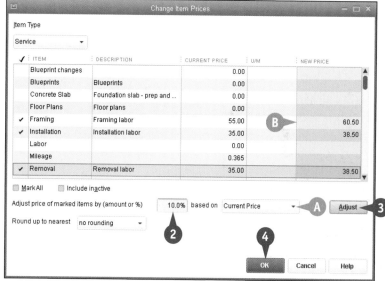

TIPS

When I update prices, where do I see the effects?
The new price appears in the Edit Item window as the rate or sales price for the item. The new price also appears on all new transactions, but QuickBooks does not change prices on existing transactions, including memorized transactions. To update memorized transactions, you need to edit and rememorize those transactions. For details on memorizing transactions, see Chapter 12.

How do I lower the price of items?
You type a lower number in the New Price column, or if you are updating a group of prices uniformly, you can type a negative number or a negative percentage in the **Adjust price of marked items by (amount or %)** box.

Build Assemblies

If you use QuickBooks Premier or higher, you can *assemble items* from component parts you keep in inventory. You can read about defining inventory assembly items in Chapter 3. When you build an assembly, QuickBooks reduces the number of the component parts on hand and increases the number on hand of the assembled item.

You cannot delete assembly items after you build them, so if you are uncertain about building a particular assembly, you can use the Mark Build As Pending command on the Edit menu while you decide whether to complete or delete the build transaction.

Build Assemblies

1 Click **Vendors**.

2 Click **Inventory Activities**.

3 Click **Build Assemblies**.

The Build Assemblies window appears.

4 Click ▼ and select an assembly item.

Ⓐ Quantity information for the assembly appears here.

Ⓑ Quantity information for each component appears here.

Ⓒ The maximum you can build based on available components appears here.

5 Type the quantity to build here.

6 Click **Build & New**.

QuickBooks saves the transaction and clears the window.

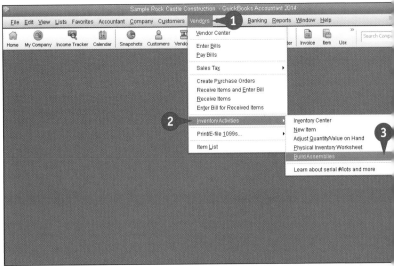

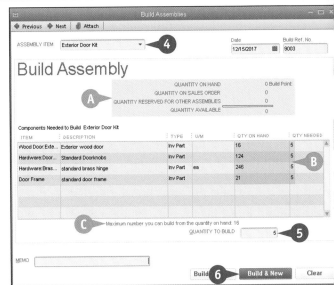

Count and Adjust Inventory Quantity or Value

Most companies that carry inventory count it, typically annually, to ensure that the physical quantity on hand matches inventory records. You can print the Physical Inventory Worksheet report to use while counting inventory, and you make adjustments to inventory records to reflect actual quantities.

When you make an inventory adjustment, you increase or decrease the item quantity (shown in this section), total value, or both. As double-entry bookkeeping requires, you must assign another account to the transaction to keep the transaction in balance. And, if appropriate, you can assign an inventory adjustment to a customer.

Count and Adjust Inventory Quantity or Value

1 Click **Vendors**.

2 Click **Inventory Activities**.

3 Click **Adjust Quantity/Value on Hand**.

4 Click ⏷ to select the adjustment type.

5 Click 🗓 to select an adjustment date.

6 Click ⏷ to select an account for the adjustment.

7 Click ⏷ to select an item.

8 Type the New Quantity or the Qty Difference.

Note: When you type one of these values, QuickBooks adjusts the other.

A QuickBooks fills in the total value and the number of adjustments.

9 Repeat steps **6** and **7** as needed.

10 Click **Save & Close** to save your changes.

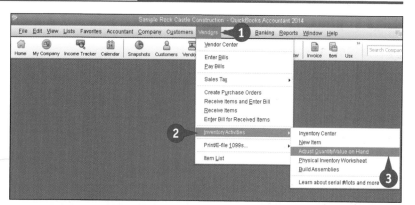

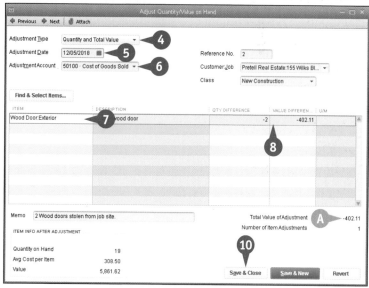

CHAPTER 11

Working with Bank Accounts

Depositing checks and paying bills may comprise most of the work you do with your bank account, but QuickBooks enables you to deal with additional account-related activities. In this chapter, you learn how to handle bounced checks you receive, reconcile your bank statement, and transfer funds between bank accounts.

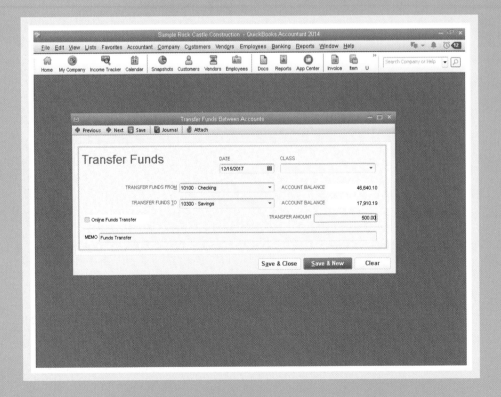

Handle NSF Checks

If you deposit a *nonsufficient funds* (NSF) check, your bank deducts the check amount and a processing fee from your bank account. The way you account for the situation depends on whether you originally recorded an invoice or a sales receipt.

To handle a bad check, you create a non-taxable Other Charge item called Bad Check and assign it to your bank account. To charge your customer a "bad check" penalty, create another non-taxable Other Charge item called Bad Check Service Charge. See Chapters 2 and 3 for help setting up an account and an Other Charge item.

Handle NSF Checks

Handle NSF Checks and Sales Receipts

1 Click **Customers**.

2 Click **Create Invoices**.

The Create Invoices window appears.

3 Click ▼ to select the customer.

4 Click ▼ to select the Bad Check item.

5 Type the amount of the NSF check.

6 Click **Save**.

7 Click **New**.

8 Repeat steps **3** to **5**, selecting the Bad Check-Service Charge item and the original item the customer purchased.

Note: Make the line for the original item non-taxable.

9 Click **Save & Close**.

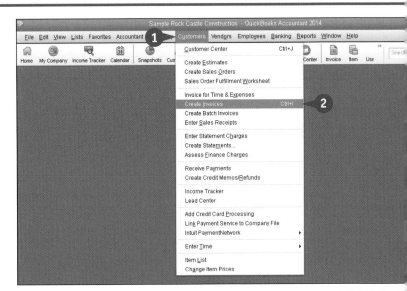

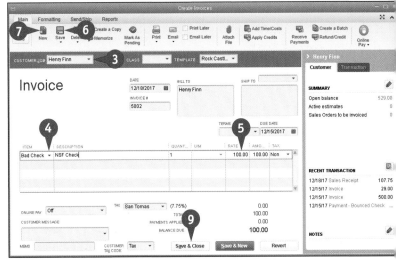

Handle NSF Checks and Invoices

1 Click **Customers**.

2 Click **Receive Payments**.

The Receive Payments window appears.

3 Display the transaction that recorded the bounced check on-screen by clicking **Find** or using the Previous (◀) and Next (▶) arrows.

4 Click **Record Bounced Check**.

The Manage Bounced Check window appears.

5 Type the fee your bank charged you here.

6 Click 📅 to select a date for the transaction.

7 Click ▼ to select the account for the bank charge.

8 Type the fee you want to charge the customer.

9 Click **Next**.

QuickBooks displays the Bounced Check Summary.

10 Click **Finish**.

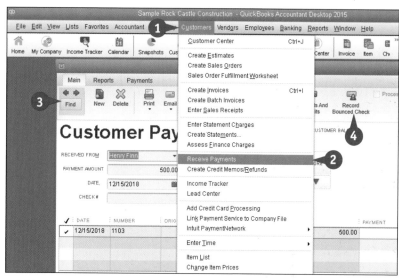

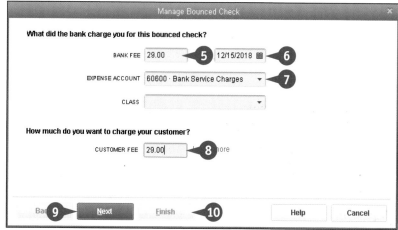

TIPS

What happens with the invoice in the subsection "NSF Checks and Sales Receipts"?

The invoice with the Bad Check item reverses the effects the recorded sales receipt and subsequent deposit. A second invoice passes the bank's penalty along to the customer, recharging for the item. The line containing the original item non-taxable balances your sales tax liability.

What are the Bounced Check Summary actions?

QuickBooks marks the original invoice as unpaid and deducts it and the bank's service charge from your bank account. QuickBooks then creates an invoice for the amount you opted to charge the customer in step **8**.

Reconcile a Bank Statement

Each month, you should reconcile the bank statement you receive with your QuickBooks bank account activities to ensure that you and the bank agree on your account balance. The statement you receive includes checks, deposits, and actions the bank takes, such as charging you for nonsufficient funds checks. The statement balance should match the QuickBooks balance; if they do not match, you resolve the discrepancies, as described in the section "Resolve Discrepancies."

The bank statement displays cleared transactions. To reconcile your account, you adjust the bank statement balance by adding and subtracting uncleared transactions. QuickBooks automates this process.

Reconcile a Bank Statement

1 Click **Home**.

2 Click **Reconcile** to display the Begin Reconciliation window.

3 Click ▾ to select an account.

4 Click 📅 to select a statement date.

5 Type the ending balance listed on the statement here.

Ⓐ You can type service charges and interest earned here.

Ⓑ You can click 📅 to select dates and click ▾ to select accounts for service charges or interest earned.

6 Click **Continue**.

The Reconcile window appears.

7 Click next to each deposit and check that appears on the bank statement (☐ changes to ☑).

Ⓒ The Difference on the bank statement should equal zero.

Note: If this value is not zero, see the section "Resolve Discrepancies."

8 Click **Reconcile Now**.

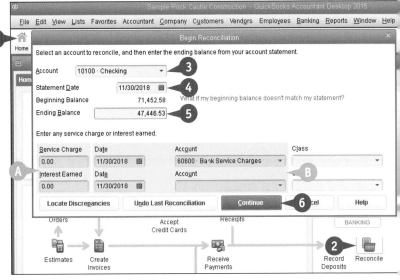

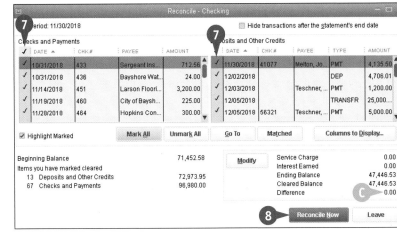

QuickBooks marks the selected transactions as reconciled and displays the Select Reconciliation Report window.

9 Click a report type option (◉ changes to ◉).

Note: This example shows **Both** selected.

10 Click **Display**.

The reconciliation reports appear.

11 Review the reports.

12 Click **Print** on either the Reconciliation Summary or the Reconciliation Detail windows.

13 Click the **Close** button (☒) to close the reports.

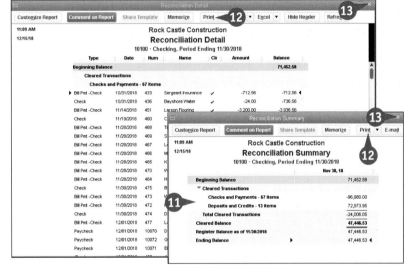

TIPS

What do the Columns to Display and the Go To buttons in the Reconcile window do?
Columns to Display selects the columns you want to see in the Reconcile window. In addition to the Date, Chk #, Payee, and Amount columns, you can display the Memo column for both the Checks and Payments side of the window and the Deposits and Other Credits side of the window. When you select a transaction and click **Go To**, QuickBooks displays the transaction in the window where you originally created the transaction.

Can I reprint reconciliation reports?
Yes. Click **Reports**, click **Banking**, and click **Previous Reconciliation**. The Select Previous Reconciliation Report window lists the past reconciliation reports you can print.

Resolve Discrepancies

When you match all the transactions in QuickBooks to the transactions on your bank statement, as illustrated in the section "Reconcile a Bank Statement," and the difference is something other than 0, you must figure out why and resolve the problem. The difference may not equal 0 for several reasons. Compare transaction amounts on the statement to those in QuickBooks, and double-check the ending balance amount you entered and the beginning balance amount. You can use the Discrepancy report in QuickBooks to help you find transactions that may be causing the problem.

Resolve Discrepancies

① Click **Banking**.

② Click **Reconcile**.

The Begin Reconciliation window appears.

③ Click **Locate Discrepancies**.

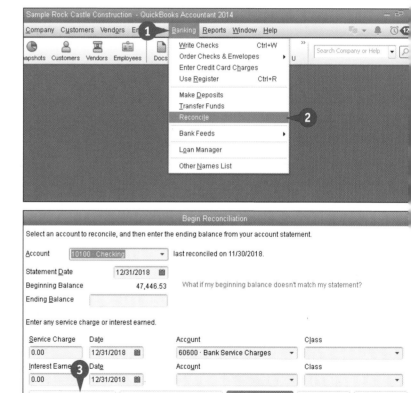

The Locate Discrepancies window appears.

④ Click ▼ to select an account.

⑤ Click **Discrepancy Report**.

The Discrepancy Report appears, showing transactions modified since reconciliation.

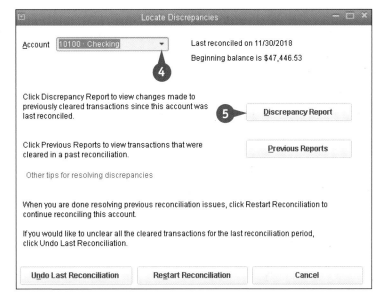

Ⓐ You can double-click a transaction to display it in the window where you created it and modify it.

Is there an easy way to determine what is causing the difference to be something other than 0?
You can eliminate one of the potential reasons if you use the Sum of the Digits rule. Add the digits of the difference to see if they equal 9 or a multiple of 9. If so, you probably transposed digits while recording one or more checks or deposits.

Does the Discrepancy Report show only those transactions that help resolve reconciliation problems?
No. The report shows all cleared transactions that have changed, including changes to the date of a cleared transaction. You might want to compare previous reconciliation reports to the current report to ensure that previously cleared transactions are still cleared. You also can have QuickBooks print those reports showing cleared transactions plus changes made since reconciliation.

Move Funds Between Accounts

You can move funds between accounts in QuickBooks using two different windows: the Transfer Funds window or the Make General Journal Entries window. The Transfer Funds window facilitates moving money between balance sheet accounts. For example, use the Transfer Funds window to move money between your checking account and your savings account or to record ATM withdrawals.

To transfer funds between two accounts that are not balance sheet accounts, create a journal entry. For example, to record depreciation expense, use a journal entry. The only rule for journal entries is that total debits must equal total credits.

Move Funds Between Accounts

Transfer Funds

1. Click **Banking**.
2. Click **Transfer Funds**.

   The Transfer Funds window appears.

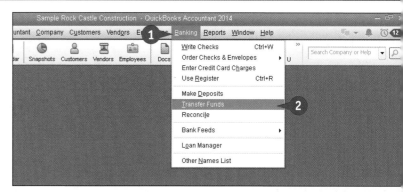

3. Click 📅 to select a date for the transfer.
4. Click ▾ to select the account from which to transfer funds.
5. Click ▾ to select the account to which you want to transfer funds.
6. Type the transfer amount here.

   Ⓐ You can type a memo here.

7. Click **Save & Close**.

   QuickBooks transfers the funds.

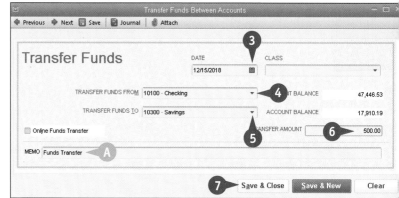

Make a Journal Entry

1. Click **Company**.

2. Click **Make General Journal Entries**.

   The Make General Journal Entries window appears.

   Ⓑ Previous journal entries appear here; you can click ▾ to select a time frame to display.

3. Click ▦ to select a date for the entry.

   Ⓒ You can type a number for the entry here.

4. Click ▾ to select an account.

5. Type a debit amount here.

6. Repeat steps **4** and **5**, typing an amount in the Credit column when you repeat step **5**.

7. Repeat steps **4** to **6** to enter additional lines.

8. Click **Save & Close**.

   QuickBooks records the journal entry.

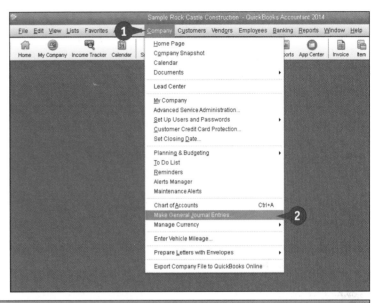

TIPS

Can I only use the Transfer Funds window when working with bank accounts?

No. You can use the Transfer Funds window to move money between bank, Other Current Asset, Fixed Asset, Other Asset, Credit Card, Other Current Liability, Long Term Liability, and Equity accounts. For example, you can use this window to move money from a line of credit account into your bank account.

How do I know whether to debit or credit an account?

In general, debits increase asset and expense accounts and decrease liability, equity, and income accounts. Credits increase liability, equity, and income accounts, and decrease asset and expense accounts. To make journal entries using unusual accounts, such as contra-asset accounts, consult your accountant.

CHAPTER 12

Performing General Tasks

In this chapter, you learn to perform tasks that do not fall into a particular category. For example, you learn to find and view transaction information and use the Memorize feature to save and use transactions you create regularly. You also learn techniques to calculate sales commissions. And, QuickBooks Pro users learn a technique to track back orders.

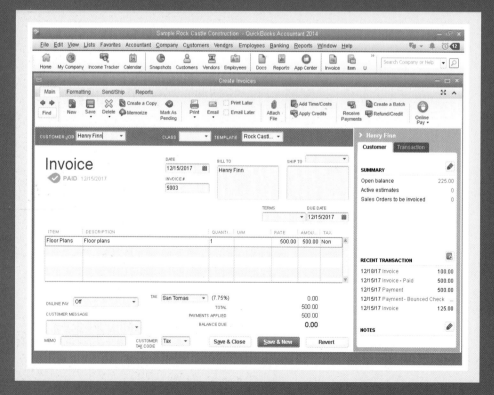

Find a Transaction

You need to find transactions you entered if you want to double-check, examine the history of, or perhaps correct a transaction. You can search in a variety of ways, but the Find feature is undoubtedly the most robust.

QuickBooks contains a Simple Find feature and an Advanced Find feature, and the two features differ in the options they make available. You can specify fewer criteria using the Simple Find feature than you can when using the Advanced Find feature. Use the Advanced Find feature when trying to search by criteria not available for the Simple Find feature.

Find a Transaction

Perform a Simple Search

1 Click **Edit**.

2 Click **Find**.

QuickBooks displays the Simple tab of the Find window.

3 Click ▼ and select a transaction type.

4 Click ▼ to select a name.

Note: The type of name changes depending on the transaction type selected.

A You can click 📅 to select starting and ending dates.

B You can type a transaction number to search for a specific transaction or type an amount for which QuickBooks should search.

5 Click **Find**.

C QuickBooks displays the search results; you can click **Go To** to view the transaction in the transaction window.

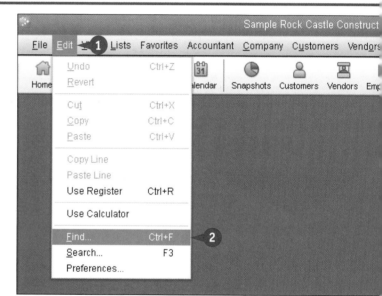

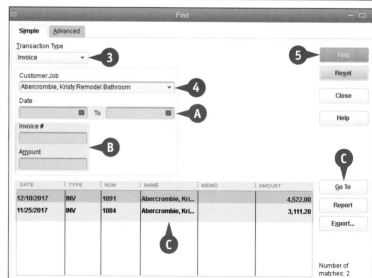

Perform an Advanced Search

1 Click **Edit**.

2 Click **Find**.

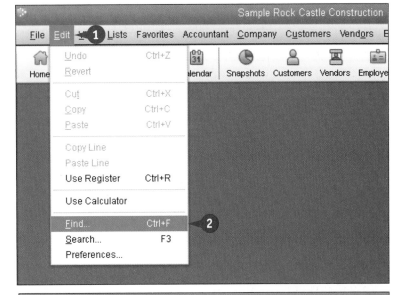

3 Click the **Advanced** tab.

4 Click a filter.

5 Select criteria for the filter.

Note: The way you select available criteria changes, depending on the selected filter.

6 Repeat steps 3 and 4 to add additional filters.

7 Click **Find**.

D QuickBooks displays the results of the search here, and you can click a transaction and click **Go To** to display it in the transaction window.

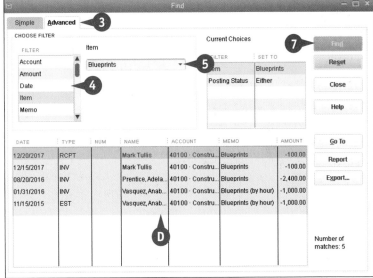

TIPS

What are some of the other ways I can search for transactions?

Open the window where you created the transaction and click the ◀ and ▶ buttons until you find the transaction. Or, open the register for an account affected by a transaction and scroll to find the transaction. Alternatively, you can create a custom report that includes the transaction, which Chapter 13 discusses.

My search turned up no results. What did I do wrong?

Either no transactions exist, or you specified too many criteria. To see more transactions, try eliminating some of the filter criteria you specified; for example, eliminate a transaction number or a date range or a filter.

View Transaction Details

Sometimes, viewing the actual transaction is not sufficient to solve problems. You may need to know what other transactions are tied to the transaction in question. For example, you may want to see payments associated with a customer invoice or checks tied to a vendor bill. In QuickBooks, you view transaction history to obtain this information. You also can view the accounts affected by a transaction and the associated debits and credits.

Be aware that you might see a message telling you that no history exists for a transaction; this message appears when no related transactions exist for the transaction you are viewing.

View Transaction Details

1 Display a transaction.

Note: See the section "Find a Transaction" or use the ➡ and ⬅ arrows in the appropriate transaction window to display a transaction.

2 Click the **Reports** tab.

3 Click **Transaction History**.

Ⓐ You can click **Transaction Journal** to view a report that shows the debits and credits QuickBooks created for the current transaction.

QuickBooks displays the Transaction History window.

4 Click a transaction.

5 Click **Go To**.

QuickBooks displays the selected transaction in the window where it was created.

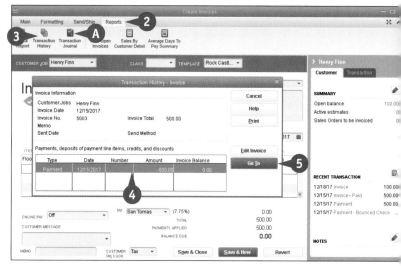

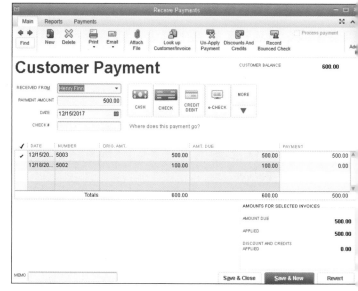

Delete or Void a Transaction

Occasionally, you need to eliminate the effects of the transaction. In most cases, you have three choices: You can enter a transaction that reverses the original transaction, you can delete the transaction, or you can void the transaction.

Entering a transaction to reverse the original transaction can be difficult and confusing, so most users avoid this option. Many users delete transactions, but deleting transactions can make tracking down a problem difficult. Whenever possible, you should void transactions instead of deleting them to set the amount to $0, negating the transaction's effect on your company's books.

Delete or Void a Transaction

1 Display a transaction.

Note: This section uses an invoice as the example.

Note: See the section "Find a Transaction" or use the and arrows in the appropriate transaction window to display a transaction.

2 Click **Edit**.

3 Click **Delete Invoice** or **Void Invoice**.

If you click **Delete Invoice**, QuickBooks removes the transaction from your company data file.

If you click **Void Invoice**, QuickBooks removes the effects of the transaction from your company file.

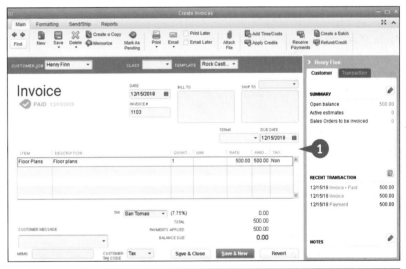

Memorize a Transaction

If you prepare a transaction on a repetitive basis, you can use the *Memorize* feature to make QuickBooks "remember" the information you enter. You can save time the next time you need to enter the transaction by using the memorized transaction. Suppose, for example, that you pay the same amount each month for insurance. You can memorize this bill to enter it quickly each month.

You can memorize most types of transactions: sales orders, sales receipts, credit memos, statement charges, purchase orders, bills, checks, and credit card transactions. You cannot memorize time tracking transactions, customer receipts, employee paychecks, inventory adjustments, or assembly builds.

Memorize a Transaction

1 Display a transaction.

Note: See the section "Find a Transaction" or use the ➡ and ⬅ arrows in the appropriate transaction window to display a transaction.

2 Click **Edit**.

3 Click **Memorize Bill**.

Note: If you are memorizing a different transaction type, click the Memorize command for that transaction type.

The Memorize Transaction dialog box appears.

4 Type a name for the transaction here.

5 Click **Add to my Reminders List** (◯ changes to ◉).

6 Click ▾ to select a frequency.

7 Click 📅 to select the next date for the transaction.

8 Click **OK**.

QuickBooks memorizes and redisplays the transaction.

9 Click **Save & Close**.

Enter a Memorized Transaction

When you create a memorized transaction as described in the section "Memorize a Transaction," you establish a date on which QuickBooks affects accounts. But QuickBooks does not affect accounts until you enter a memorized transaction that you previously created. The process, therefore, is two-part: You first create a memorized transaction and, when you are ready to affect your accounts with the transaction, you enter the memorized transaction. You can tell QuickBooks to automatically enter a memorized transaction on a specified date, or you can enter the transaction yourself, as shown in this section.

Enter a Memorized Transaction

1 Click **Lists**.

2 Click **Memorized Transaction List**.

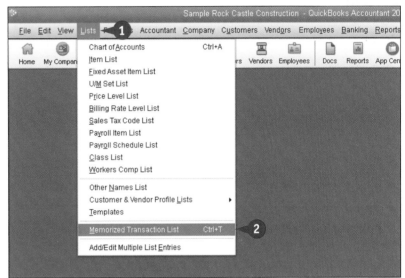

3 Click the transaction you want to enter.

Ⓐ The date of the transaction appears here.

4 Click **Enter Transaction**.

The transaction appears in the window where you created it.

Ⓑ The date of the transaction matches the next date based on the memorized criteria. You can change this date if you want.

5 Click **Save & Close**.

QuickBooks records the transaction and updates your accounts.

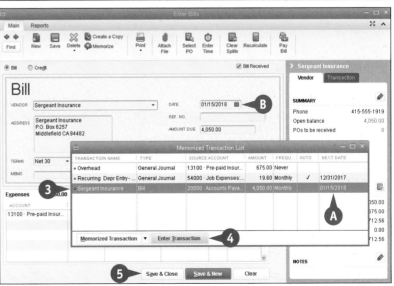

Work with a List Window

In addition to editing or viewing list information, you can make a list window itself work for you. You can sort and arrange records in a list window. For example, you may want to view the Item List in the order of quantity on hand or by price.

As for arranging lists, QuickBooks displays list information in a hierarchical view by default, where all sub-items appear indented under the parent item's name. But, you can switch to a flat view, where sub-items are listed using the parent item name, a colon, and then the sub-item name.

Work with a List Window

Sort a List

1 Click **Lists**.

2 Click **Item List**.

A The list window appears in hierarchical view.

The list appears in its default sort order.

3 Click any column heading.

Note: This section uses the Price column.

B QuickBooks sorts the list in the order of the selected column heading.

Note: This section shows the window sorted by the Price column heading from highest price to lowest price.

C This diamond (⧫) identifies the column by which the list is sorted and the direction of the sort: from alphabetically or from lowest to highest or the reverse order.

D You can click here to return the window to its default sort order.

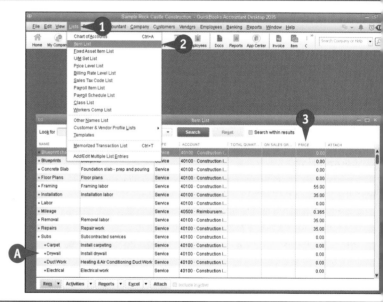

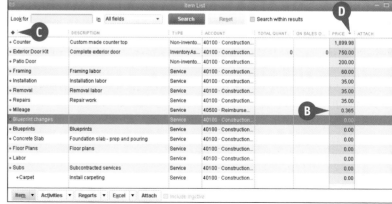

Switch Views

① Perform steps **1** and **2** on the previous page.

② Click **Item**.

③ Click **Flat View**.

QuickBooks changes the look of the list from a hierarchical presentation to a flat presentation.

Ⓔ Sub-items appear using first the parent item's name, then a colon (:), and then the sub-item name.

TIP

If I no longer need a list entry, can I delete it?

Yes, you can, but only if you did not use the entry in any transactions. You can hide entries used in transactions. Right-click the entry and click **Make Inactive**. You can display hidden entries if you click the left-most button at the bottom of the window and then click **Show Inactive**. QuickBooks displays hidden entries with an X beside them. To use a hidden item again, right-click it and click **Make Active**.

Track Back Orders Using Pending Invoices

If you have QuickBooks Pro, you can use pending invoices to track back orders.

Pending invoices do not affect your company's accounts, do not appear in registers, and do not appear on any reports except the Pending Sales report. Instead, they act as placeholders to remind you that you have made a sale but simply cannot fulfill your obligation to deliver the merchandise at the present time. After you receive the goods, you can change the status of the pending invoice to a regular invoice; at that time, QuickBooks does update your company's accounts to reflect the sale.

Track Back Orders Using Pending Invoices

1 Click **Customers**.

2 Click **Create Invoices**.

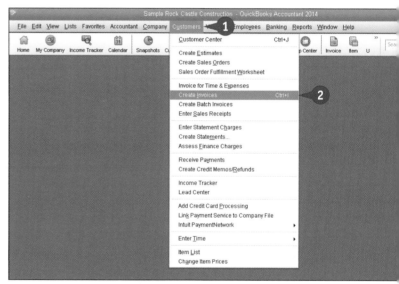

The Create Invoices window appears.

3 Click ▼ to select a Customer:Job and fill in the window as you usually would complete an invoice.

Note: See Chapter 8 for details on completing an invoice.

Ⓐ When you try to invoice more of an item than you have on hand, QuickBooks displays the Not Enough Quantity dialog box.

4 Click **OK**.

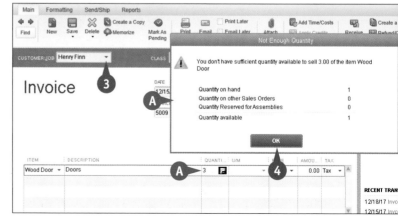

The Create Invoices window reappears.

5 Change the quantity on the invoice to match the quantity on hand and complete the rest of the invoice.

6 Click **Save & New**.

7 Repeats steps **1** to **4**, selecting the same customer and the item and quantity you need to back order.

Note: When the Not Enough Quantity dialog box appears, click **OK**.

8 Click **Edit**.

9 Click **Mark Invoice As Pending**.

B QuickBooks marks the invoice as pending.

10 Click **Save & Close**.

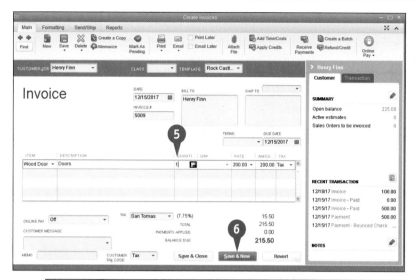

TIP

After I receive the merchandise, do I need to reenter the information from the pending invoice onto a real invoice to fill the order?

No. You can change the status of a pending invoice so that it becomes a regular invoice. Click **Reports**, click **Sales**, and then click **Pending Sales**. Set the date range to **All** so that you do not miss any pending sales. Double-click the pending sale you intend to fill. Change the invoice date to the current date. Then, click **Edit** and then **Mark Invoice as Final**. QuickBooks removes the Pending stamp from the invoice. When you save the invoice, QuickBooks updates your sales and Accounts Receivable accounts with the information on the invoice.

Calculate Sales Commissions

If you pay sales commissions, you need to determine the commission amount to pay. Most companies pay commissions only on paid sales; that way, the company does not pay a commission for a sale that may later become uncollectible.

Use the Rep field to assign a sales representative to every invoice, sales receipt, and credit memo. (If the Rep field does not appear on your templates, see Chapter 14 for details on adding the field.) Use the Sales by Rep Summary report to identify the collected amount for each sale. Then, export the report to Excel to calculate the commission amount.

Calculate Sales Commissions

Report on Sales

1 Click **Reports**.

2 Click **Sales**.

3 Click **Sales by Rep Summary**.

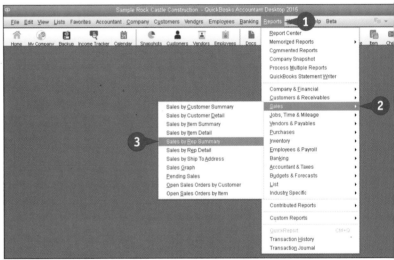

The report appears on-screen.

4 Click ▼ or 📅 to select the report period.

5 Click the **Customize Report** tab.

The Display tab of the Modify Report dialog box appears.

6 Click **Cash** (◯ changes to ◉).

7 Click **OK**.

The report reappears on-screen.

Note: Some amounts might not be assigned to sales reps. You typically do not assign finance charge, sales tax, or discount transactions to sales representatives.

8 Click **Excel**.

9 Click **Create New Worksheet**.

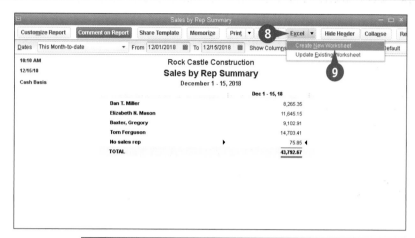

The Send Report to Excel dialog box appears.

10 Click **Create new worksheet** (◯ changes to ◉).

11 Click **in new workbook** (◯ changes to ◉).

12 Click **Export**.

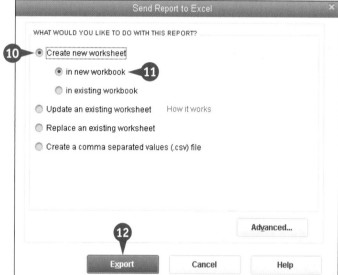

TIP

What is the easiest way to find the transactions to which I need to add a sales representative?
Print the Sales by Rep Detail report by clicking **Reports**, **Sales**, and then **Sales by Rep Detail**. All transactions that you entered but did not assign to a sales representative appear under the heading "No sales rep." Double-click a transaction to display it in the window where you created it. Add a sales representative and save the document. QuickBooks prompts you to assign the sales representative to the Customer:Job permanently. Click **Yes**, and QuickBooks saves the transaction and assigns the same rep to future documents for that customer.

continued ▶

By default, QuickBooks displays the Sales by Rep Summary report on an accrual basis, which includes all sales made by each sales representative. To display only sales your company has collected, you modify the report to display on a cash basis.

After you change the basis of the report, it shows the total collected sales but does not show the commission amount you should pay each sales representative. QuickBooks cannot calculate the sales commission due to a sales representative, but by exporting the report to Excel, you can easily determine a sales representative's commission amount using some very basic formulas.

Calculate Sales Commissions (continued)

Calculate Commissions

Excel opens and displays the report.

13 Click here and type a title for the percentage column.

14 Click here and type a title for the commission amount column.

15 Type sales commission rates as decimals in this column.

16 Click here and type an equal sign (=).

17 Click here and type an asterisk (*).

18 Click this cell.

19 Click ☑ or press Enter.

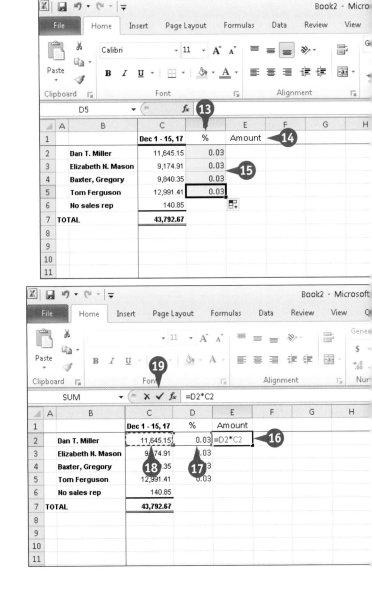

Excel stores the formula and displays the commission amount.

20 Click in the cell containing the formula.

21 Click **Copy** (🔲).

22 Click and drag to select the cells in column E that should contain commission amounts.

23 Click **Paste** (🔲).

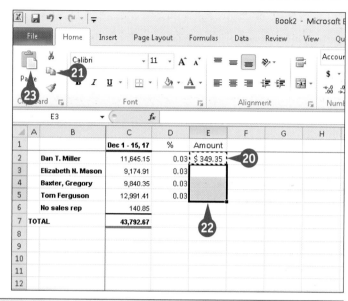

A Excel copies the formula to the selected cells.

24 Click anywhere to finish copying and pasting.

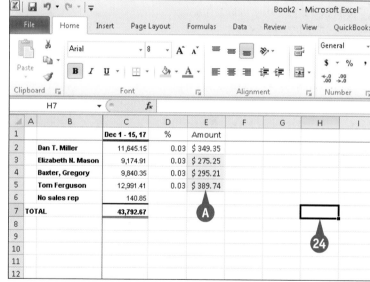

TIPS

How do I ensure that I do not pay a sales representative for the same sale twice?

Most businesses pay commissions once each month for the preceding month. Keep copies of prior reports and make sure that report date ranges do not overlap.

If the commission rate is different for each sales representative, will the formula for the commission amount be accurate if I copy it?

Yes. By default, Excel adjusts a formula you copy. If you copy a formula in Cell E2 that multiplies the contents of D2 by C2 to Cell E3, Excel adjusts the formula in E3 to multiply D3 by C3.

Track Unpaid Invoices by Salesman

If you require your sales representatives to follow up on uncollected sales, you can create a report for each sales representative to use to track down uncollected sales. The report is a variation of the Collections Report, which shows unpaid invoices for a specified period. The report includes the terms, due date, age, and balance of each open invoice, and customer contact information that the sales representative can use to get in touch with the customer.

You filter this report for one sales representative so that you can print separate reports for each sales representative.

Track Unpaid Invoices by Salesman

1 Click **Reports**.

2 Click **Customers & Receivables**.

3 Click the **Collections Report** tab.

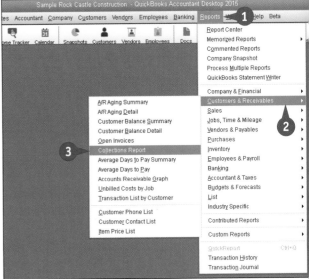

The Collections Report dialog box displays.

4 Click the **Customize Report** tab.

The Modify Report dialog box displays.

5 Click the **Filters** tab.

6 Click **Aging**.

7 Click **Remove Selected Filter**.

8 Repeat steps **6** and **7** for the **Due Date** filter.

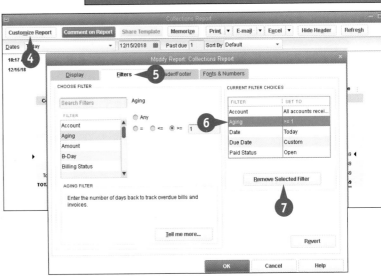

9 Click **Rep**.

10 Click ▾ to select a rep.

A You can click the **Header/ Footer** tab, and in the **Report Title** field, type a more meaningful report title, such as "Unpaid Invoices For" followed by the sales rep's name.

11 Click **OK**.

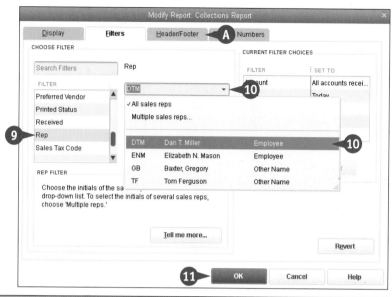

The report for the selected sales representative appears.

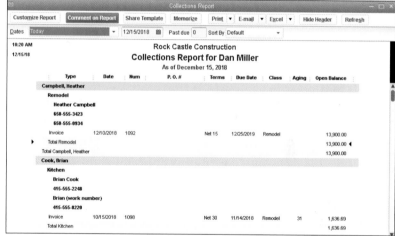

TIP

Is there an easy way to modify the existing report for another sales representative or must I re-create it from scratch?
While viewing the current version of the report, you can click **Customize Report**. In the Modify Report dialog box, click the **Filters** tab. Click the **Rep** field in the Current Filter Choices list on the right side of the tab. Click ▾ in the middle of the tab and select a different sales representative. Do not forget to change the report title on the Header/Footer tab if you included the sales representative's name in the report title. You might want to memorize one report for each sales representative; see Chapter 13.

Working with Reports

This chapter focuses on using reports in QuickBooks. You learn to find, customize, and print a report. You also learn to use the Memorize feature to make QuickBooks remember changes you make to settings and to print reports using settings you memorize. In addition, you work with the Document Center and the Income Tracker.

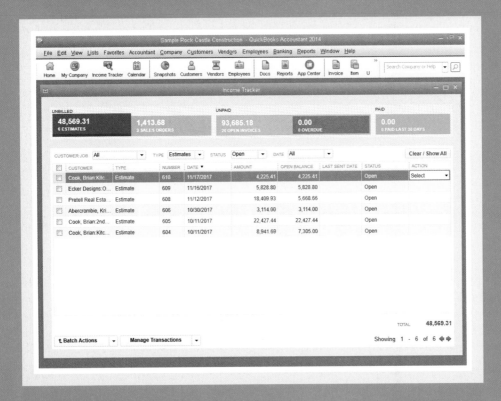

Find and Print a Report

You can find and print reports containing your company's information. QuickBooks contains the Reports menu and the Report Center. The Report Center helps you identify the report you want to print by providing a sample image and a brief description of the information found in each report. When you run a report, it appears on-screen, and you can set criteria to display the information you need and then print the report.

The Report Center window organizes reports into groups, and these groups also appear on the Reports menu, so you can print the report without using the Report Center window.

Find and Print a Report

1 Click **Reports** to display the Report Center.

A These groups appear on the Reports menu.

B The categories in the Standard group appear on the Reports menu.

2 Click a group and then a category to view the reports in it.

C You can type keywords that describe the report for which you want to search and click (🔍); QuickBooks displays search results on a Search tab.

D You can click **Carousel** (▣), **Grid** (▤), or **List** (▦) in this area to change the way you view report samples.

E You can click · to hide report categories.

3 In Grid or List view, click any report's Info button (🔳).

F QuickBooks displays a larger preview image and a description of the report.

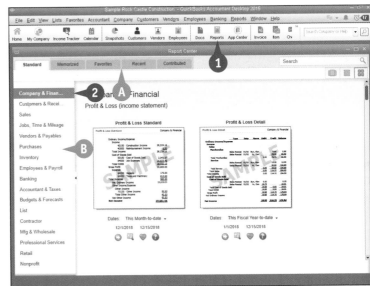

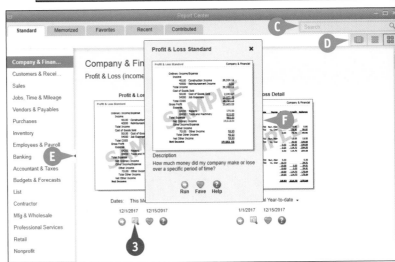

G You can click ✕ to close the image preview and redisplay the Report Center.

4 Click **Run** (⊙).

The report appears on-screen.

H You can use these buttons to customize the appearance of the report.

I Clicking **Print** displays printing options and prints the report.

J You can click **E-mail** to email a report as an Excel file or as a PDF file.

K You can click **Excel** to export the report to Excel.

Note: The Collapse button hides subaccounts and reduces the length of your report.

5 When you finish, click ✕ twice to close the report and the Report Center.

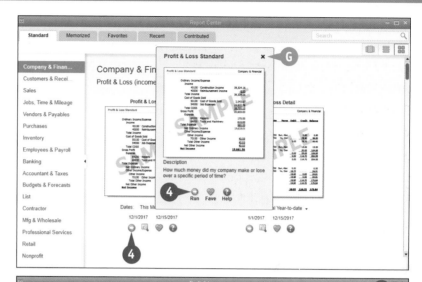

TIPS

Is there another way to select a report to print?

Yes. You can click the **Reports** menu. The menu lists the same categories as those that appear on the **Standard** tab in the Report Center, and also contains options to view and print memorized reports, reports you have marked as favorites, and contributed reports.

What are contributed reports?

Contributed reports are templates for custom reports created by Intuit and other QuickBooks users. The person who creates the report uploads it to make it available for others to use by clicking the **Share Template** button that becomes available when you customize any report by making changes to the date range, the report columns, or the report filters.

Memorize a Report

You can save time by using the Memorize feature to save customized settings for a report. When you memorize a report, QuickBooks stores the settings to create the report but not the data that appears on the report. Each time you print a memorized report, QuickBooks uses the saved settings.

This section demonstrates how to memorize a version of the Profit & Loss Standard report and include it in an existing report group. You can print all reports in a group simultaneously, as described in the section "Print Memorized Reports" later in this chapter.

Memorize a Report

1 Click **Reports**.

2 Click **Company & Financial**.

3 Click **Profit & Loss Standard**.

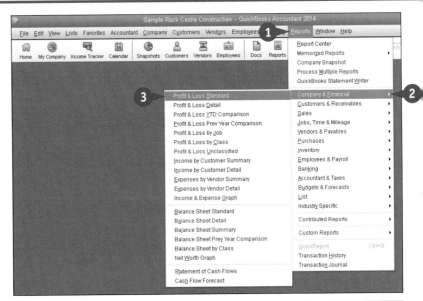

The report appears on-screen.

4 In this area, click either ▼ or 📅 to change the report dates.

A You can click ▼ to change the columns displayed.

B You can click ▼ to sort the report in another order.

C You can click the **Customize Report** tab to make other changes to information on the report.

5 Click the **Memorize** tab.

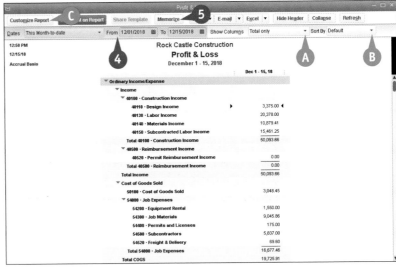

The Memorize Report dialog box appears.

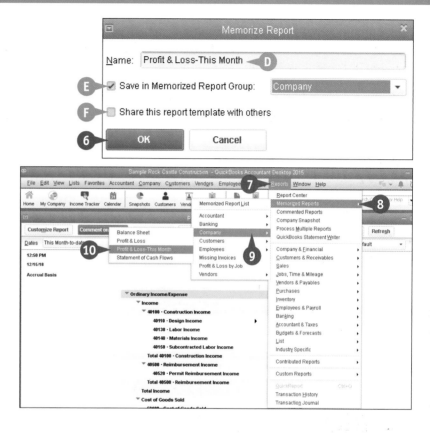

D You can change the report name here.

E You can save the report in a memorized report group if you click here (☐ changes to ☑), and then click ▾ to select the group.

F You can click here (☐ changes to ☑) to share the report template with others.

6 Click **OK**.

QuickBooks memorizes the report.

7 Click **Reports**.

8 Click **Memorized Reports**.

9 Click the group in which you placed the report.

The report appears on the Memorized Report menu in the group you selected.

10 Click the report to display it on-screen.

TIPS

Can I delete a memorized report?
Yes. Use the Memorized Report List window, which looks just like the Memorize Report dialog box shown in this section. Click **Reports**, click **Memorized Reports**, and click **Memorized Report List**. In the Memorized Report List window, click the report you want to delete, click **Memorized Report**, and then click **Delete**.

After I memorize a report, can I change the name I assigned to it?
Yes. Click **Reports**, click **Memorized Reports**, and click **Memorized Report List**. In the Memorized Report List window, click the report you want to rename, click **Memorized Report**, and click **Edit**. In the Edit Memorized Report dialog box, type a new name for the report.

Print Memorized Reports

You can print any memorized report, and if you place your memorized reports in groups, you can display the entire group on-screen simultaneously and then print each item in the group individually. For more information on memorizing a report, see the section "Memorize a Report."

Most people create memorized report groups to organize reports by subject. For example, you might create a memorized report group that you print at the end of the month. You can print the reports individually, or you can print the entire group. You also can move existing memorized reports into a new group.

Print Memorized Reports

1 Click **Reports**.

2 Click **Memorized Reports**.

3 Click **Memorized Report List**.

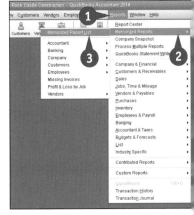

The Memorized Report List window appears.

4 Click a report group heading.

Note: Report group headings appear in bold type.

5 Click **Display**.

The Process Multiple Reports window appears.

Ⓐ You can click next to any report to exclude it from printing (☑ changes to ☐).

❻ Click **Display**.

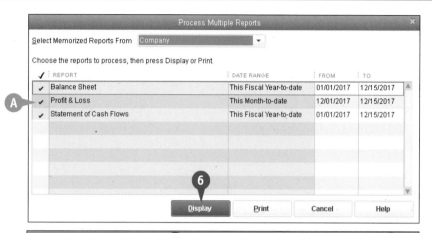

QuickBooks displays all selected reports on-screen.

❼ Click any report title bar to view that report.

Ⓑ While viewing a report, you can click **Print** to print the report.

❽ Click the **Close** button (☒) to close each report.

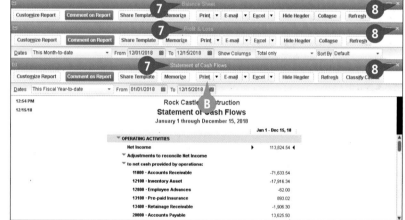

TIPS

Can I create a new report group?

Yes. Click **Reports**, click **Memorized Reports**, and click **Memorized Report List** to display the Memorized Report List window. Click the Memorized Report button at the bottom of the window and then click **New Group** to display the New Group dialog box. Type a name for the new group and click **OK**. QuickBooks places the new group alphabetically in the Memorized Report List window.

How do I move a memorized report from one group to another?

Drag the small diamond (◈) to the left of each report until the report appears in the appropriate group. You also can reorganize groups in the window by dragging the diamond beside a report group name.

Create a Custom Summary Report

On occasion, you might not find the report you want to print listed in the Report Center window or on the Reports menu. In these cases, you can create custom reports. The Custom Summary Report shows sums of numbers instead of the details behind the sums.

The Custom Summary Report gives you great flexibility. Down the left side of standard reports, you can print only accounts, but down the left side of a custom report, you can include just about any field. This section illustrates an example of a custom summary report that shows Income by Class and Customer Type.

Create a Custom Summary Report

1. Click **Reports**.

2. Click **Custom Reports**.

3. Click **Summary**.

   The Custom Summary Report and the Modify Report dialog box appear.

4. In this area, click ⏷ or 🗓 to set a reporting time frame.

5. Click ⏷ to select report columns; this example uses Class.

6. Click ⏷ to select report rows; this example uses Customer Type.

A. You can click ⏷ to select a specific sort order.

B. You can click these options (☐ changes to ☑) to add comparison columns.

7. Click the **Header/Footer** tab.

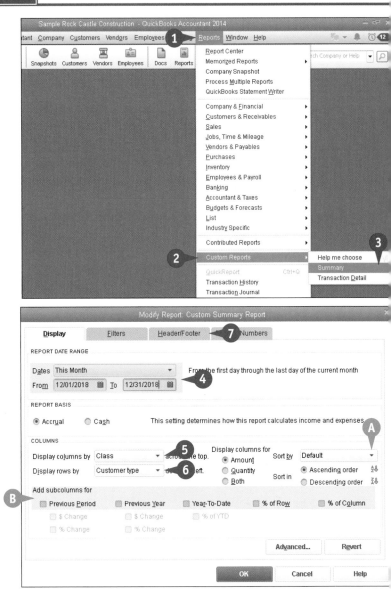

8 Click here, delete the current title, and type a new title.

C You can remove any header or footer information from the report by clicking these options (☑ changes to ▢).

D You can click the **Filters** tab to exclude information from the report.

E You can click the **Fonts & Numbers** tab to change the font for individual report elements and control the appearance of numbers.

9 Click **OK**.

The report appears on-screen.

10 Click ✖ to close the report.

Note: When you close the report, QuickBooks prompts you to memorize it to avoid having to set it up in the future; see the section "Memorize a Report" for details.

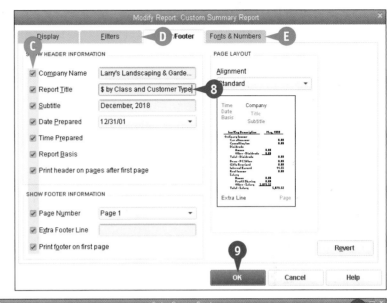

TIP

Should I select Cash or Accrual as the Report Basis?

The answer depends on whether you want to see money you have spent or collected, or money you owe to vendors or are owed by customers. Accrual-basis reports include unpaid invoices and bills, whereas cash-basis reports include only cash spent or collected. For example, a cash-basis report on vendor-related information includes checks, credit card, and bill payments (check) transactions; the same report on an accrual basis also includes bills.

Create a Custom Transaction Detail Report

When you cannot find a report that provides you with transaction detail, you can create a Custom Transaction Detail Report. This report shows the details behind numbers on a summary report. Although you can create a Custom Transaction Detail Report for almost anything you want, this section shows an example of payments made during a specific time frame to each vendor type.

The rows on a Custom Transaction Detail Report are the transactions, and you specify the report columns, date range, the field by which you total the report, and the report sort field and order — ascending or descending.

Create a Custom Transaction Detail Report

1 Click **Reports**.

2 Click **Custom Reports**.

3 Click **Transaction Detail**.

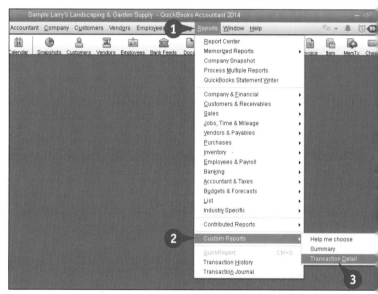

The Custom Transaction Detail Report and the Modify Report dialog box appear.

4 Click ⏷ or 📅 to select a report date range.

5 Click to remove or add report columns; for this example, remove **Clr** and **Split** (☑ changes to ☐).

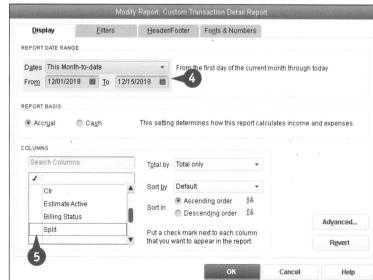

6 Click ⏷ to select a field by which to total; for this example, select **Vendor type**.

Ⓐ You can click ⏷ to change the sort order.

7 Click the **Filters** tab.

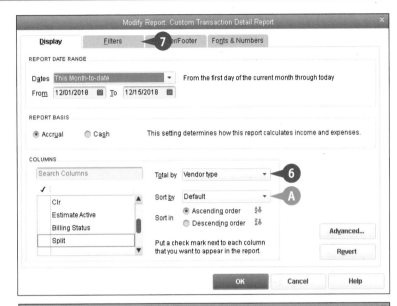

Ⓑ You set a filter by selecting the field on which you want to filter and then setting the parameters for that field.

Ⓒ Existing filters appear here.

Ⓓ You can remove a filter by clicking it and then clicking **Remove Selected Filter**.

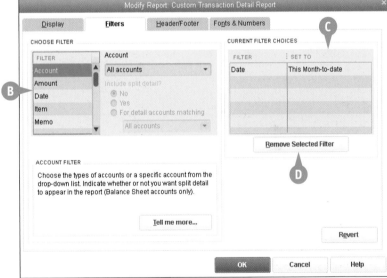

TIP

What report basis should I choose?

The answer depends on the information you want on the report. Choose a cash basis to report only money that has come into or gone out of your business. The cash basis report does not report money owed to you, which appears on your A/R Aging report, or money you owe, which appears on your A/P Aging report. The accrual basis report shows unpaid customer invoices and vendor bills as well as money you collected and paid out during the time period.

continued ▶

You can limit the transactions that appear on the Custom Transaction Detail Report by setting a report date range or by filtering information using the Filters tab.

On the Filters tab, the fields available to limit the report appear on the left side. As you click a field, QuickBooks displays criteria available to limit the report information; the criteria change, depending on the field you select. Filters you use appear on the right side of the Filters tab; if a particular field does not appear on the right, you have not limited the report for a particular field.

Create a Custom Transaction Detail Report (continued)

⑧ Click a field; for this example, click **Account**.

⑨ Set the criteria for the field; for this example, click ▾ to select **All bank accounts**.

Ⓐ The filter appears here.

⑩ Click the **Header/Footer** tab.

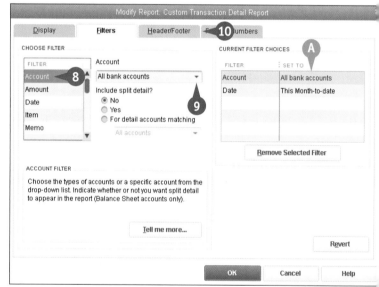

⑪ Click here, delete the default title, and type a new title.

Ⓑ You can remove any header or footer information from the report by clicking an option (☑ changes to ▢).

⑫ Click the **Fonts & Numbers** tab.

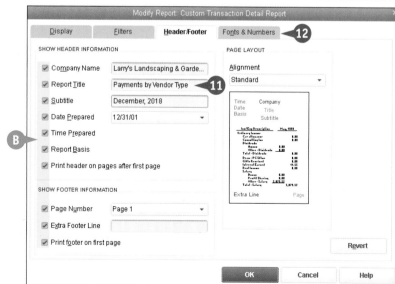

C You can click a report element and then click **Change Font** to select a different font for that report element.

D You can click an option to control the appearance of negative numbers (◯ changes to ◉).

E You can click an option to control the appearance of all numbers (☐ changes to ☑).

13 Click **OK**.

The report appears on-screen.

Note: You can memorize this report to avoid having to set it up in the future; see "Memorize a Report" for details.

14 Click ✖ to close the report.

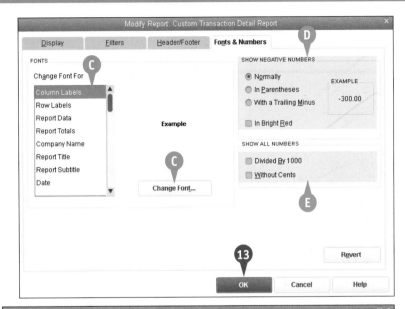

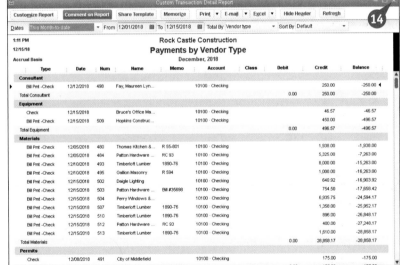

TIP

What happens when I click Advanced on the Display tab?
In the Advanced Options dialog box that QuickBooks opens, you can set two options. First, you can choose to include all accounts even if no transactions affected the account during the report time frame, or you can choose to include only accounts affected by transactions during the report time frame. Second, you can select the method for showing balances. If you choose Current, QuickBooks shows balances as of today. If you choose Report Date, QuickBooks calculates balances through the report date. The Current option is the faster method.

Work with the Doc Center

You can use the Doc (short for "document") Center to keep track of locally stored documents like expense reimbursement receipts or bills you receive electronically. You can add documents stored on your computer to the Doc Center, as shown in this section, or you can scan documents into the Doc Center. You also can remove documents from the Doc Center.

You can also attach documents from the Doc Center to QuickBooks transactions like invoices or bills, or records such as a particular customer or item. If you change your mind, you can detach documents. Using the Doc Center is free.

Work with the Doc Center

1 Click **Company**.

2 Click **Documents**.

3 Click **Doc Center**.

The Doc Center appears.

Ⓐ You can type search text and click the magnifying glass (🔍) to find a particular document.

4 Click **Add a Document** or click **Add**.

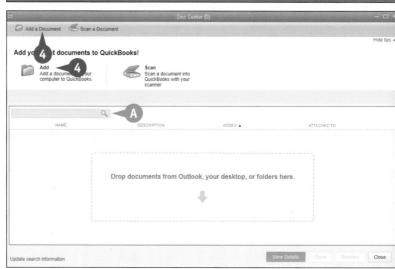

Windows Explorer or File Explorer appears.

5 Navigate to the folder containing the document you want to add.

6 Click the document.

7 Click **Open**.

B The document appears in the Doc Center.

8 Click here to select the document (☐ changes to ☑).

C You can click these buttons to view the document's details, open it, or remove it from the Doc Center.

9 Click **Close** to close the Doc Center.

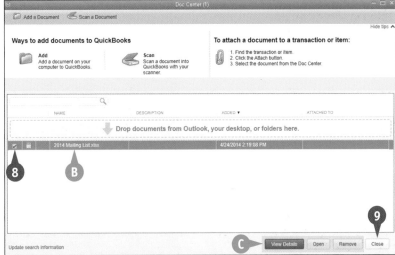

TIP

How do I attach a document to a QuickBooks record?

Display the transaction and click **Attach File** Ⓐ. Or, click a customer or vendor in the appropriate center and click the Attach button (📎) on the right side of the screen. In the Item List, click an item and click **Attach** at the bottom of the window.

Using the Income Tracker

Although not exactly a report, the Income Tracker helps you easily find and work with open estimates, sales orders, and invoices, and income you have received through paid invoices and sales receipts.

The Income Tracker window initially shows a high-level view of all transactions organized into groups. You can view the transactions of each group individually so that you can focus on a particular type of transaction, such as estimates or open and unpaid invoices. You can create new transactions or edit existing transactions from the Income Tracker window. You also can print or email any row in the window.

Using the Income Tracker

1 Click **Customers**.

2 Click **Income Tracker**.

The Income Tracker window appears.

Ⓐ All unbilled, unpaid, and paid transactions appear.

Ⓑ Summary totals for each group of transactions appear here.

Ⓒ You can click ▾ to filter the list to view transactions that meet selected criteria.

Ⓓ You can click beside any transaction to include that transaction (☐ changes to ☑) in a batch action and then click **Batch Actions**.

Note: You can batch-print transactions of the same type. You cannot print estimates, but you can mark a batch inactive.

3 Click any summary total. This example selects the first estimate.

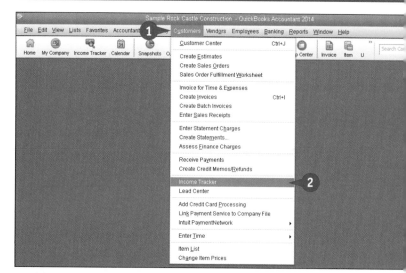

E QuickBooks displays the transactions that make up that summary total.

Note: You can double-click any transaction to open and edit it in its transaction window.

4 Click **Clear/Show All** to redisplay all transactions.

5 Click **Manage Transactions**.

QuickBooks displays a menu of transaction types.

F You can click a type of transaction to open that transaction window and create a new transaction.

6 Click ☒ to close the Income Tracker.

TIP

TIP

What actions are available when I click ▼ in the Action column?

The available actions vary, depending on the group of transactions you are viewing at the time. You can always print or email a row.

Select ▼
Convert to Invoice
Convert to Sales Order
Mark as Inactive
Print Row
Email Row

CHAPTER 14

Working Your Own Way

You can customize much of the appearance and behavior of QuickBooks. In this chapter, you learn to set up custom fields, work with reminders and To Do notes, set a variety of preferences, customize the icon bars, and work with form templates.

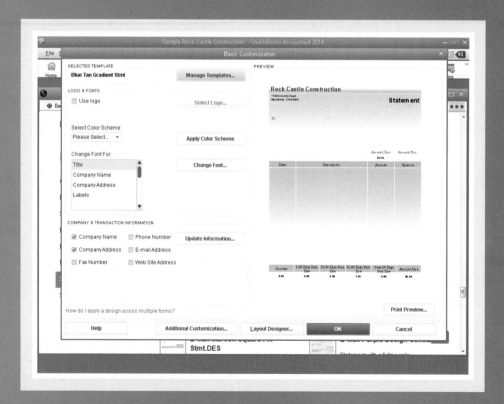

Define Custom Fields

QuickBooks provides *custom fields* for customers, vendors, employees, and certain items that you can use to store information for which no fields exist. For example, if your business operates from two locations, you can create an Office custom field and then assign the appropriate office to each customer, vendor, and employee.

You create labels for custom fields that appear in the records of customers, vendors, employees, and items. Then, in the appropriate record, you supply the information. You can create custom fields from any customer, vendor, employee, or item record; this section starts from a vendor record.

Define Custom Fields

1 Click **Vendors**.

2 Click **Vendor Center**.

The Vendor Center appears.

3 Double-click any vendor to edit that vendor.

A You can create a new vendor by clicking **New Vendor** and then **New Vendor** again.

The Edit Vendor dialog box appears.

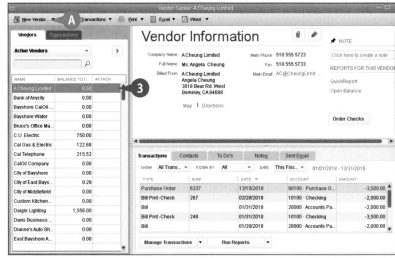

4 Click **Additional Info**.

5 Click **Define Fields**.

The Set up Custom Fields for Names dialog box appears.

6 Type a field label here.

7 Click options (☐ changes to ☑) to activate the field for the appropriate record type.

8 Repeat steps **6** and **7** to create additional custom fields.

9 Click **OK** to save the custom fields.

A message appears describing how to use custom fields in transactions. Click **OK**.

10 Fill in custom field information as appropriate.

11 Click **OK**.

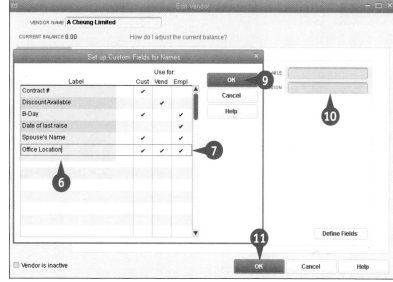

How do I set up custom fields for items?
Open the Item List (click **Lists** and then click **Item List**) and double-click any item to edit it. Then, click the **Custom Fields** button. You can set up custom fields for Service, Inventory, Non-Inventory, Inventory Assembly, Other Charge, Group, Discount, and Payment items.

Are custom fields available on transactions and reports?
Yes. You can include custom fields on both the on-screen and printed versions of transaction templates; see the section "Customize the Data Layout of a Form." You also can sort and filter most list and detail reports on which you include custom fields according to one custom field.

Work with Reminders

You can use the Reminders feature in QuickBooks to remind you of almost any event. For example, QuickBooks can remind you to pay bills, make a bank deposit, or print forms. If you use memorized transactions that QuickBooks does not automatically enter, QuickBooks can remind you to enter memorized transactions.

Information in the Reminders window appears in one of three formats: a custom format that you define in the Preferences dialog box, a summarized list of reminder categories, and a detailed list of both categories and all reminders within each category. Alerts, generated by QuickBooks, also appear on the Reminders List.

Work with Reminders

Create Reminders

1 Click **Edit**.

2 Click **Preferences**.

The Preferences dialog box appears.

3 Click **Reminders**.

Ⓐ On the My Preferences tab, you can click here (☐ changes to ☑) to display the Reminders List when you open QuickBooks.

4 Click the **Company Preferences** tab.

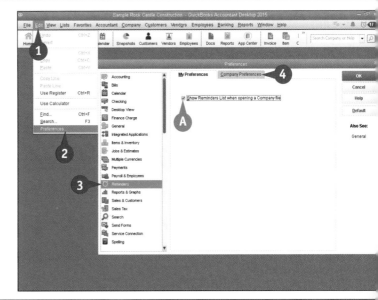

5 Click an option to specify each reminder's appearance in the Reminders window (☐ changes to ◉).

6 As appropriate, type the number of days QuickBooks should remind you prior to the event.

7 Click **OK**.

QuickBooks saves your settings.

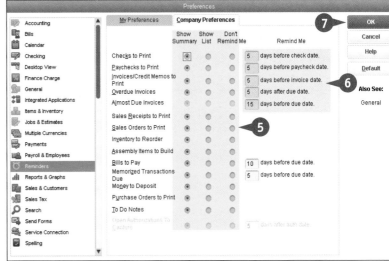

View Reminders

1 Click **Company**.

2 Click **Reminders**.

The Reminders window appears.

B You can click the expand arrow (▶) to view details of reminder category.

C You can click the collapse arrow (▼) to hide reminder categories.

3 Click the **Close** button (✕) to close the window.

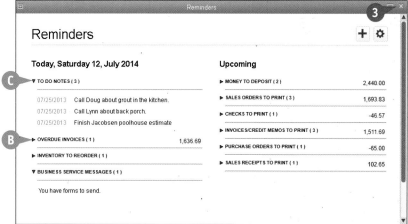

TIPS

Can I view the details of a particular reminder?

Yes. Follow steps 1 and 2 in the subsection "View Reminders" and click to display the category of reminders. Then, double-click the reminder, and QuickBooks opens the reminder in the window where you created it.

What is an alert and how does it differ from a reminder?

Alerts, generated by QuickBooks, are important business events often external to your day-to-day operation of QuickBooks. For example, QuickBooks generates an alert if an update to QuickBooks exists that you need to download. Reminders, created by you, focus more on tasks you perform within QuickBooks, such as making loan payments, paying bills, or making deposits.

Create a To Do Note

When you need to accomplish a task that does not appear as one of the tasks about which QuickBooks reminds you, you can use To Do notes, which are free-form notes not tied to any particular event in QuickBooks.

You can tie To Do notes to calendar dates, customers, vendors, employees, or leads. When you finish the To Do note action, you can mark it completed. You also can delete To Do notes or change their status to inactive. And, you can print the To Do Notes report from the To Do window or from the Reports menu.

Create a To Do Note

1. Click **Company**.

2. Click **To Do List**.

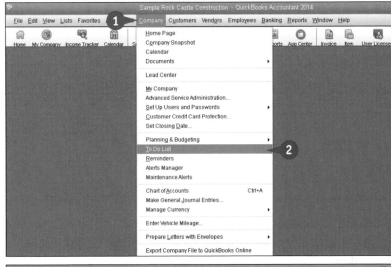

The To Do List window appears.

Ⓐ You can filter the To Do List window using these lists.

3. Click the **To Do** ▾.

4. Click **New To Do**.

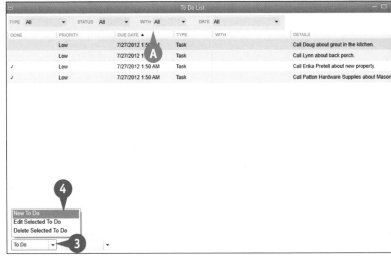

The Add To Do dialog box appears.

⑤ Click ▾ to assign a priority to the To Do.

🅱 You can click the **WITH** option (☐ changes to ☑) and then click ▾ to select a customer, vendor, employee, or lead with which to associate the To Do.

⑥ Type the To Do message here.

Note: To display a summary of a lengthy To Do note, type a summary of the note on the first line, press ⬐t, and type the rest of the note.

⑦ Click 📅 to select a reminder date.

⑧ Click **OK**.

The To Do List window reappears.

🅲 The new To Do appears in the window.

⑨ Click ✖ to close the window.

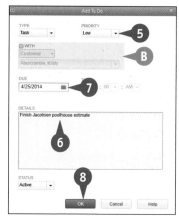

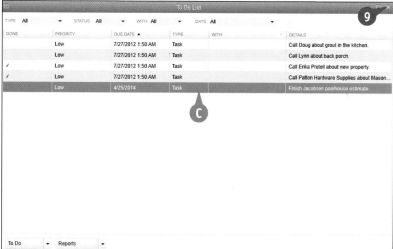

TIP

How do I get rid of a To Do note?
Double-click a To Do note to display it in the Edit To Do dialog box, and click ▾ to change its status from Active to Done or Inactive. Completed notes remain in the To Do List window, but QuickBooks displays a check mark (☑) beside them. Inactive To Do notes remain in the window, but you can hide them by filtering by status. You can delete a To Do note by right-clicking it and clicking **Delete Selected To Do**. In this case, QuickBooks removes the To Do note from your company data file.

Set Desktop View Preferences

You can set Desktop preferences to enable QuickBooks to display the desktop view of your choice, and you can have QuickBooks save those settings when you make changes or when you close a QuickBooks company, or you can have QuickBooks ignore changes you make.

You can choose to have QuickBooks maximize every window you open and hide other open windows, or you can have QuickBooks display multiple windows. You can choose to display the Home page, which helps you find your way around QuickBooks, and you can control the QuickBooks color scheme.

Set Desktop View Preferences

1 Click **Edit**.

2 Click **Preferences**.

The Preferences dialog box appears.

3 Click **Desktop View**.

4 Click an option to control window behavior (◉ changes to ◉).

5 Click an option to control saving the QuickBooks desktop (◉ changes to ◉).

6 Click this option (☐ changes to ☑) to display the Home page when you start the program.

7 Click this option (☐ changes to ☑) to display light-colored icons on the Top Icon Bar.

8 Click ▼ to select a color scheme.

9 Click **OK** to save your settings.

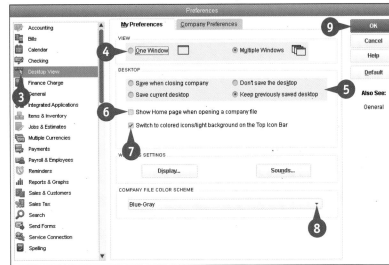

Set Up Favorite Features

You can use the Favorites menu to store menu choices you use most often. That way, you do not need to remember the menu QuickBooks uses for the choice; you can simply open the Favorites menu and click the option you want to display.

For example, suppose that you regularly use menu options such as the Items List, the Create Invoices command, the Receive Payments command, the Use Register command, the Enter Bills command, and the A/P Aging Summary report. You can pin all these commands to the Favorites menu so that they appear in one place.

Set Up Favorite Features

① Click **Favorites**.

② Click **Customize Favorites**.

Note: If the Favorites menu does not appear, click **View** and then click **Favorites Menu**.

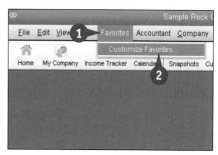

The Customize Your Menus dialog box appears.

Ⓐ QuickBooks organizes available menu items in this list in the same order they appear on the QuickBooks menu bar.

③ Click an option.

④ Click **Add**.

Ⓑ Options you have selected appear in this area.

⑤ Click **OK**.

The next time you click **Favorites**, the commands you added appear on the menu.

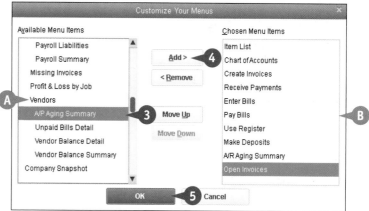

Set Email Preferences

If you intend to email forms to customers or vendors, you can set up an email address that QuickBooks can use to send email. Identify whether you use web mail or have a subscription to the QuickBooks Email service; this section assumes you use web mail.

Provide your email address and web mail provider; for common web mail providers such as Gmail, Yahoo!, and Hot Mail, QuickBooks fills in typically used outgoing server information for you. For other web mail providers, you supply the outgoing server information. QuickBooks emails forms as PDF files to customers, vendors, employees, or other names.

Set Email Preferences

1. Click **Edit**.

2. Click **Preferences** to display the Preferences dialog box.

3. Click **Send Forms**.

Note: Unless you have a QuickBooks Email Subscription, Web Mail is selected by default.

4. Click **Add** to display the Add Email Info dialog box.

5. Type your email address here.

6. Click ▼ to select an email provider.

Note: QuickBooks supplies outgoing server information for common web mail providers.

Ⓐ If necessary, supply outgoing server information.

7. Click **OK** twice to save your settings.

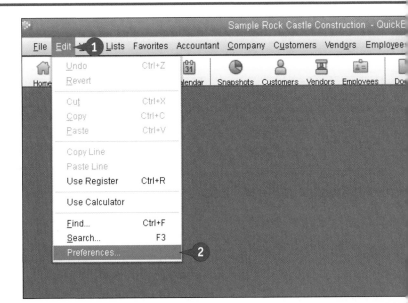

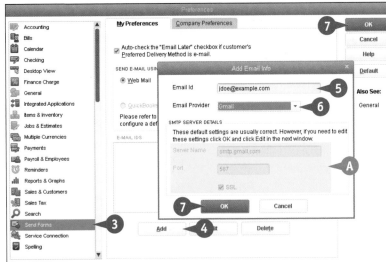

Set Preferences for Finance Charges

Y ou can calculate *finance charges* on unpaid customer balances that you can include on customer invoices and statements. You can specify the way QuickBooks calculates the finance charge.

You can specify an annual percentage to charge on the unpaid balance, and you can specify a grace period before QuickBooks charges a finance charge. You can calculate finance charge amounts for the unpaid balance from the due date or from the invoice date. You also can specify a minimum finance charge amount; if the calculated percentage finance charge is less than the minimum finance charge amount, QuickBooks charges the minimum amount.

Set Preferences for Finance Charges

1 Click **Edit**.

2 Click **Preferences**.

The Preferences dialog box appears.

3 Click **Finance Charge**.

4 Click the **Company Preferences** tab.

A You can change the finance charge rate here.

B You can change the grace period by typing here.

5 Click ▾ to select an account for finance charge income.

6 Click an option to determine the date from which QuickBooks calculates finance charges (◯ changes to ◉).

7 Click **OK**.

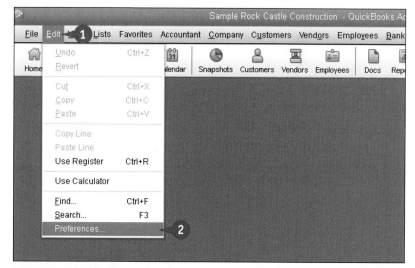

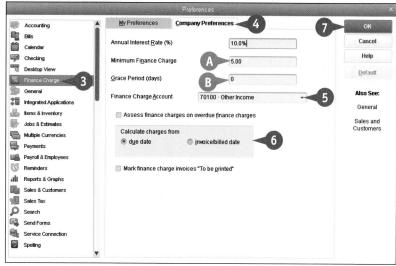

Set Preferences for Reports and Graphs

You can set preferences for the way QuickBooks handles reports and graphs. For example, if you modify most reports every time you print them, you can avoid displaying a report you will not use, and have QuickBooks automatically display the Modify Report dialog box before it prepares the report.

You also can specify whether QuickBooks should display summary reports on a cash or an accrual basis. Because the accrual basis recognizes revenues and expenses when they occur instead of when you receive payment or pay bills, the accrual basis generally provides a more accurate picture of where your company stands financially.

Set Preferences for Reports and Graphs

1 Click **Edit**.

2 Click **Preferences**.

The Preferences dialog box appears.

3 Click **Reports & Graphs**.

Ⓐ You can click this option to display the Modify Report dialog box each time you open a report (☐ changes to ☑).

4 Click a refresh option (◯ changes to ◉).

Ⓑ You can click these options to speed up graph presentation and use patterns instead of colors on graphs (☐ changes to ☑).

5 Click the **Company Preferences** tab.

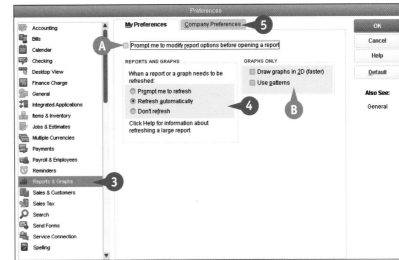

6 Click to select the default basis for reports (⊙ changes to ⊙).

7 Click a report aging option (⊙ changes to ⊙).

8 Click an option for the appearance of items and accounts on reports (⊙ changes to ⊙).

9 Click **Format**.

The Report Format Preferences dialog box appears.

10 Deselect these options so that the corresponding information does not appear on reports (☑ changes to ☐).

11 Click ▼ to select a report alignment.

C You can click the **Fonts & Numbers** tab to control the appearance of numbers and establish default fonts for selected report sections.

12 Click **OK** to close the Report Format Preferences dialog box.

13 Click **OK**.

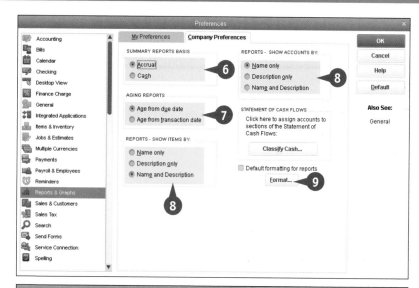

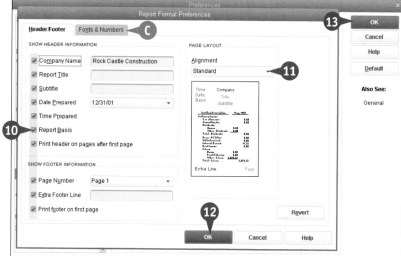

Why does QuickBooks includes refresh options?

Typically, QuickBooks updates reports you are viewing if you make changes that affect the data on the report. Sometimes, however, QuickBooks cannot automatically incorporate the changes you make. In these cases, QuickBooks needs to *refresh* the report by regenerating it from scratch. If your company data file is large, regenerating a report can be a lengthy process. So, QuickBooks enables you to set options to automatically refresh, prompt you before refreshing, or not refresh at all. Select the option that works best with the amount of data in your company data file.

Customize the Top Icon Bar

You can customize the Top Icon Bar, located immediately below the menu bar, to ensure the availability of the icons you use most often to quickly open windows. This section assumes you are displaying the Top Icon Bar; see Chapter 1 for details on selecting an icon bar.

The length of the icon bar cannot exceed the width of your screen; if the Top Icon Bar contains many icons or uses long text descriptions, some icons may not be visible. You can use the small carat at the right end of the icon bar to display hidden icons.

Customize the Top Icon Bar

1 Click **View**.

2 Click **Customize Icon Bar**.

The Customize Icon Bar dialog box appears.

3 Click an option to control the appearance of icons on the Icon Bar (⊙ changes to ⦿).

Ⓐ You can add a line to the right of an icon if you click the icon in the list and then click Add Separator. In the list, the separator appears as "(space)."

Ⓑ You can click and drag the diamond (◆) beside an icon to reposition it. As you drag, a dotted line helps you identify the current position.

4 Click the icon that should appear to the left of a new icon.

5 Click **Add**.

Note: You can click **Edit** instead of **Add** to change the icon's label and description using the steps that follow.

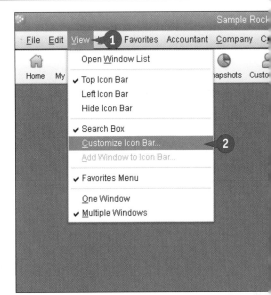

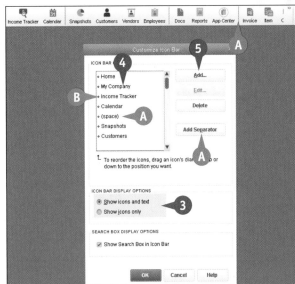

The Add Icon Bar Item dialog box appears.

6 Click the icon you want to add.

C You can change the icon picture by clicking in this list.

D You can change the icon label and description by typing in these boxes.

Note: You can type up to 30 characters for an icon's name.

7 Click **OK**.

The Add Icon Bar Item dialog box closes and the Customize Icon Bar dialog box reappears.

E The new icon appears in the Icon Bar Content list and on the Icon Bar.

8 Click **OK**.

QuickBooks saves the changes.

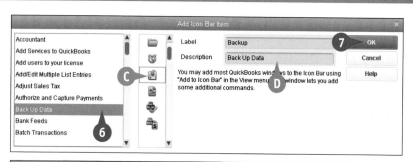

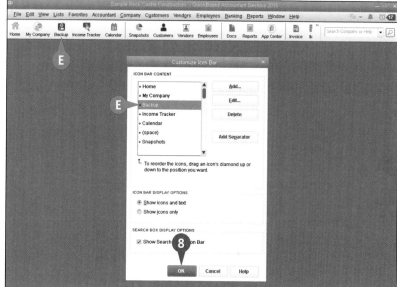

TIP

Is there a way to add the Pay Bills window to the Top Icon Bar?

Open the window to add to the Top Icon Bar. Then:

1 Click **View**.

2 Click **Add to Icon Bar**.

3 In the Add Window to Icon Bar dialog box, change the icon, label, and description as needed.

4 Click **OK** to add the icon.

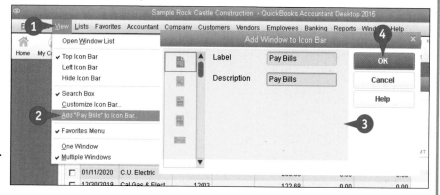

Customize the Left Icon Bar

You can customize the Left Icon Bar to ensure the availability of icons you use most often to quickly open windows. This section assumes you are displaying the Left Icon Bar; see Chapter 1 for details on selecting an icon bar.

You can customize the My Shortcuts section of the Left Icon Bar to ensure that shortcuts for the windows you use most often appear in the My Shortcuts section. You also can customize the View Balances section to display the balances of accounts of your choice so that you can easily monitor the balances of those accounts.

Customize the Left Icon Bar

Customize Shortcuts

① Click **My Shortcuts**.

② Right-click any entry in the My Shortcuts list.

③ Click **Customize Shortcuts**.

The Customize Icon Bar dialog box appears.

Note: See the section "Customize the Top Icon Bar" for details on adding a shortcut to the My Shortcuts list.

Customize Balance Information

1 Click **View Balances**.

2 Click **Customize view balances**.

The Customize Account Balances dialog box appears.

3 Click ▼ to select the type of account.

4 Click an account.

5 Click **Add**.

6 Repeat steps **3** to **5** to add more accounts.

Note: To reposition an account, select it in the Selected Accounts List, and then click **Move Up** or **Move Down** until it appears where you want it.

7 Click **OK**.

The accounts appear in the View Balances section.

TIP

Is there a way to add the Pay Bills window to the Left Icon Bar?

Open the window to add to the Left Icon Bar. Then:

1 Click **View**.

2 Click **Add to Icon Bar**.

3 In the Add Window to Icon Bar dialog box, change the icon, label, and description as needed.

4 Click **OK** to add the icon.

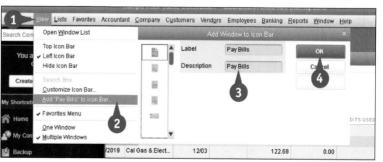

Switch to a Different Form Template

Each window in which you enter transactions uses a *form template* that contains the fields you fill in as you complete the transaction. You can switch between form templates in any transaction window; templates are available for all printable forms, including Invoices, Sales Receipts, Estimates, Sales Orders, Credit Memos/Refunds, Statements, and Purchase Orders.

QuickBooks comes with several predefined form templates, and this section demonstrates using the QuickBooks sample product-based company Rock Castle Construction. The examples illustrates switching from the Rock Castle Invoice form template to a different form template in the Create Invoices window.

Switch to a Different Form Template

1 Click **Customers**.

2 Click **Create Invoices**.

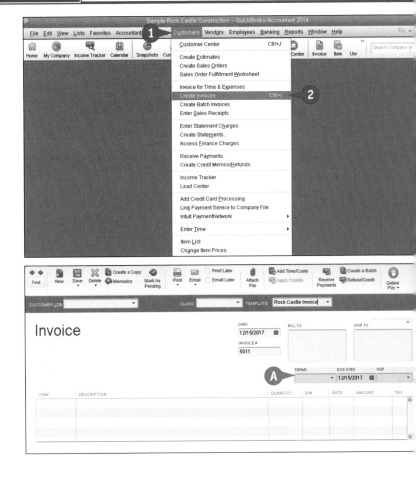

The Create Invoices window appears.

A The Rock Castle Invoice form contains only three options in this section of the invoice.

3 Click ▾ to display the list of available invoice form templates.

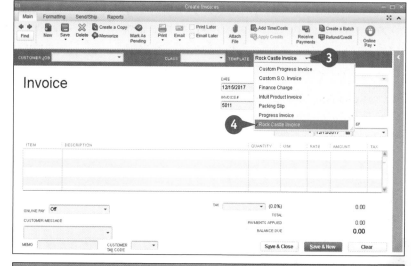

4 Click a form template.

B QuickBooks changes the appearance of the Create Invoices window to use the fields on the selected form template.

TIP

Can I make changes to a form template?

Yes. You can add fields to or remove fields from a form template, as described in the section "Customize the Data Layout of a Form." You also can use the Layout Designer to move fields around on a form template. You cannot save changes to any predefined form template that comes with QuickBooks, so you must duplicate that template and change the duplicate. Click **Lists** and then click **Templates**. In the Templates window, click the **Templates** button and then click **Duplicate**.

Download a Form Template

Intuit offers a gallery of more than 100 predesigned form templates to help you find form templates that suit your needs. The gallery contains form templates for invoices, credit memos, estimates, statements, sales receipts, sales orders, purchase orders, and donations. You will also find form templates specific to particular industries. You can use the gallery while you work in QuickBooks to download templates that interest you.

After you download a template, you can use it without making any changes to it, or you can modify it as described in the section "Customize the Data Layout of a Form."

Download a Form Template

1 Click **Lists**.

2 Click **Templates**.

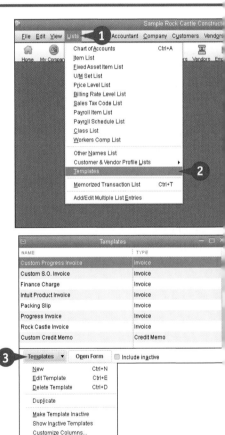

The Templates window appears.

3 Click **Templates**.

4 Click **Download Templates**.

The QuickBooks Support window appears.

⑤ Click the type of form template to download.

⑥ Click a form template download link.

A Windows File Download dialog box appears. Click **Open** to download the template.

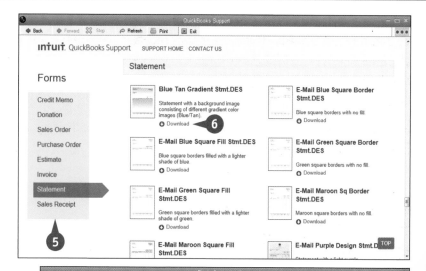

QuickBooks downloads the form and displays the Basic Customization dialog box.

⑦ Click **OK**.

The QuickBooks Support window reappears; click ⊠ in the upper right corner to close the window.

The Templates window reappears and displays the downloaded template in the list.

TIP

What do the buttons at the top of the QuickBooks Support window do?

The QuickBooks Support window is actually a browser window, so the buttons at the top behave like typical browser buttons. You can navigate back and forward to different browser pages, and you can refresh a browser page and stop the page from loading. The **Print** button prints the contents of the window, and the **Exit** button closes the QuickBooks Support window the same way that clicking ⊠ closes the window.

Customize the Data Layout of a Form

You can customize the appearance of a form template by adding or removing fields. Suppose, for example, that your company has two locations and you have defined a custom field to assign to customers to associate them with a particular location. You can include the location on estimates, sales orders, invoices, and purchase orders, as shown in this section.

You cannot make changes to any of the default form templates that come with QuickBooks, but you can duplicate them and then make changes to the duplicate. When you try to modify a default template, QuickBooks prompts you to duplicate it.

Customize the Data Layout of a Form

① Click **Customers**.

② Click **Create Invoices**.

The Create Invoices window appears.

③ Click the **Template** ▼.

④ Click the form template to modify.

⑤ Click the **Formatting** tab.

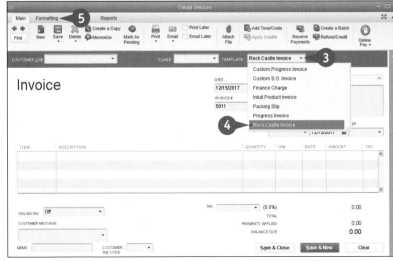

6 Click **Customize Data Layout**.

Note: If you selected a default form template in step **4**, QuickBooks displays a message asking you to make a copy. Click **Make a Copy**.

The Additional Customization dialog box appears.

A A preview of the printed form appears here.

B Fields in the header area of the form appear here.

C Tabs representing parts of the form appear in this area.

7 Click these options (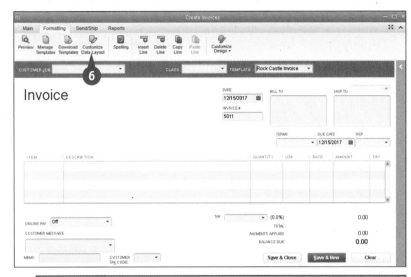 changes to ☑) to add fields to the on-screen and the printed forms.

D You can change the description for selected fields in this area.

8 Click the **Columns** tab.

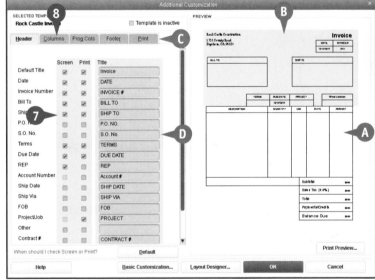

TIPS

What does the Customize Design button on the Formatting tab do?
Clicking **Customize Design** opens the Intuit Forms window, where you can customize a form design for a fee. You can select a form background, add a company logo, and control colors, fonts, and grid styles.

Can I add my company logo to the form?
Yes. Click **Basic Customization** while viewing the Additional Customization dialog box. Then, click **Use Logo** (☐ changes to ☑). The Select Image dialog box appears, and you can navigate to the folder containing your logo, select it, and click **Open**. For best results, your logo image should be square because QuickBooks fits your logo in a square space.

continued ▶

Customize the Data Layout of a Form (continued)

You can add or remove fields from the on-screen version of a form template, from the printed version of a form template, or from both versions of the form template. You can add or remove fields from a form's header area, the columns where you provide item details, and the footer area. You also can specify print settings for a form template, or you can assign the settings specified in the Printer Setup dialog box to the form.

If you add more fields than will fit across a printed page, QuickBooks warns you and offers ways to fix the problem.

Customize the Data Layout of a Form (continued)

The Columns tab appears.

(A) Fields in the Columns area appear here.

(9) Click these options (☐ changes to ☑) to add fields to the on-screen and the printed forms.

(10) For selected fields, type numbers to specify the order of the fields, from left to right, in the column area.

(B) You can change the description QuickBooks displays in this area.

(11) Click the **Prog Cols** tab.

Note: This tab appears if you use progress invoicing. If you do not use progress invoicing, skip to step **13**.

(C) Fields in the Prog Cols area appear in the same area where Columns fields appear.

(12) Repeat steps **9** and **10** as appropriate.

(13) Click the **Footer** tab.

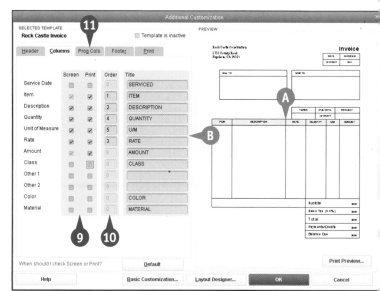

The Footer tab appears.

Ⓓ Fields in the Footer area appear here.

⑭ Repeat steps **9** and **10** as appropriate.

⑮ Click the **Print** tab.

The Print tab appears.

⑯ Click an option to specify printer settings QuickBooks should use (◯ changes to ◉).

⑰ Click this option to print page numbers on transactions that are longer than two pages (☐ changes to ☑).

Ⓔ You can click this option (☐ changes to ☑) to align amounts on printed forms using the decimal point.

⑱ Click **OK** to save your settings.

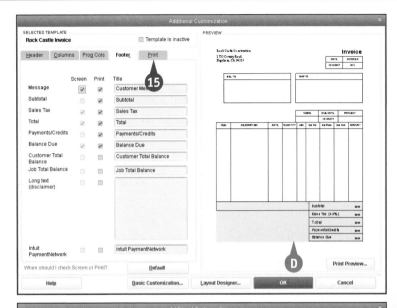

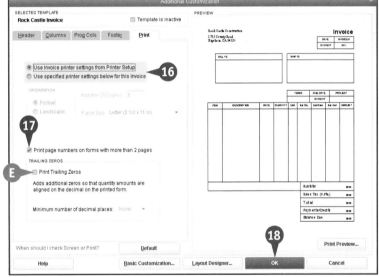

When I was assigning order numbers on the Columns tab, the Overlapping Fields window appeared. What happened and why?

QuickBooks allocates a certain field length for each field. When you add more fields than will fit across a printed page, QuickBooks displays the Overlapping Fields window. If you click **Continue**, you must open the Layout Designer and manually adjust field lengths. Alternatively, click **Default Layout**, and QuickBooks adjusts the field lengths to accommodate the fields you selected. QuickBooks also displays a somewhat misleading warning that you are about to lose all changes made to the form; QuickBooks actually keeps your changes but adjusts field lengths. Click **Yes** to proceed.

CHAPTER 15

Managing QuickBooks Data

Your QuickBooks company data could turn out to be one of the most precious assets your business owns because it contains a record of all your customers, vendors, and employees along with all the transactions you have completed with those contacts. You need to protect your data, and in this chapter, you learn how.

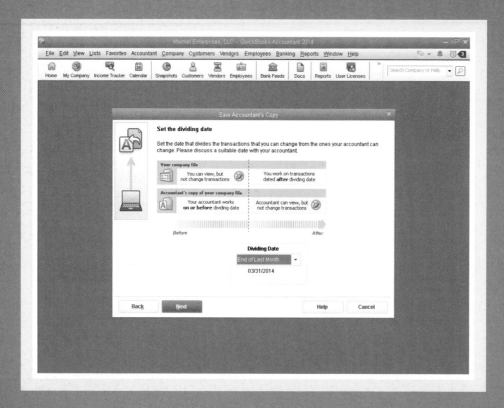

Update QuickBooks

The *Automatic Update feature* ensures that you have the latest release of your version of QuickBooks; you may want to make some changes to the functioning of the Automatic Update feature to include additional types of updates or to handle updating QuickBooks in a multiuser environment.

Periodically, Intuit releases updates to QuickBooks to address problems or add functionality to the program. These updates are not new versions of the program; they are enhancements to the program to make it function better. When you install QuickBooks, you install an update agent that checks for QuickBooks updates.

Update QuickBooks

1 Click **Help**.

2 Click **Update QuickBooks**.

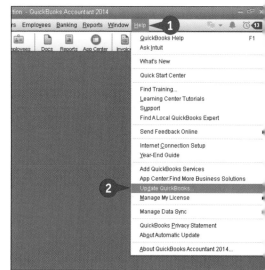

The Overview tab of the Update QuickBooks dialog box appears.

Ⓐ The status for automatic updating appears here.

Ⓑ You can click **Update Now** to update QuickBooks immediately.

3 Click the **Options** tab.

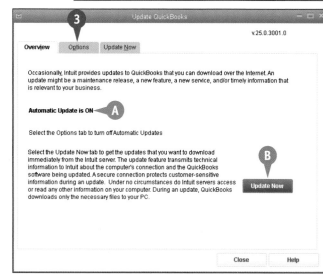

The Options tab appears.

④ Click an option to turn Automatic Update on or off (◉ changes to ◉).

⑤ Click an option to share downloaded updates in a multiuser environment (◉ changes to ◉).

⑥ Click beside each type of update you want to download (◉ changes to ☑).

⑦ Click the **Update Now** tab.

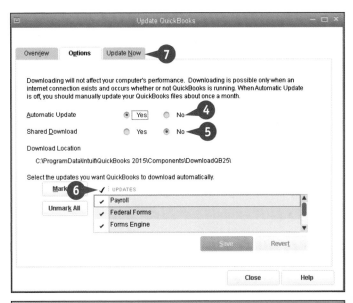

The Update Now tab appears.

ⓒ QuickBooks displays the updates it will download.

⑧ Click **Get Updates**.

QuickBooks connects to the Internet and downloads any available updates.

⑨ When QuickBooks finishes downloading updates, click **Close**.

TIP

Will I hurt anything if I turn off Automatic Update?

QuickBooks continues to function, but you do not automatically receive updates that may fix problems in the software. Turning off Automatic Update is not recommended because QuickBooks searches for updates in the background without interrupting your work. You do not even need to be using QuickBooks for Automatic Update to do its job. If you must turn off Automatic Update, make it a habit to manually check for updates at least once a month. You can set up a reminder in QuickBooks to check for updates; see Chapter 14 for details on creating reminders.

Back Up Your Company Records

No task is more important than backing up your company data file. Without a backup, recovering from a failed hard drive is a nightmare because you must re-create your company data file. With a backup, you can quickly and easily restore a backup as described in the section "Restore a Backup."

You can back up your company data file manually when you choose, or you can set up a schedule for backing up; for example, you can back up QuickBooks every evening before you leave for the day or schedule a backup for the middle of the night.

Back Up Your Company Records

Back Up Manually

1. Click **File**.
2. Click **Back Up Company**.
3. Click **Create Local Backup**.

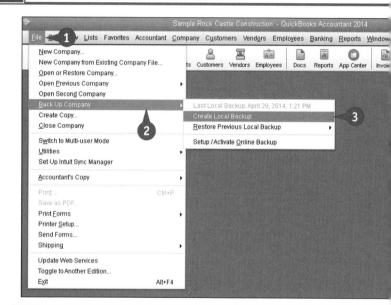

The Create Backup wizard begins.

4. Click **Local backup** (🔘 changes to 🔘).
5. Click **Next**.

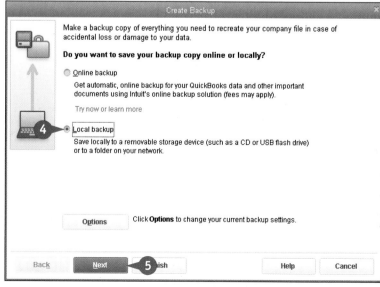

6 Click **Save it now**
(○ changes to ⦿).

7 Click **Next**.

The Save Backup Copy dialog
box appears.

8 Click ▼ to navigate to the
drive where you want to save
the backup.

9 Double-check the name
QuickBooks suggests for the
backup file and make
changes as needed.

Note: Make sure the name
includes your company name and
the backup date.

10 Click **Save**.

QuickBooks backs up your
data, and a message appears
when the backup completes
successfully. Click **OK** to
dismiss the message.

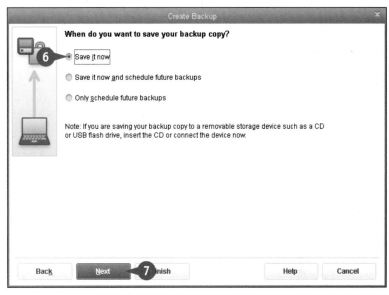

TIP

What happens if I click Options when I select Local Backup?

QuickBooks displays the Backup Options
dialog box, where you can specify options
for all backups, such as where to store a
backup Ⓐ and how many backups to
save Ⓑ.

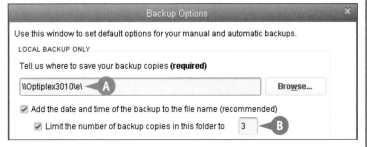

continued ▶

When you back up your company data, QuickBooks copies your data exactly as it appears at that moment. Verify the backup to ensure that you will be able to use it in case of an emergency. You can back up your QuickBooks company file to any type disk, but do not back up your company data file to the same hard drive where the company data file resides. Store a backup on removable media so you can easily take your backups to an off-site location.

Keep several backups to give yourself several chances to recover from a disaster.

Back Up Your Company Records (continued)

Schedule Backups

1. Complete steps 1 to 5 in the subsection "Back Up Manually."

2. Click **Save it now and schedule future backups** (☐ changes to ☉).

3. Click **Next**.

The Create Backup dialog box appears.

4. Click this option to turn on the automatic backup feature (☐ changes to ☑).

5. Click here and type a number to specify how often QuickBooks should save a backup.

6. Click **New**.

The Schedule Backup dialog box displays.

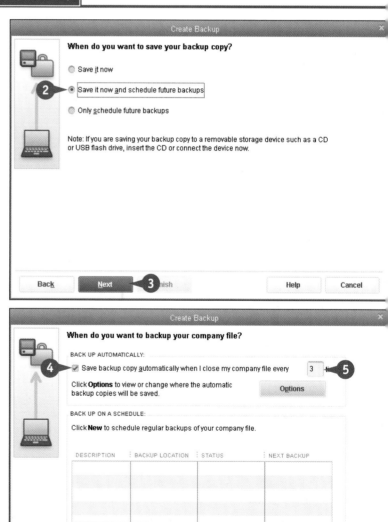

⑦ Type a name and a location for the backup or click **Browse**.

Ⓐ You can click this option (☐ changes to ☑) and type the number of backups to keep.

⑧ Click ▾ to select a backup time and specify how often to back up.

⑨ Click these options (☐ changes to ☑) to select days to back up.

⑩ Click **Store Password**.

⑪ In the Store Windows Password dialog box, type your Windows username password.

⑫ Click **OK** twice.

Ⓑ The scheduled backup appears here.

⑬ Click **Finish**.

QuickBooks displays a confirming message; click **OK**, and QuickBooks backs up your data.

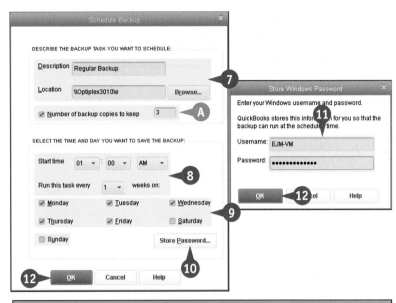

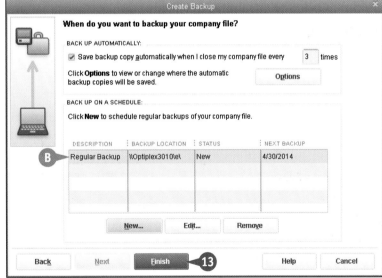

TIP

How often should I back up?

The answer is a matter of personal preference based on your risk-taking tolerance. Ask yourself the question, "If I do not back up my data today, how much effort will be required to re-create all the work I did today?" If you think that re-creating your work will take no time at all, you can skip backing up. The more time it takes you to re-create, however, the less willing you should be to skip backing up. Remember, backing up your company data files usually takes no more than five minutes. If re-creating your work takes more than five minutes, backing up is worthwhile.

Restore a Backup

I f your data becomes corrupt or your hard drive crashes and must be replaced, you can easily get your company data file back to where it was before the disaster occurred by restoring your latest backup. *Restoring* a backup is not a difficult process; you only need the location of the backup file to be up and running.

In most cases, when you restore a QuickBooks backup, you do so over an existing company file. Restoring over an existing company file completely overwrites that file and replaces the information in that company with the information from the backup.

Restore a Backup

1 Click **File**.

2 Click **Open or Restore Company**.

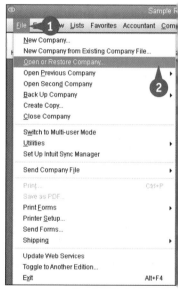

The Open or Restore Company wizard begins.

3 Click **Restore a backup copy** (◉ changes to ◉).

4 Click **Next**.

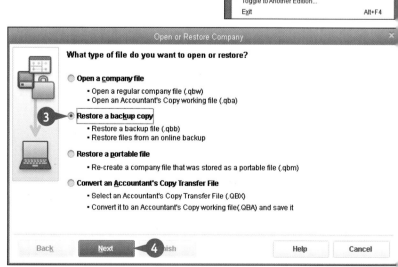

5 Click **Local backup**
(◉ changes to ◉).

6 Click **Next**.

The Open Backup Copy dialog
box appears.

7 Click a backup file to restore.

A If necessary, click ▾ to
navigate to a different folder
containing backup files.

8 Click **Open**.

A message box appears,
explaining your options
concerning the location
you choose for the restored
company; click **Next**.

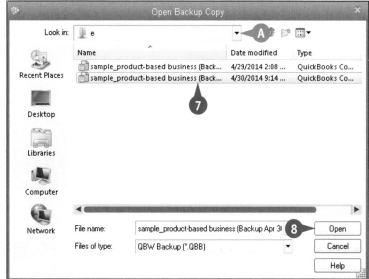

What happens if I select Online Backup?

When you select this option, you use the Intuit Data Protect service to back up your data to the cloud. This
fee-based service backs up your data in the background as you work; the backup happens automatically
once each day at a prescheduled time as long as your computer is logged in to Windows and connected to
the Internet. If your computer is off when a backup is scheduled to occur, the backup automatically runs
when you turn on your computer. The service stores each backup for 45 days, and you can restore any
backup.

continued ▶

If you restore a backup because your company data file became corrupt, it is perfectly acceptable to write over the corrupted data file. If your hard drive failed and you set up a new hard drive, you need to install QuickBooks before you can restore your data. When you open QuickBooks for the first time, QuickBooks prompts you to create a new company. You can set up the new company with minimum information, because restoring the backup replaces all information in the company with the information stored in the backup. For details on creating a new company, see Chapter 1.

Restore a Backup (continued)

The Save Company File as dialog box appears.

Ⓐ If necessary, click ▾ to navigate to a different folder for the restored company.

⑨ Click **Save**.

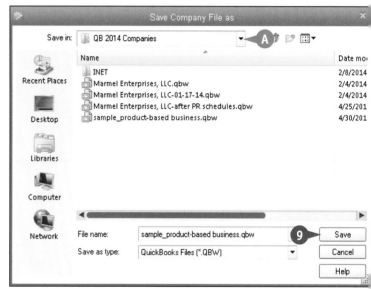

If you choose the same location where your original company file resides, QuickBooks asks if you are sure that you want to overwrite an existing company.

⑩ Click **Yes**.

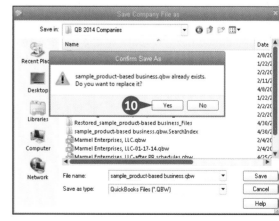

QuickBooks displays the
Delete Entire File dialog box.

11 Type **yes**.

12 Click **OK**.

QuickBooks restores your
data, and a message appears
when the restore process
completes successfully.

13 Click **OK**.

TIP

If I set up a new hard drive, is there a way to avoid creating a new company so that I can restore my backup?

Yes. You can open one of the sample companies that comes with QuickBooks and begin the restore process from that company. When you restore your data, select your company backup file, and in the Save Company File As dialog box, navigate to the folder where you want to store your company file. When QuickBooks restores the data, you will not see either of the dialog boxes that ask you to confirm overwriting a company file.

Create an Accountant's Copy

You can create an accountant's copy of your company file so that both you and your accountant can work with your QuickBooks data at the same time. As you create the accountant's copy, you set a *dividing date*; you can work freely with transactions dated after the dividing date, but you cannot make changes to transactions dated before the dividing date. Your accountant can work with transactions dated on or before the dividing date.

When your accountant finishes making changes to your company file, you import the changes into your company file; see the section "Import Accountant's Changes" for details.

Create an Accountant's Copy

1 Click **File**.

2 Click **Send Company File**.

3 Click **Accountant's Copy**.

4 Click **Client Activities**.

5 Click **Save File**.

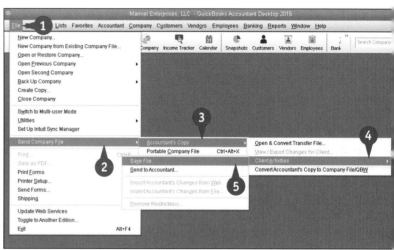

The Save Accountant's Copy wizard begins.

6 Click **Accountant's Copy** (◯ changes to ◉).

7 Click **Next**.

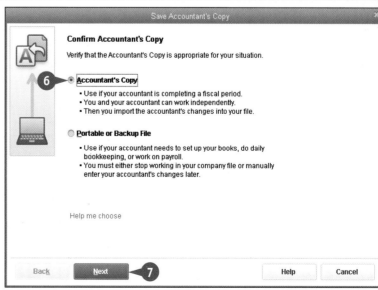

The Set the Dividing Date window appears.

8 Click ▼ to select a dividing date.

9 Click **Next**.

The Save Accountant's Copy dialog box appears.

10 Select a location to save the copy.

Ⓐ You can click ▼ to navigate to a folder.

11 Click **Save**.

QuickBooks creates the Accountant's Copy file and displays a message telling you that it was successfully created; click **OK** to dismiss the message, and give the Accountant's Copy file to your accountant.

Note: The QuickBooks title bar indicates your company file's status as Accountant's Changes Pending.

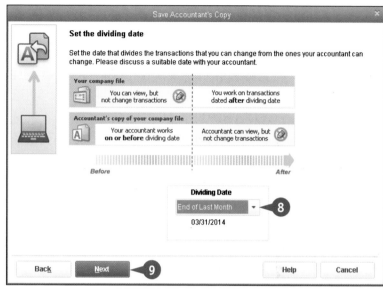

TIPS

Does creating an accountant's copy restrict my work?

Yes, some. In addition to adding and changing transactions dated after the dividing date, you also can add or edit list entries, but you cannot merge or delete list entries. Similarly, you can add accounts, but you cannot edit, merge, or deactivate accounts and you cannot add subaccounts.

Is my accountant's work restricted?

Your accountant can add, edit, void, or delete transactions dated on or before the dividing date and add accounts and entries to some lists. Your accountant also can reconcile periods that end before the dividing date or change the cleared status of reconciled transactions. Your accountant cannot work with payroll, transfers, sales tax payments, non-posting transactions like estimates, and inventory assemblies.

Import Accountant's Changes

Typically, when you give your accountant an Accountant's Copy, he or she returns a file that contains changes you import into your QuickBooks company file. QuickBooks does not overwrite your company file during this process, but instead merges the data your accountant gives you with the data in your company file.

Importing your accountant's changes is very similar to restoring a backup, and QuickBooks closes all open windows during the process. You can save open windows using Desktop Preferences; see Chapter 14. Once you import the changes your accountant provides, QuickBooks removes editing restrictions from your company data file.

Import Accountant's Changes

Ⓐ This information appears in the program title bar when you have created an accountant's copy.

① Click **File**.

② Click **Send Company File**.

③ Click **Accountant's Copy**.

④ Click **Client Activities**.

⑤ Click **Import Accountant's Changes from File**.

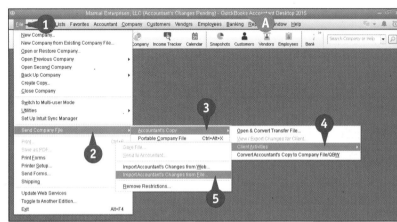

The Import Accountant's Changes dialog box appears.

⑥ Navigate to the file your accountant sent you.

Ⓑ You can click ▾ to navigate to a different folder.

⑦ Click the file.

⑧ Click **Open** to display the Incorporate Accountant's Changes window.

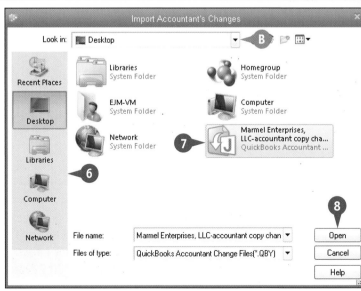

9 Review the changes the accountant made.

Note: You can review details by clicking the plus sign (+) beside a change (+ changes to –).

10 Click **Incorporate Accountant's Changes**.

QuickBooks displays a message indicating it will close all open windows; click **OK**.

QuickBooks indicate you must back up; click **OK**.

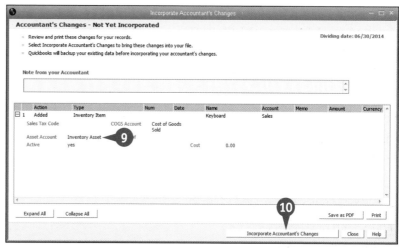

QuickBooks displays the Create Backup window.

11 Click **Local backup** (◉ changes to ◉).

12 Click **Next**.

QuickBooks displays the Save Backup Copy dialog box; navigate to the location where you want to save the backup file and click **Save**.

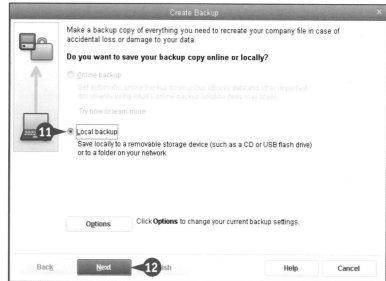

TIP

What should I do if my accountant has no changes to make to my company file?
You can cancel the Accountant's Copy restrictions. Complete steps **1** to **3** in this section, and then on the Client Activities menu, click **Remove Restrictions**. QuickBooks changes the status of your company — the title bar no longer contains the "Accountant's Changes Pending" message — and QuickBooks removes the editing restrictions placed on transactions dated before the dividing date.

continued ▶

Before you import, QuickBooks prompts you to back up your company file. You find overview steps in this section to handle backing up; for details on backing up, see the section "Back Up Your Company Records" earlier in this chapter. QuickBooks also creates a PDF file of the changes it incorporates, and places that PDF file in the same folder that contains your company file.

After importing, QuickBooks prompts you to set a closing date and password; if you choose to do so, QuickBooks displays accounting preferences in the Preferences dialog box, where you set the closing date and password.

Import Accountant's Changes (continued)

QuickBooks saves the backup and displays a message indicating the backup was successful. Click **OK**.

⑬ When QuickBooks displays a message explaining that a PDF file containing change information was created, click **OK**.

Ⓐ QuickBooks also displays the Incorporate Accountant's Changes window showing that changes were successfully merged into your company file.

⑭ Click **Close**.

Ⓑ The program title bar no longer contains information about the accountant's copy.

QuickBooks displays the Closing Date dialog box, prompting you to update the company file's closing date and password.

⑮ Click **Yes** or **No** as appropriate.

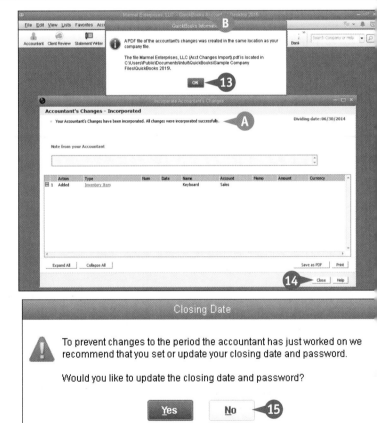

Condense Data

A s you work, your company data file grows. You can *archive* and *condense* data to speed up processing. During the process, QuickBooks removes data from the company file prior to the date you specify, as long as the transactions dated before the specified date do not affect transactions dated after the specified date. QuickBooks replaces the detailed information it removes with summarizing transactions, leaving numbers and balances in your company file unaffected. The only changes are in the size of your company file and the level of detail you can view.

QuickBooks makes a copy of your company file before condensing.

Condense Data

① Click **File**.

② Click **Utilities**.

③ Click **Condense Data**.

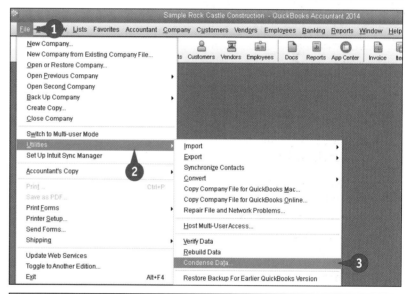

The Condense Data wizard begins.

④ Click an option (◯ changes to ◉) to identify the transactions to remove.

Ⓐ If you select the first option, click 🔳 and select the latest transaction date QuickBooks should remove.

⑤ Click **Next**.

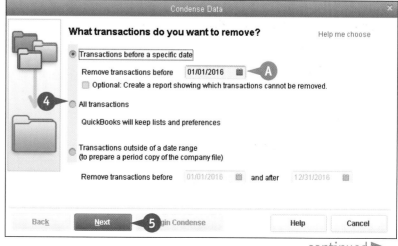

continued ▶

Condense Data (continued)

Q uickBooks removes transactions that are complete, such as a bill and the bill-payment checks that pay the entire bill, as long as the check has cleared the bank. When you select the recommended option, QuickBooks tends to condense fewer inventory transactions than other types of transactions. And, QuickBooks does not condense payroll transactions dated in the current calendar year. QuickBooks condenses only those estimates associated with jobs designated as closed in the Customer:Job list.

QuickBooks condenses billed time data if you do not pay employees based on it, time data you mark "not billable," and time data for closed jobs.

Condense Data (continued)

6 Click an option (changes to) to specify how QuickBooks should summarize transactions.

Note: You click the second option to preserve the ability to produce monthly or quarterly historical financial statements.

7 Click **Next**.

8 Click an option (changes to) to specify how to condense inventory.

9 Click **Next**.

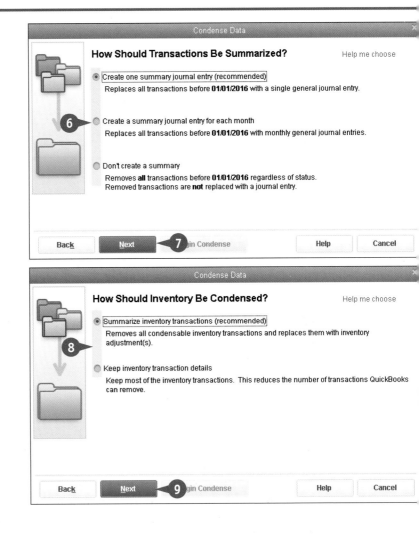

10 Click options (☑ changes to ☐) to avoid removing transactions.

11 Click **Next**.

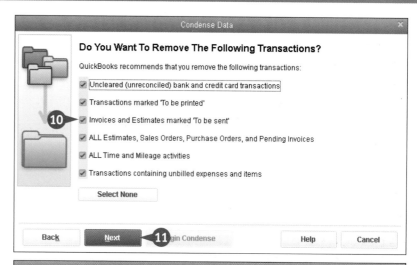

12 Click options (☑ changes to ☐) to avoid removing unused list entries.

13 Click **Next**.

The Begin Condense screen appears, telling you that condensing will take a while; click **Begin Condense**.

QuickBooks makes a copy of your company file, removes the transactions you specified, and displays a message when condensing completes, telling you where the original company file is located so that you can open it if you need transaction details.

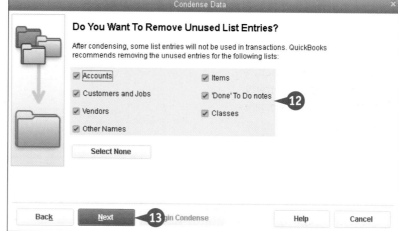

TIP

How should I choose to summarize transactions, condense inventory, and remove transactions?
In most cases, summarizing transactions with a single journal entry works well unless you need to produce monthly or quarterly financial statements. QuickBooks summarizes very few inventory transactions and retains all open inventory transactions, so, summarizing inventory transactions is safe. Condensing does not affect account balances, so you can safely remove the types of transactions the wizard suggests. Remember, QuickBooks works only with transactions dated before the date you specify on the first wizard screen.

Verify or Rebuild Data

Y ou can verify and rebuild your data if you see errors such as Invalid Protection Faults or Fatal Errors, or if strange events occur in QuickBooks. For example, you might notice that payments you already deposited reappear in the Payments to Deposit window, names do not appear in lists, or transactions are missing from reports.

QuickBooks stores the results of data verification in a file named qbwin.log that you can open to view its information. If rebuilding does not fix your problems, restore from a backup or contact Intuit Technical Support, who can, for a fee, repair your data.

Verify or Rebuild Data

Verify Data

1 Click **File**.

2 Click **Utilities**.

3 Click **Verify Data**.

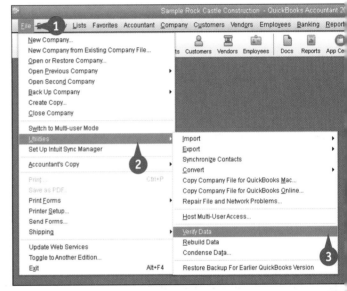

QuickBooks verifies your data and displays a message with the results.

4 Click **OK**.

Rebuild Data

1 Complete steps **1** to **3** in the subsection "Verify Data," but in step **3** click **Rebuild Data**.

A message appears, explaining that you must back up your data before rebuilding.

2 Click **OK**.

The Save Backup Copy dialog box appears.

3 Type a filename.

A You can click ▼ to navigate to a location for the backup.

4 Click **Save**.

QuickBooks backs up your data and rebuilds it, and when the process completes, a message appears, explaining the results.

5 Click **OK**.

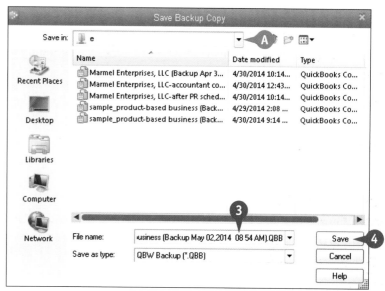

TIP

How do I open the qbwin.log file to read it?

While working in your company:

1 Press F2 to display the Product Information dialog box.

2 Press Ctrl + 2 to display the Tech Help window.

3 Click the **Open File** tab.

4 Click **QBWIN.LOG**.

5 Click **Open File**.

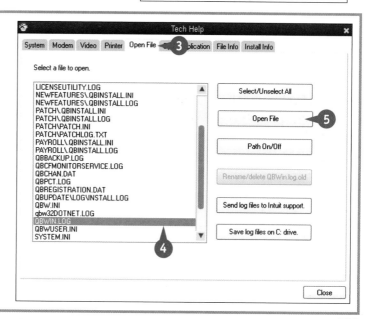

Set Up Security

You can set up security in QuickBooks to protect a QuickBooks data file from unauthorized access by requiring each user to type a unique username and password to open the data file. You also can limit each user's access to only those areas of the company data file that you specify, and you can identify the types of functions the user can perform. For example, you can permit a user to run reports but not view payroll information.

You should also set up the QuickBooks Administrator — the Admin user — who has unrestricted access to QuickBooks.

Set Up Security

Create a User and Assign Privileges

1 Click **Company**.

2 Click **Set Up Users and Passwords**.

3 Click **Set Up Users**.

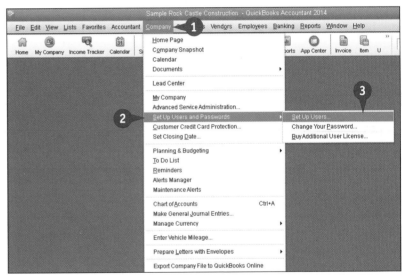

The User List window appears.

Note: If you have not set up a password for the administrator, you can edit the Admin user and follow steps **6** and **7** to create the administrator's password and provide a challenge question and answer.

4 Click **Add User**.

The Set Up User Password and
Access wizard begins.

5 Type the username here.

6 Type a password here.

7 Retype the password here.

8 Click here (☐ changes to ☑)
to add the user to your
QuickBooks license.

9 Click **Next**.

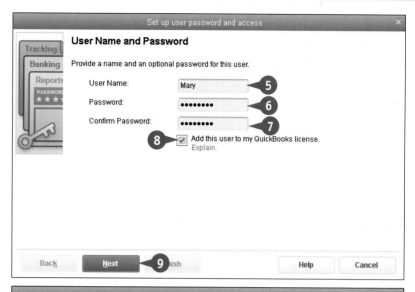

The Access for User screen
appears.

10 Click an option to establish
security for the selected user
(◯ changes to ◉).

Note: This section sets up security
to selected areas of QuickBooks.

11 Click **Next** to display the Sales
and Accounts Receivable
screen.

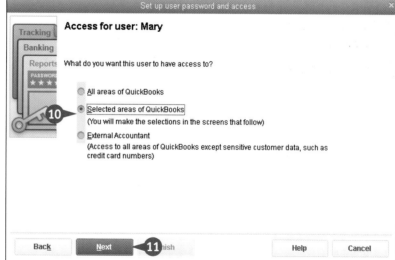

continued ▶

TIP

How many users can I set up in my QuickBooks data file?
You can set up as many users as you want. However, the number of users that can simultaneously access
your company file depends on your QuickBooks licensing agreement. If you use QuickBooks Pro or Premier,
up to five users can work in a company file simultaneously, based on the number of user licenses you
purchase. To find out how many user licenses you own, press your keyboard's **F2** key. The number of
licenses you own appears in the top left corner of the Product Information window.

Set Up Security (continued)

W hile logged into your company as the Admin user, set up all other usernames and passwords and assign their security privileges using a wizard. You can give a user no access, full access, or selective access for the functional areas of Sales and Accounts Receivable, Purchases and Accounts Payable, Checking and Credit Cards, Inventory, Time Tracking, Payroll and Employees, Sensitive Accounting Activities, and Sensitive Financial Reporting. This section shows the settings on the Sales and Accounts Receivable screen.

Once you set up users and assigns passwords, QuickBooks prompts you to log on each time you open your company data file.

Set Up Security (continued)

12 Click an option to control the user's access to QuickBooks information (🔘 changes to 🔘).

Ⓐ If you click **Selective Access**, click one of these options (🔘 changes to 🔘).

Ⓑ If you accept customer credit cards, you can click here (☐ changes to ☑) to permit the user to view credit card information.

13 Click **Next**.

14 Repeat steps **12** and **13** for all functional areas of QuickBooks until the Changing or Deleting Transactions screen appears.

15 Click an option to control the user's ability to change or delete transactions dated both before and after the closing date (🔘 changes to 🔘).

16 Click **Next**.

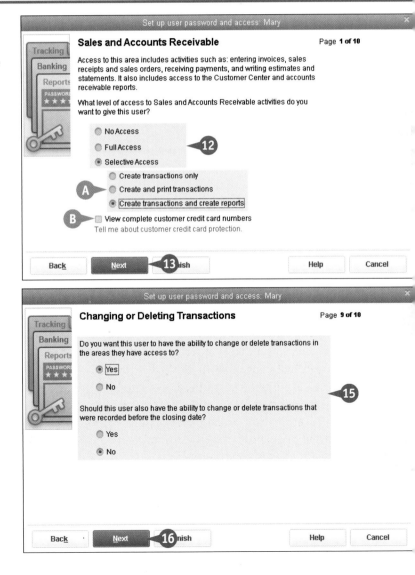

A summary of permissions for the selected user appears.

17 Click **Finish**.

The User List reappears with the user's name in it; you can click **Close** to close the User List window.

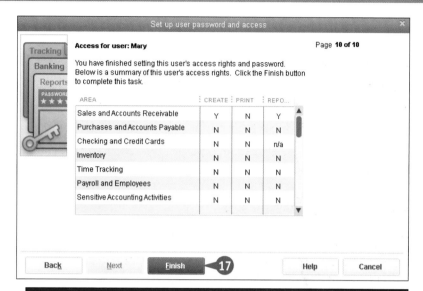

Open QuickBooks

Note: When you open the company, the QuickBooks Login dialog box appears.

1 Type your username here.

2 Type your password here.

3 Click **OK**.

QuickBooks opens.

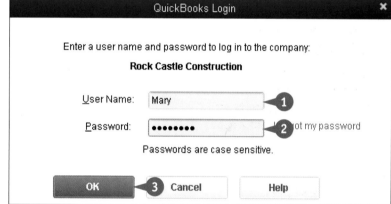

Index